The Invisibilities of Political Torture

The Presence of Absence in US and Chilean Cinema

Berenike Jung

EDINBURGH
University Press

Edinburgh University Press is one of the leading university presses in the UK. We publish academic books and journals in our selected subject areas across the humanities and social sciences, combining cutting-edge scholarship with high editorial and production values to produce academic works of lasting importance. For more information visit our website: edinburghuniversitypress.com

© Berenike Jung, 2020, 2022

Edinburgh University Press Ltd
The Tun – Holyrood Road
12 (2f) Jackson's Entry
Edinburgh EH8 8PJ

First published in hardback by Edinburgh University Press 2020

Typeset in 11/13pt EhrhardtMT by
Exeter Premedia Services Pvt Ltd., Chennai, India,

A CIP record for this book is available from the British Library

ISBN 978 1 4744 3699 1 (hardback)
ISBN 978 1 4744 3700 4 (paperback)
ISBN 978 1 4744 3701 1 (webready PDF)
ISBN 978 1 4744 3702 8 (epub)

The right of Berenike Jung to be identified as author of this work has been asserted in accordance with the Copyright, Designs and Patents Act 1988 and the Copyright and Related Rights Regulations 2003 (SI No. 2498).

Contents

List of Figures   v
Acknowledgements   vi

Introduction   1
   The Image of Torture   2
   Why Torture Now?   3
   Accountability, Impunity, Amnesty   6
   Thinking through Torture with Films   10
   Matter and Form   14

1. **Visible Torture: The Case of *Zero Dark Thirty***   24
   The Torture Debates   25
   Double Binds   27
   The Torturers and Us   37

2. **Witnessing Torture, and Mediated Witnessing in War-on-Terror Films**   50
   Witness Politics and Failing Witnesses   53
   Crossing Over to 'the Dark Side'   60
   Visual Regimes   65

3. **Television Torture, Made in the USA**   72
   24: Torture on Repeat   74
   Homeland   78
   A Crisis of Epistemology   80

4. **Television Torture, Made in Chile**   90
   Los Archivos del Cardenal   91
   Memory Formations   96
   Los 80: Media Memories on Television   101

CONTENTS

5. **Negotiating Evidence** — 109
   - The Abu Ghraib Images — 109
   - *The Unknown Known* — 116
   - *Standard Operating Procedure* — 120

6. **The Presence of Absence in Contemporary Chilean Cinema** — 132
   - Social Hauntings — 134
   - The Absent Signifier — 137
   - Sensual Visualities: Sound, Breath and Touch — 141

7. **The Politics of Realism in Chilean Cinema** — 153
   - *Post Mortem* — 157
   - *Tony Manero* — 164
   - *La Danza de la Realidad* — 165

8. **Cinema as Poetic Archive** — 172
   - Rethinking Indexicality — 172
   - *Nostalgia de la luz* — 176
   - *NO* — 183

Conclusion — 196
   - The Invisibilities of Torture in US and Chilean Cinema — 196
   - The Politics of Affect — 198
   - Epistemological Quests — 199
   - The Spectator and the Torture of Others — 202

Bibliography — 204
Filmography — 233
Index — 235

Figures

I.1	Memorial for the disappeared, *Nostalgia de la luz*	14
I.2	Coup of 11 September 1973: bombing of *La Moneda*	15
I.3	Quema de Libros/Chile, 1973	15
I.4	Poster protesting disappearances	16
1.1	*Zero Dark Thirty*	33
1.2	*Zero Dark Thirty*	45
2.1	Crucified prisoner in *Rendition*	55
2.2	Western witnesses in *Rendition*	55
2.3	'The Situation Room'	58
2.4	*Body of Lies*	59
2.5	*Syriana*	64
2.6	*Body of Lies*	67
2.7	*Zero Dark Thirty*	68
3.1	*Homeland*	85
4.1	*Los Archivos del Cardenal*	91
4.2	*Los Hornos de Lonquén*	94
4.3	*Los 80*	103
5.1	*The Unknown Known*	119
5.2	*Standard Operating Procedure*	121
5.3	*Standard Operating Procedure*	125
6.1	*NO*	138
6.2	*Pena de Muerte*	139
6.3	*Carne de Perro*	147
6.4	*Carne de Perro*	148
7.1	*Post Mortem*	158
7.2	*Post Mortem*	161
7.3	*Post Mortem*	163
7.4	*Tony Manero*	165
8.1	*Nostalgia de la luz*	178
8.2	*Nostalgia de la luz*	178
8.3	*NO*	186
8.4	*NO*	188

Acknowledgements

This book would not have been possible without the generous support and unfailing guidance of my PhD supervisors, Professor Stella Bruzzi and Professor John King, whose advice in and out of class was invaluable. Their wisdom, encouragement, wealth of experience and knowledge has shaped and inspired both me and this book in numerous ways.

Further, I am deeply grateful to my examiners and first readers, Professor Nikolaj Lübecker and Professor Alison Ribeiro de Menezes, who have improved and advised this work, as well as Professor Fabienne Manicom and Professor Karl Schoonover for their sagacious counsel. Special thanks must go to Professor David Martin-Jones and Professor Walter Metz, for their support of and confidence in my intellectual capabilities at critical times.

I would also like to thank the University of Warwick for their generous Chancellor's Scholarship, an IAS Early Career Fellowship and various grants that allowed me to organise a conference and to conduct field work in Chile. I am further grateful to King's College London, the Institute of Media Studies at the University of Tübingen, the PG community at Warwick and, of course, the patient publishers at Edinburgh University Press, for their support in creating this volume.

Too many people have offered intellectual and emotional input along the way to mention them all – but some must be named and thanked emphatically: Dr Ivan Girina, Dr Sarah Griswold, Dr Derilene Marco, Dr Marta Wasik, Dr Paraskevi Gikopoulou, Dr Omololu Akanji, Dr Anuja Jain, Dr Stefanie Rauch, Dr Ali Saqer, Dr Charlotte Stevens, Dr Owen Weetch, Dr Matthew Denny, Dr Geli Mademli, and Dr Selma Kadi – thank you for joint explorations of academic resilience, for smart comments and inspiring conversations. I am deeply indebted to Professor John King, Dr Tomás Peters and Rodrigo Rojas for introducing me to many wonderful scholars and practitioners in Chile, such as Professor Ignacio Agüero, Professor Carlos Flores Delpino, Tevo Díaz, Xavier Guerrero, Fernando Guzzoni, Catalina Palma Herrera, Professor Orlando Lübbert, Dr Carolina Urrutia; the Cineteca Nacional de Chile and the *Museo de la Memoria y de los Derechos Humanos*.

With all my love and gratitude to my wonderful family, both living and passed, who have led me here, and to my amazing family of friends – shout-outs to Nomsa Buchholz, Ian Dayang, Sven Dukat, Eva Gauss, Jan Gerken, Martin Gloss, Laetitia Kiener, Tobias Kunisch, Param Thind, Femke Winkels and Klaudia Ziomek.

Thank you to all those who were there during this journey. Thank you for your encouragement, for inspiring and incubating new ideas, for challenging and nurturing my thinking, for inspiring me with your example and your presence.

Some of the issues and films discussed in Chapters 6, 7 and 8 have been published as: 'History, Fiction and the Politics of Corporeality in Pablo Larraín's Dictatorship Trilogy', in Jennie Carlsten and Fearghal McGarry (eds) *Film, History and Memory* (2015); 'Surface Meanings: A Media Archaeological Analysis of *NO* (Pablo Larraín, 2012)', in *Cinergie Libri* (2019); and '"Within the limits of the possible": Realist Aesthetics in Larraín's Dictatorship Trilogy', in Laura Hatry (ed.), *ReFocus: The Films of Pablo Larraín* (forthcoming). Full publication details are supplied in the Bibliography.

Introduction

In 2004, when the Abu Ghraib images went viral online, I was horrified, nauseated and strangely confused in my shock: I realised that, as a West Berlin native, I had still retained some of my childhood image of 'America' – the collectively inherited sense of a benevolent superpower protecting my city from those who encircled our tiny city island. Years later, living in Chile, I was immersed in a world where I seemed to be constantly missing bits of what was being communicated. I could sense that there was something more being said beyond the words spoken, something that went beyond language skills and *chilenismos*. I recognised those sensations as related to the social feeling I had grown up with in Cold War Berlin, expressed in a speech heavy with subtext and silences, a kind of pressure in the air, a sense of suspicion, fear, a low-level threat.

Years later, the Chilean writer Diamela Eltit helped me make sense of this memory when she described what is necessary to live in *and to come out of* a dictatorship:

> Tú tienes que desaprender para reaprender a vivir bajo la dictadura … Necesitas olvidar ciertas cosas. No puedes hablar mucho … Debes pasar a una sociedad de la sospecha … salir de la dictadura también fue un problema. Uno se había disciplinado en la dictadura. Uno tuvo que volver a hablar, a decir palabras que antes no decía.
>
> You have to unlearn everything and relearn how to live … You need to forget certain things. You cannot talk much … You move … to [a society] of suspicion … leaving the dictatorship was also a problem. One had disciplined oneself during the dictatorship. One had to return to actually talk again, to say words that we had no longer said before.[1]

These connections began to make sense when I learnt more about Chile's history, especially the history of torture under the Pinochet dictatorship. In contrast to the Abu Ghraib images which had affected me so much, nothing about the torture in Chile's past was readily, visibly available. I had to go and look for the places and find the people – but once I did, traces and histories emerged everywhere. In this book, I have tried to explore both of these cases, which have haunted me, through cinema and its ability to make us blind or to make us see and feel, in order to comprehend not only how what happened could have happened, but also how we make – or fail to make – sense of it.

The Image of Torture

The starting point for this book was the startling contrast between the momentary ubiquity of the images that emerged from the Abu Ghraib prison in Iraq and the seeming absence of visual documentation of the torture committed during the military dictatorship in Chile. Where the images that emerged from Abu Ghraib[2] ricocheted in visual public culture, the systemic, extensive and institutionalised system of torture in thousands of torture centres in Chile and neighbouring countries[3] remained much less visually documented and much less publicly visible, even after the end of the dictatorship.[4]

Yet, as public memory often organises around a few iconic exemplars, the dominance of just a few images may reflect the paucity but also the excess of documentary evidence. In a comparison explicitly drawn between the 'amnesiac' memory culture in Chile and the omnipresence of the Abu Ghraib photographs, Macarena Gómez-Barris has argued that hypervisibility may be 'an alibi for invisibility', a manifestation of the same phenomenon.[5]

These dynamics of visibilities and invisibilities invite the exploration of the limits and potential of the image. Both hypervisibility and absence point to the limitations of the visual as epistemological strategy. Therefore, this book moves beyond issues of selective, incomplete, distorted representation, tied mostly to the visible sphere, towards an epistemological dimension. The ethical question of 'visual complicity' is reframed as a question of how to create believable categories of historical truth, beyond a representation-based surface analysis or strict binaries of documentary and fiction.

This book investigates the interaction between factual torture cases, their visual documentation and their fictional portrayal in key contemporary US and Chilean films and television shows. Taking a cue both from Slavoj Žižek, who asks in reference to *Zero Dark Thirty*, 'why has such a film been made now?',[6] and from Robert Rosenstone's suggestion to look at both what the films say about the present moment of their production and what they say about the history they depict,[7] the focus lies on how contemporary cinema re-examines the past, distinct or recent, and how this relates to the present moment. The aim of such a historically informed and transnational approach is to help understand something fundamental not only about torture, but also about how we relate to our current reality through our images. Especially considering the exponential increase in visual information in the contemporary media landscape, the belief in the political power of the image through aspirational visibility must be adjusted. Showing the (right) images is not enough, and yet I suggest that films can play a key role in better understanding the visibilities and invisibilities inherent in the subject matter of torture.

Why Torture Now?

In public discourse, torture is narrowly defined as an isolated event, an exceptional measure, generally alien to 'Western', 'civilised' values. Both in political rhetoric and in cinema, torture tends to be paired as response to (or pre-emptive measure against) terrorism. Constructed as provoked, contained and eventually productive, torture is transformed into a legitimate act of defence against aggression.[8]

As documented by human rights groups, torture takes place in countries regardless of political ideologies and economic systems, but it is not part of every war, contrary to the claims of an exculpatory narrative. A wilful and hypocritical amnesia denies the historical and continuing use of torture by democracies and protects the invisibility of ongoing torture sponsorship. *Why torture here and why now?* urges us to analyse both when and where torture, a historically recurring 'social practice, not a legal policy'[9] takes place and how it spreads in a 'global economy of punishment and discipline':[10] fifty-four countries participated in the CIA's rendition programme; and events similar to those at Abu Ghraib have been replicated throughout the so-called 'coalition of the willing'.[11]

Guantánamo Bay and black sites across the globe created spatial and legal 'black holes'[12] into which people vanished: by interpreting international treaties as only applicable to US territory, captives were effectively stripped of their human rights. Held at these 'spaces of exception',[13] outside any domestic or international legal protection, the prisoners became 'publicly invisible'. This power to make people vanish followed the same logic as mass disappearances in Latin America during the dictatorship decades. Literally rejecting any shared ground, such spaces constitute the logical climax of dehumanising discourses that construct the enemy as a disease, a political (Marxist/Islamist terrorist) 'cancer'.

In some ways, such enforced fields of invisibility are specific to this contemporary moment: from drone warfare, the use of 'clean' torture[14] and rendition as 'surrogacy',[15] the routine inhumanity of mass incarceration[16] in US prisons to the cultural practices of concealment in the manipulation and censorship of images to win the propaganda war. Hidden in plain view, these practices facilitate interpretative denial of responsibility while maintaining their threatening impact.

In other ways, the forms of torture are historically rooted, echoing colonial violence, concentration camps, both lynching at home and US military interventions around the world.[17] The US history with torture also includes funding torture in and exporting techniques to Latin America.[18] The Army School of the Americas for instance brought Latin American military officers to the US for advanced training that encompassed torture techniques, including Chile's dictator Pinochet himself.

Considering these entanglements, it is perhaps not surprising that William Cavanaugh, comparing torture in Chile and torture in post-9/11 America, finds both 'significant differences and distressing similarities'. The latter include similar torture techniques, documented in two reports, one from Chile 1975, one from Red Cross 2004 on the treatment of detainees by US forces in Iraq. In both cases, 'information was rarely at stake'; and torture's primary purpose was the production of enemies in a situation of what Anne McClintock called an 'enemy deficit'.[19] Visible enemies were conspicuously absent both after the terror attacks of 11 September 2001 – where the hijackers died in the crash – and after the coup d'état in Chile – where the military, met with little resistance, gained control within twenty-four hours. In order to justify the already realised coup as the only way to save the nation 'from a diabolical Marxist conspiracy', the Chilean military needed to create an 'atmosphere of war': 'Wars are about the imaginary dividing of the world into friends and enemies. And enemies must exist in sufficient abundance and sufficient monstrosity if a war is to be sustained'.[20]

Political torture helped to create that enemy – be they in Chile's torture centres, where the demonisation of the prisoners as 'terrorists' justified their maltreatment, or in the prisons of Iraq and black sites around the world, where 'torture was also a way to coercively produce the Arab subject and the Arab mind'.[21] The 'War on Terror' discursively constructed a framework of an unprecedented struggle against a uniquely barbaric, hidden enemy.

Further uniting these two specific countries is the struggle to increase accountability and to open up public memory to incorporate a more encompassing, and truthful, history. Both the US and Chile manifest national narratives of exceptionalism,[22] which frame the moment that permitted or fostered torture as an outlier, a fall from grace, an exceptional response to a state of emergency.

In Ken Loach's piece for *9'11"01* (Youssef Chahine et al., 2002), Chilean poet and playwright Ariel Dorfman writes an empathetic letter to the US public after the terror attacks of 11 September 2001 (9/11) reminding them of the Chilean 'once de septiembre' and asking them not to forget historical responsibility even in times of crisis, grief and anger. By pairing the bellicose rhetoric of the US administration under George W. Bush with images of the Chilean coup, Loach alerts the viewer to distressing similarities and reminds us of a particular moment in history when the US was supporting state terrorism.

In Chile, torture helped to instal the ideology of corporate capitalism. As is well documented now, the US destabilised Chile economically before the CIA helped direct the military coup. Exported through the so-called 'Chicago Boys', Chile emerged as a petri dish for an extreme version of unchecked neoliberalism. Torture played a necessary part in this

> social war against a broad popular political bloc ... that gave strong support to [Chile's President] Allende and his project of a parliamentary 'Chilean Road to Socialism'. The whole apparatus of torture and disappearance ... simulated the atmosphere of war that the regime needed to justify its policies.[23]

As a means of control, torture spreads fear, disrupts social relations and establishes 'the ability of the state to impose its narrative'[24] by targeting the 'social imagination'. It is a discourse of power enacted through bodies, and its intended targets are not individuals but 'social bodies'.[25] As Joseph Brodsky concludes, rather soberingly, by him- or herself 'no individual is worth an exercise in injustice (or for that matter, in justice) ... it's the echo that counts'.[26]

And yet, in political discourse, mirrored and fortified in cultural products, we pretend that it is truth – perhaps recast as information or intelligence – we are after. Unravelling this misrepresentation is necessary because misapprehending the nature of torture means misapprehending the incentive to resort to it, creating the conditions that enable the continuation of torture.[27] Thus, at least part of an answer to Žižek's question – why such films are being made now – would be that in some ways the torture has never really ended: we still live in an age of impunity.

By reframing the definition of torture, this book seeks also to expand the limited public debate. As the study of selected films will show, films can broaden our understanding of the nature of torture, by inviting us to perceive or to feel aspects neglected in the periodically recurring 'torture debates', such as the collective and emotional aftermath. Before laying out the structure and scope of this argument, however, it is necessary to give a brief account of the facts, and the attempts at accountability made by both countries.

Accountability, Impunity, Amnesty

Where do we stand on torture today? When I was carrying out the research that would lay the foundation for this book, the official status of the use of torture seemed to be in limbo, banned by an executive order of the Obama administration, but without sufficient and public working through. Today, the US commander-in-chief declares that he 'loves' waterboarding, that he 'feels' torture works (and 'even if it doesn't work, they deserve it') and he has vowed to keep the detention camp Guantánamo Bay open.[28] Meanwhile, in Chile, Pinochet-era anti-terrorist emergency laws continue to be invoked whenever there is a political crisis.[29] While this was largely ignored as long as it mainly affected Chile's indigenous population,[30] the recent social unrest has thrown these relics of the past into strong relief. In 2019, a protest against increased subway fares for the Santiago metro turned into nationwide demonstrations against economic injustice and demands to change the dictatorship-era constitution, which enshrines social inequalities beneath the political rhetoric of Chile as an economic miracle. The images of military forces clashing with civilians strongly evoke the political repressions of the dictatorship period. With astonishing speed, the government regressed into a discourse of 'war' against parts of its citizenry. At the time of writing, the response of security forces have left 26 people dead and hundreds severely injured. The National Human Rights Institute has 'filed 442 criminal complaints on behalf of victims, with prosecutors alleging police-inflicted injuries, cruel treatment, torture, sexual violence, attempted killings, and killings'.[31]

Such impunity and political backlash are typically expected and blamed on absence of evidence or lack of transparency. Yet it seems clear that neither the ubiquitous presence nor the marginalisation of images of factual torture can explain the collective failure to create a fundamental shift in our global understanding of and attitude towards torture after the revelations of either country's commissions tasked with coming to terms with the past.

The UN Convention Against Torture and Other Cruel, Inhuman or Degrading Treatment or Punishment (UNCAT, 1984/1987), which was ratified by Chile in 1988 and by the US in 1994, defines torture as 'any act by which severe pain or suffering, *whether physical or mental*, is intentionally inflicted on a person for such purposes as obtaining from him or a third person *information or a confession*'.[32]

UNCAT includes treatment intended to humiliate, and the threat of torture or execution; it does not allow the practice of rendition and requires prosecution of any acts of torture. In 2002–03, lawyers in the Department of Justice and the Pentagon drew up what came to be called 'torture memos', which redefined legal precedent,[33] arguing that international treaties applied only to acts carried out on US soil, and that 'severe pain or suffering' qualified as torture only when resulting in 'permanent and serious physical injury, organ failure, or even death'.[34] Even according to this twisted definition, the US tortured: the interrogation and detention regime implemented by the US has resulted in the deaths of at least 100 detainees in US custody. There is evidence of institutional collusion and medical collaboration, such as the revival of prisoners for further torture, or the falsification of death certificates.[35] Most of those who were being held cannot be linked to terrorist activity. A Red Cross report concludes scathingly 'the policy of brutalisation was and is systematic, approved and justified all the way up to the highest levels of the administration'.[36]

After almost half a dozen previous investigations into the 'prisoner abuse scandal' at Abu Ghraib, the US Senate launched a final report into the interrogation programme. The Executive Summary of the *Committee Study of the Central Intelligence Agency's Detention and Interrogation Program* (the so-called 'Torture Report') was released, after eleven months of prolonged discussions, in December 2014 – *ten years* after the pictures went viral. The report was limited in scope, covering only prisoners held by the CIA (excluding Guantánamo and detainees handed over to foreign governments),[37] and it focused on documenting the programme as ineffective, unnecessary and wasteful, rather than illegal in nature. It did not offer recommendations or acknowledgements of internal dissent and resistance within the agency.[38] Yet what the report illustrated clearly was a disquieting pattern of misrepresentation, denial, obstruction of evidence, culminating in the destruction of ninety-two videotapes of 'enhanced interrogation sessions' in 2005.[39]

No criminal charges have ever been brought against any CIA officer running the programme. Many of those involved moved on to leading the CIA drone programme.[40] In June 2017, the Trump administration, including the FBI and the CIA, returned the copies of the Senate Intelligence Committee so-called 'Torture Report' to Congress; in 2018, the International Criminal Court (ICC) was declared to be 'illegitimate' and the visa of one of the court's chief prosecutors was revoked in response to her intention to investigate potential war crimes by US soldiers in Afghanistan.[41]

Gina Haspel, a top CIA official who is linked not only to the torture programme but also directly to the destruction of evidence in 2005, was confirmed as the new head of the agency;[42] tellingly, during her confirmation, the dreadful euphemism 'enhanced interrogation' continued to be used. Haspel is a product of a culture that legalised and rebranded torture, and that would not admit wrongdoing in a meaningful and consequential way.

Both in the US and in Chile, such lack of accountability has toxic social consequences. Antagonistic memories may persist in the face of historical documents, of course, but a false democracy of facts is harder to maintain after official contradiction. Yet when documentation – such as the findings of Chile's Truth Commission or the full US Senate report – is censored, buried or classified, what should be grounded in fact becomes a matter of opinion. This issue may have returned with new urgency, but the accountability gap was a problem before the 45th US presidency ushered in the age of the post-factual. The Obama administration's executive order banning torture did not address the sponsoring of torture overseas, nor did it engage in finding an appropriate paradigm for transparency and accountability with regards to the programmes, which remain instead as 'fully loaded weapons'[43] on the shelf. The administration's call to 'turn the page', an approach which Amnesty International has characterised as 'engaging in a de facto amnesty', uncomfortably echoed the received wisdom of 'looking forward and not backward' ('*salir adelante*') in Chile's post-dictatorship process. The Obama administration also continued its predecessor's broad claims that lawsuits would divulge state secrets, and so far, courts have sided largely with the Justice Department on these claims. As fundamental legal issues remain unresolved, from permissible evidence to the rights of Guantánamo defendants,[44] it appears impossible to prosecute any high-level detainees without allowing them to tell all about their torture.[45] The living presence of the survivors of US torture thus seems to limit the scale of judicial consequences, and the 'disruptive memory of torture' impedes the ability to construct a coherent *legal* memory for 9/11.[46]

This question of accountability and memory is also a question of *wanting* to know what is going on in the present moment: as Timothy Melley has argued, a 'security state' depends on 'a dynamic of collective repression or disavowal', creating an atmosphere of public half-knowledge and what Michael Rogin called 'motivated forgetting'.[47] In this situation of absence and disavowal, films, as expressions of what Melley calls the 'cultural imaginary' offer audiovisual bodies to be questioned for what they make visible, what they hide and what they make known to our own bodies and senses.

* * *

Chile's first National Commission for Truth and Reconciliation, *La Comisión Nacional sobre Verdad y Reconciliación* (CNVR), named Rettig after its chairman, took place almost immediately after the return to democracy and ran from April 1990 until March 1991. The Commission explicitly excluded from its investigation any human rights violations that did not result in death, based on the claim that torture was unprovable, but its final report nevertheless acknowledged torture as a recurrent and institutionalised event. While the Commission debunked some myths, its narrow focus impeded a more nuanced understanding of the multifaceted repressions of the dictatorship. Few copies of the final report were printed, and as late as 1996, mentioning the Human Rights abuses was considered in 'bad taste'.[48]

Set up in 2003 and publishing in 2004, a second Truth Commission, *La Comisión Nacional sobre Prisión Política y Tortura* – again named after its chairman, Sergio Valech – was to finally address the previously excluded issues of political imprisonment and torture. Operating under severe time pressure, the Valech Commission accepted testimony from over 28,000 people, and concluded that the torture had been systematic, continuously advancing in its methods, supported by the judiciary, the army and the security apparatus. Torture was shown to have preceded most of the executions and 'disappearances' of victims, 94 per cent of all political detainees were tortured and nearly all female victims reported that they had suffered sexual torture.

Given their limited time frames and mandates, both reports suffered from numerous shortcomings: they could not name those responsible or initiate investigations; they were restricted to cases where prisoners could prove that their detention was politically motivated; the responsibility of providing evidence was located with the victims; detention in a country other than Chile or other than one of the 1,200 official detention centres was excluded, as was detention for less than five days. (In 2011, a third instalment, 'Valech II', amended some of the most egregious omissions and added almost 10,000 more cases.)[49] None of the official reports features clear recommendations for the future. Further to be examined are the roles of the judiciary, civilian collaborators, bystanders and moderates, the corruption of other branches of society and government and the combined failure of institutions to stop the propagation of narratives of denial, which often led to re-victimisation – and also where there was resistance within the military and low-level dissenters.

Unquestioned amnesty and de facto impunity erase the distinction between forgiving and forgetting[50] and allow revisionist narratives to fester and to spin history. What Steve Stern called a stagnation or impasse of public memory was only broken in 1998 with Pinochet's detention in London, which lead to a seminal moment for universal, international human rights jurisdiction and created terms – such as 'the disappeared' – to describe similar or analogous cases of human rights abuses worldwide.

Following Pinochet's arrest, Chilean courts became moderately more active.[51] The Truth Commissions' Reports, the subsequent Report of the Armed Forces and the army's official recognition in 2004 somewhat deflated the political right's revisionist history, which describes pre-coup Chile as bankrupt, close to civil war, and accordingly framed human rights violations as a lamentable, rare and necessary evil.[52] A national Museum of Memory, the *Museo de la Memoria y de los Derechos Humanos*, was inaugurated in 2010, twenty years after the end of the dictatorship. However, most torture centres were dismantled at the beginning of the 1990s, with little regard for public and private memory; even today, the task of preserving the memory these spaces contain remains mostly in private hands.[53] Although 'official memory' slowly expands its acknowledgements, conflicting memory narratives to this day shape the social net of Chile.[54]

Thinking through Torture with Films

What role can films play in supporting the social memory of torture, in the public debates, in healing these social divisions? By explaining my methodology and what I see lacking in the current literature on torture in movies, I will also outline the political place I see for cinema on this topic.

To represent torture means always also speaking about or approximating 'the fact that torture is the extreme example of incommunicability'.[55] Yet precisely because torture deliberately cuts people off from their communities and threatens to become unspeakable, because it is experienced and publicly framed as abject, it is essential to render public what Joanna Bourke called the 'pain event' of torture.

In light of often unreliable, biased or contested documentation, of absent, 'publicly forgotten' or censored images of factual political torture, there is an ethical urgency to provide evidence of atrocity. This need coincides with renewed scrutiny directed towards (moving) images' relation to the real, as the digital turn has challenged the dominant theoretical basis of linking cinema to reality. 'The ways in which digital technologies break down whatever remains of our inherited faith in the indexical relationship between the photograph and its object are ... of obvious importance to the epistemology and politics of an image-saturated culture'.[56]

Prompted by technological and social changes, scholars describe new forms of seeing and propose new visualities, aesthetics and even ontologies of the cinematic image.[57] Such aspects have not been discussed in relation to torture, however, which tends to be discussed as a corollary of other forms of violence, especially terrorism. This book therefore fills a gap in critical attention on this specific form of violence.

* * *

Torture on film comes with a substantial history. Even excluding documentaries, rape-revenge cycles and the 'torture porn' horror subgenre, several cinematic masterpieces include famous torture scenes: *Rome, Open City* (Roberto Rossellini, 1945), *Battle of Algiers* (Gillo Pontecorvo, 1966) and *Night and Fog* (Alain Resnais, 1955), to name but a few. As far as torture *specifically* is analysed in these, as well as the spate of recent Hollywood movies, scholars have tended to focus on representational and historical veracity or on the potential for identification and the resulting emotional or ideological effects on audiences.[58] Compare Rachel Walsh's critique that the ending of *Rendition* 'demands very little of its viewers politically' with James Agee's remarkably similar criticism of *Rome, Open City* as a film which, for a postwar US audience, erodes culpability and absolves viewers into a comfortable 'self-satisfied smugness … about his or her own place in the world'.[59]

These analyses have generated a useful language to describe patterns, tropes, images and formulas which clutter and inhibit a deeper understanding and fortify ideological constructs. For instance, Paul Kahn analyses torture's symbolic potency,[60] and Darius Rejali outlines the 'torture folkore', which includes the framing of torture as the 'lesser evil' of an assortment of violence,[61] the notion that there is a 'science' to torture, and a potential for 'productive' torture, so deeply ingrained in political and legal narratives.[62] While the analyses of torture in post-9/11 Hollywood films have generated important insights, they are often intertwined with a general suspicion of popular cinema as escapist, ideology-driven and violence-generating entertainment. Especially the quantitative increase in images of torture,[63] and the alleged invitation to 'identify' with torturers rather than their victims, is said to normalise and increase acceptance of torture, with the films functioning as 'ad hoc mass indoctrination'.[64] In these films, the politics of torture are individualised, abstracted from institutional contexts, while historical and socio-cultural specificity and complexity are reduced to 'simple, often psychological causes which, in turn, lend themselves to apparently easy (and mostly violent) solutions'.[65] As Faisal Devji points out, 'in its conventional narrative [torture] plays the role of a mere supplement to politics, one that lacks any ontology of its own. The confession or resistance of the torture victim is also therefore non-political.'[66]

However, underlying much of the representation-centred criticism is the assumption that art compels us to revolt when showing revolting things, that showing torture in the *appropriate* form would 'shock' the spectator into action. Making torture *visible* is intended to raise awareness, lead to protest and thereby help eradicate the practice. Yet seeing does not equal understanding, nor does knowledge necessarily result in political action. Jacques Rancière writes that 'the current scepticism ... was generated by the disappointed belief in a straight line between perception, affection, comprehension and action'.[67] This scepticism then extends to the political capacity and suspicion of *any* image. At its heart seems to be a misunderstanding of the relationship between images, emotions, beliefs and action, based on a relatively straightforward link from cinematic representation via audience identification towards audiences' behaviour and opinions on factual torture. The 'pedagogical model'[68] of art misrecognises the cinematic experience and the relationship between film and audience. It grants both too much transformative power to the film – neglecting how a film may crystallise already existing social debates – and too little agency to the spectator. Underestimating viewers (and overestimating the exception of the critic) leaves little space for potential changes in viewers' responses, both within a film, or with repeated viewings, as both film and spectator move through time. While there are legitimate concerns over power dynamics and the weight of privilege present in compassion, as well as the threat of de-politicising political or juridical claims through a personal dimension,[69] much scholarship on film violence tends to view the arousal of affective emotions in cinema with suspicion. Compare Michelle Aaron's damning conclusion that 'externally displayed emotions and ... emotive reactions are 'our bit' in the economy of spectatorship and visual culture; in a sense, we relinquish ethical investment by shedding tears [which] disavow us of any potential responsibility for those images'.[70]

Perhaps the disappointment derives at least in part from expecting too much of the wrong thing of cinema, such as behavioural change. After all, even the seemingly innocuous assumption that empathy with the victim will foster ethical and pro-social behaviour is surprisingly difficult to verify empirically.[71] The question of emotions is often resolved by distinguishing between the instinctual affective response of a spectator who enjoys screen torture as guilty pleasure, stilling a 'primitive urge for retributive justice'[72] or indulging in self-righteous 'empty empathy',[73] and the evocation of refined empathy as a 'higher-evolved'[74] emotional state, genuine empathy for the other person, empathy with awareness and choice.[75] But it is not convincing that our affects or instincts should be more easily tricked than our cognitive – potentially ideologically deluded – faculties.[76] Accordingly, this book considers both affects and emotions as sociocultural constructs *as well as* neurological categories, as distinctive yet interacting 'points on a continuum going from body to mind'.[77]

Likewise, film scholarship has expanded a rigid, passive and one-way model of 'identification' towards more fluid, non-binary concepts of subjectivity, and reframed forms of vision in ways that do not equate seeing with a possessive gaze.[78] Violent images in particular often seem to grasp us affectively. A focus on the affective dimension of the cinematic experience pays attention to what is invisible beyond 'the conventional claim of making visible the invisible' – to overcome an optical imperative which 'overlook(s) the complex interrelationship of seeing and not seeing',[79] to go beyond a structurally inbuilt complicity. This book operates with a conception of spectatorship that seeks to account for cultural differences in the reception and impact of an image or film. Departing from an embodied viewer and informed by the affective turn in contemporary scholarship, throughout this book I ask how the films offer a potential, an opening to link an individual spectator's subjectivity and personal memory to a collective history.

In contemporary memory scholarship, a number of terms have emerged to describe various memory modes, to help account for diverse ways of experiencing and remembering, and the shifting state of memory/-ies. This volume also operates with memory as a malleable figure: the term is used not to denote a personal storage of truth, or a realistic registration of past events, but a pool of cultural images and narratives that are changing with each re-telling, overlap with cultural knowledge and factual history, that do not replace but exist alongside individual or collectively asserted memories. Such 'liquid' memories may be shared among various pools of audiences. The requirement to appeal to and allow for different points of access for diverse groups finds expression, especially in the hybridity of certain cinematic texts. While the films are produced and consumed in a global world, they also remain historically and politically grounded in specific cultural and national situations. Especially in the scholarship on Chilean film, memory remains a key figure both in the film texts and in their reception context, linking the social to the personal level.[80] Transnational pointers reside alongside national or social imaginaries, local meanings. Linking textual analysis to a contextual reading of the historical and social context, to the presence and reception of existing iconographies in the public sphere, helps us explore how a treatment of torture looks and feels, offering a way to 'think not *against* the movies or *about* them but *with* them'.[81]

Figure I.1 Memorial for the disappeared, *Nostalgia de la luz*.

Matter and Form

As examples of existing documentation in the public sphere, the Abu Ghraib images are examined in detail, as well as archive material on the violence committed by the Pinochet dictatorship. This material includes footage of the presidential palace being bombed, and images of the estimated 3–4,000 *detenidos desaparecidos*, known as the 'disappeared' in English.[82] Changes in the 'careers' of these iconic images over time – new and additional images and information, recontextualisation and reframing in films – have now also become part of their biography, alongside the original events they are based on.[83] Reading films in conjunction with such other visual texts highlights common concerns around how historical experiences, factual evidence and memories can be represented. The analysis of media content, practices and cultures asks us to be mindful of the specificities of each form, but the ongoing dialogues and interrelations between these forms are just as important, as people experience culture in a transmedia form and as cultural products inseminate one another.

In his volume about war films, David LaRocca argues that the relationship between war and film encompasses a variety of aesthetic phenomena and poses a combination of ethical quandaries that go far beyond definitional problems in terms of genre.[84] Following LaRocca's strategy, I have expanded the scope of what counts as a film 'about' torture. This has allowed me to include films that address issues such as social impunity or emotional pain; films which indict the system that allows or fosters torture; films which enable us to perceive the long-term effects of torture on perception, thought and language.

Similarly, despite the tendency to discuss ethics in documentary and fiction on entirely different terms, the ethical urgency of the subject matter affects both fiction and nonfiction films. Striking a balance between real

Figure I.2 Coup of 11 September 1973: bombing of *La Moneda* (© licensed under the Creative Commons Attribution 3.0 Chile; Biblioteca del Congreso Nacional).

Figure I.3 Quema de Libros/Chile, 1973 (© public domain, Wikimedia Commons).

Figure I.4 Poster protesting disappearances (Mujeres de la Agrupación de Familiares Desaparecidos se manifiestan frente al Palacio de Gobierno durante el Régimen Militar de Pinochet © Kena Lorenzini – Museum of Memory and Human Rights, CC BY-SA 3.0)

and imagined, between poetic truth and historical accuracy, is precisely what the films chosen here are engaged with, transcending a dichotomy of documentary truth versus fictional imaginary. These films are either identified as fiction, but explicitly engaging with factual events, or they fall under the heading of documentaries but prominently include fictional elements in their aesthetic strategies. Besides this referential aspect, the selected films are further demarcated by their relatively recent production, with occasional forays into later productions when appropriate.[85] The demarcation lines were set between 2004 and 2014: in 2004 the images from Abu Ghraib images went viral, while a Chilean film set during the dictatorship, the first after a long hiatus in such topics in fiction film, became a sudden hit (*Machuca*, Andres Wood, 2004).

* * *

In the first instance, this book is organised as a movement from visually present torture towards such films in which the visual *presence* of torture is not the main access point, or rather, which feature the *presence of absence* or the process of *being made invisible*. The first half of this book begins with the representation of torture, with films that grapple with the visual material presence of images of torture in the collective pool of memory. Given that this kind of documentation is absent in Chile, the first Chilean films will appear relatively late in this volume. Yet the analyses of the lateral approaches towards these absences and ways of making absences present and felt eventually helps us rethink the absences in the US films as well.

Chapter 1 is dedicated to one of the most contested post-9/11 films, *Zero Dark Thirty* (Kathryn Bigelow, 2012). Building on existing scholarship both on torture – especially Elaine Scarry, Jennifer Ballengee and Page DuBois – and on the film itself, my analysis links detailed close readings with an evaluation as to its adherence or departure from the structure of torture's hypocrisies and double binds. Further analytical emphasis is paid to the alliance of documentary and fictional aesthetic and the kind of cinematic experience generated through the film's protagonist, Maya, as affective, and affectively empty, proxy for the audience. Textual analysis demonstrates how the film is strategically laced with ambivalences, which helps us understand why the film's position on torture has been subject to so much controversy.

Beyond the potential invitations to 'identify' either with torturers or with victims, Chapter 2 expands on the theme of the witness – key to torture and to cinema – through protagonists, viewers, diegetic truth-telling machines, the film itself. Close readings of *Rendition* (Gavin Hood, 2007) and *Body of Lies* (Ridley Scott, 2008) explore how the films address this key visual metaphor, supported by research on the witness and mediated witnessing, and scholarship on how current films express contemporary violence through different kinds of images that reflect 'a regime change in media as well as military control'.[86]

Chapters 3 and 4, on torture in television series, provide the link between US and Chilean audiovisual production. A show like *24* (Fox, 2001–10), whose legacy was partly renegotiated in *Homeland* (Showtime, 2011–20[87]), had an undeniable impact on the public imagination of torture, while popular Chilean television shows such as *Los Archivos del Cardenal* (TVN, 2011–14) and *Los 80* (Canal 13, 2008–14) clearly addressed social memories of the dictatorship, which remain largely absent from the movie screen. Precisely the characteristics of contemporary serial television – its breadth of audience reach, its 'rhetoric of discussion', and its sophisticated narratives – allow for wider audiences and the kind of emotional involvement through which the political can be worked into a public space.

As the second half of the book moves towards epistemological territory, Chapter 5 discusses the changing status of the image in relation to the infamous digital photographs of torture that emerged from Abu Ghraib, and their exploration in *Standard Operating Procedure* (Errol Morris, 2008). Read alongside the director's subsequent *The Unknown Known* (Errol Morris, 2013), I analyse how both films investigate the ways in which media create and shape our perception of the event 'torture at Abu Ghraib' and the role played by language in this process, applying research by Elizabeth Dauphinée, Seymour Hersh and Anne McClintock, among others.

Both US and Chilean films explore the capacity of their own medium in the making and telling of historical events. Where the US films discussed here reflect on and negotiate the changes in our mediated ocularcentric epistemology mainly through a changed visual imagery to accommodate today's 'radically changed logistics of perception that includes many more types of images',[88] as well as camerawork and continuity, the Chilean films employ various aesthetic strategies to reconfigure what is considered unspeakable. Some of these films seek to not only render visible the missing referents, but to even translate 'the erasure of the erasure', the processes of being made invisible. Here, the affective turn in memory and film scholarship helps frame how these films invite different ways of seeing and understanding both history and contemporary social toxicity; while the analysis of Chilean film generally is supported by brilliant Latin American scholars such as Verónica Cortínez and Manfred Engelbert, Macarena Gómez-Barris, Nelly Richard, Carolina Urrutia, Miriam Haddu and Joanna Page.

The textual analysis of *Pena de Muerte/Death Penalty* (Tevo Díaz, 2012), and *Carne de Perro/Dogflesh* (Fernando Guzzoni, 2012) in Chapter 6 employs Davina Quinlivan's expansion of Laura Marks's concept of haptic visuality and Sara Ahmed's model of the circulation of emotions. By activating sensual modes of seeing, these films help to expand our parameters of 'seeing' and thereby connecting to the past.

Recent Chilean cinema is frequently read in historical lineage with post-traumatic melancholy or in line with a general realist tendency in 'world cinema',[89] but should also be contextualised with contemporary cultural, economic and social factors that influence and limit the selection and aesthetic treatment of subject matter in Chilean cinema. The analysis of the dominant use of realist aesthetics in *Post Mortem* (Pablo Larraín, 2010), *Tony Manero* (Pablo Larraín, 2008) and *La Danza de la Realidad/The Dance of Reality* (Alejandro Jodorowsky, 2013) in Chapter 7 is complemented by such a contextual reading, providing transnational and historical connections, local supplementary associations and specific alienations in a neoliberal society, to explore the conditions that generate these striking aesthetic choices as well as the possible meanings they evoke.

Chapter 8 explores how *Nostalgia de la luz/Nostalgia for the Light* (Patricio Guzmán, 2010) and *NO* (Pablo Larraín, 2012), made by the two most internationally famous Chilean directors, employ profilmic people, spaces, objects but also the material body of the films themselves in order to anchor their link to the 'real'. Contextualised with academic work on the role and ontology of cinema after the digital turn, I discuss these films as responses to a crisis of faith in dominant epistemological systems, set within a debilitating moment in the global and local memory landscape, building on Jaimie Baron's work on the archive and research on the 'nostalgic turn'.

The focus on epistemological strategies that are not based on the visual inevitably lends a self-reflexive dimension to these films. In different ways, they all expound the difficulty of accessing historical truth and doing justice to memory. But they can also be read as statements about the ethical potential of cinema. For the analyses presented here, the recalculations of the affective turn have provided venues of interventions that might help formulate a different kind of (visual) politics, which seeks to escape some of the overly politicised tendencies parameters in either cinema's scholarship. If history in postmodern time is defined as fact-based but nevertheless mainly as experience, expanding on Fredric Jameson's 'history is what hurts',[90] one might be tempted to say, 'history is how it feels'. Yet the films do not offer *History* per se – clearly limiting claims to capital-letter truth – but an invitation to establish a different relationship with and a personal connection to the past through an emotional experience, in a way that is responsible and responsive to the facts of this past. These films expose and tap into deep fissures in their respective societies in this regard, speaking both about the history they depict and to the present moment of their production, reminding us that memory is always about the present because 'we do not remember the past ... we "remember" what remains living within our situations now'.[91]

Notes

1. Eltit and Jung, 'Pain and Writing', pp. 206–7 and pp. 216–17.
2. As 'Abu Ghraib' has become a shorthand for the entire CIA programme and the torture that happened under US occupation, I will use the umbrella term as a reference point to the visual documentation of these events in various places.
3. For instance, Collins, 'State Terror and the Law'.
4. Cf. Draper, 'The Business of Memory'.
5. Gómez-Barris, *Where Memory Dwells*, p. 100.
6. Žižek, 'Hollywood's Gift'.
7. Rosenstone, *History on film/film on history*.
8. Schillings, *Enemies of All Humankind*. Kahn, 'Torture and the Dream of Reason'.
9. Cf. Rejali, 'Convenient Truths', p. 234.
10. DuBois, *Torture and Truth*, p. 154.

11. Cf. Williams, *A Very British Killing*. Devji, 'Torture at the Limits of Politics'.
12. Sands, *Torture Team*, p. 22. Black sites have become spaces devoid of law, where 'legal exceptionalism' is enacted via 'spatial exceptionalism'. Marks, 'Logic and Language of Torture', p. 67–8.
13. Agamben, *Homo Sacer*.
14. The increasing preference for 'clean' or 'lite' techniques which do not leave easily traceable physical signs, make it harder for survivors to seek legal consequences, cf. Rejali, 'Convenient Truths', p. 229.
15. Del Rosso, *Talking about Torture*, p. 23.
16. Gordon, 'The United States Military Prison'; Cusac, *Cruel and Unusual*; Carby, 'A Strange and Bitter Crop'.
17. The British army tortured in Kenya, the French in Algeria, the French and USA in Vietnam; the USA used torture against Native Americans, during interventions in Central America, the Caribbean and the Philippines. Cf. Rejali, *Torture and Democracy*; Kleinhans, 'Imagining Torture'. British intelligence used techniques against the IRA that at least bordered on torture. Cf. Pitzer, *One Long Night*.
18. Cf. Bass, 'Counterinsurgency and Torture'.
19. McClintock, 'Paranoid Empire'.
20. Cavanaugh, 'Making Enemies', pp. 312–14.
21. Butler, *Frames of War*, p. 126.
22. Chilean sociologist Tomas Moulian deconstructed the discourse on Chile as political, social and racial/ethnic exception. Similarly, Lessie Jo Frazier suggested that to isolate the violence under the Pinochet dictatorship as a traumatic aberration in Chilean history obscures continuities in the process of nation-state formation. Moulian, *Chile Actual*; Frazier, *Salt*, p. 17; cf. Portales, *Los Mitos De La Democracia Chilena*. For a reading on how the discourse of American exceptionalism permits to condemn torture while affirming superiority, cf. Adelman, 'Tangled Complicities', p. 367.
23. Beverley, 'Torture and Human Rights', p. 312. Cf. Klein, *The Shock Doctrine*.
24. Cavanaugh, 'Making enemies', p. 308.
25. Gordon, *Ghostly Matters*, p. 124.
26. Brodsky, *On Grief and Reason*, p. 144.
27. Reyes et al., *Tortura durante la transición a la democracia*, p. 23.
28. Executive Order No. 13,823 (30 January 2018); Jacobs, 'Donald Trump on waterboarding'.
29. Sznajder and Roniger, *The Politics of Exile in Latin America*, p. 160.
30. In March 2016, Chile's National Institute for Human Rights (*Instituto Nacional de Derechos Humanos* [*INDH*]) accused the police of using torture against indigenous people. 'INDH presenta querella por torturas'.
31. 'Chile: Police Reforms Needed'.
32. UN General Assembly Convention Against Torture, *CAT* (emphasis added). For criticism on the exclusions and limitations of law with regards to torture,

see Shue and Luban, 'Mental Torture'. Williams, 'Atrocity and the Pain in Law'.
33. For instance, the US had prosecuted Japanese for the use of 'water treatment' in World War Two.
34. After being leaked in 2004, most of these memos were 'withdrawn'. Cf. Farrell, *The Prohibition of Torture*.
35. Greenwald, 'The Suppressed Fact'.
36. Cavanaugh, 'Making enemies', p. 314.
37. A concession made to the Republican minority on the Committee, which eventually refused to participate anyway.
38. Cf. Soufan, *The Black Banner*; Mayer, 'The Black Sites'.
39. The CIA offered false information to the Department of Justice, to Congress, which was supposed to oversee it, and to the executive branch, about the efficacy of their clandestine programmes.
40. Timm, 'CIA's Torture Experts Now Use Their Skills in Secret Drones Program'.
41. Mazzetti and Savage, 'Trump Administration Returns Copies of Report'; Bowcott, Holmes and Durkin, 'Bolton threatens sanctions'.
42. Rosenberg, 'Gina Haspel'; Sorkin, 'Gina Haspel and the Enduring Questions About Torture'.
43. Anthony Romero in Savage, 'Harsher Security Tactics?'.
44. Rosenberg, Carol, *Guantánamo Trials*.
45. Hutchings, 'Spectacularizing Crime', p. 13. Lithwick, 'Throwing Away the Key'.
46. Bond, *Frames of Memory*, p. 145.
47. Melley, 'Zero Dark Democracy', p. 19.
48. Cf. Verdugo, *De la tortura no se habla*; Hayner, *Unspeakable Truths*; Collins, 'Prosecuting Pinochet'; Stern, *Reckoning with Pinochet*.
49. Behind these odd rules was the attempt to frame Valech in a way that allowed the creation of a second commission without recanting on the previous claim that torture was unprovable. As these testimonies have been classified as confidential (the names of the perpetrators are redacted), they cannot be used in trials concerning human rights violations and associations of ex-political prisoners have been denied access.
50. Simms, *Paul Ricoeur*, p. 120.
51. For instance, constitutional reforms got under way, such as an amendment in 2005 that abolished appointed senators. Cf. Collins, 'Human Rights Trials in Chile'; Fajardo, *Los militares que se opusieron al golpe*. Collins, 'Human Rights Trials in Chile During and after the "Pinochet Years"'; Collins, 'State Terror and the Law'.
52. Stern, *Reckoning with Pinochet*. Marking a position distinctly different from earlier negations, the army's commander-in-chief Emilio Cheyre admitted to massive and systematic torture under the dictatorship and characterised the practice as unjustifiable. Cheyre, 'Ejército de Chile'. Winn suggests that this

mea culpa was more significant for the dismantling of such narratives than the report itself. Winn, 'El pasado'.
53. Villa Grimaldi was saved from destruction by private groups; Londres 38, situated in the heart of Santiago, is funded modestly and privately; the National Stadium was unsentimentally re-purposed, only a little plaque reminds of its role during the dictatorship. Cf. Draper, 'The Business of Memory', p. 128. Jacobsen and Lorenzo, *La imagen quebrada*; Villarroel and Mardones, *Señales contra el olvido*.
54. Cf. Mitnick, 'La persistencia'; Richard and Arrate, 'Las derrotas'.
55. Bourke, *The Story of Pain*, p. 30.
56. Peter Lunenfeld in Sobchack, 'The Charge of the Real', p. 259.
57. For instance: Doane, 'The Indexical and the Concept of Medium Specificity'; Elsaesser, 'Digital Hollywood'; Gunning, 'Moving Away from the Index'; Rodowick, *Virtual Life of Film*.
58. For instance, Murray Smith, '*The Battle of Algiers:* Colonial Struggle and Collective Allegiance'. See also Chapter 4, note 21 and Chapter 7, note 56. Some examples on more recent cinema: McCoy, 'Beyond Susan Sontag'; Chaudhuri, 'Documenting the Dark Side'; Bächler, *Inszenierte Bedrohung*; McSweeney, *The 'War on Terror' and American Film*; Flynn and Salek, *Screening Torture;* Hammond, *Screens of Terror*; Holloway, *9/11 and the War on Terror*.
59. Walsh, 'What stories we tell', p. 162; Agee cited in Schoonover, *Brutal Vision*, p. 106.
60. Kahn, 'Torture and the Dream of Reason': Kahn, *Sacred Violence*.
61. Rejali, 'Convenient Truths'; Rejali, *Torture and Democracy*.
62. Williams, *A Very British Killing*.
63. Bass, 'Counterinsurgency and Torture', p. 234; Nacos, 'The Image of Evil'.
64. McCoy, 'Beyond Susan Sontag', p. 126. Both McCoy and Chaudhuri quote a spokesman from *Human Rights First* who argued that 'today the good guys torture'.
65. Shaw, *Cinematic Terror*, p. 285; Holloway, *9/11 and the War on Terror*.
66. Devji, 'Torture at the Limits of Politics', p. 253. Cf. Shaw, *Cinematic Terror*; Nacos, 'The Image of Evil'.
67. Rancière, *The Emancipated Spectator*, p. 103.
68. Rancière, *Dissensus*, p. 136.
69. Berlant, Compassion; Brown and Rafter, 'Genocide Films'; Bond, *Frames of Memory*.
70. Aaron quoted in Straw, 'The Guilt Zone', p. 102.
71. Moses, 'Empathy and Dis-Empathy in Political Conflict', p. 136. Coplan and Goldie, 'Introduction'. There is actually no track record of even politically activist documentaries leading to social change. Cf. Gaines, 'Political Mimesis'.
72. Bacon, *Film Violence*.
73. Kaplan, *Trauma Culture*, p. 93.

74. Aaron, *Spectatorship*, p. 180.
75. Cf. LaCapra, *Writing History, Writing Trauma*; also Didi-Huberman, *Images in Spite of All*; Nowak, 'The Complicated History of Einfühlung'; Coplan, 'Understanding Empathy'.
76. As highlighted by the work of cognitivist film scholars; the challenge posed by cultural anthropologists to positioning a predominant Western conception of emotions as universal; or historical accounts of the genesis of emotions.
77. Labanyi, 'Doing Things', p. 224.
78. For this volume, this refers especially to the work by phenomenologists such as Vivan Sobchack and Laura Marks; cognitivist scholars (Murray Smith, Greg M. Smith, Carl Plantinga), Brian Massumi and Sara Ahmed, as well as the early Steven Shaviro.
79. Minh-ha, 'The Image and the Void', p. 131.
80. See, for instance Claudia Bossay, Walescka Pino-Ojeda, Zuzana Pick, Jaqueline Mouesca.
81. Aguilar, *New Argentine Film*, p. 3, emphasis in the original.
82. The initial formulation 'detenidos desaparecidos' denoted the political character of the repression. In the following, I will speak about the disappeared without quotes.
83. Cf. Mitchell on the 'Abu Ghraib Archive' in *Cloning Terror*.
84. LaRocca, 'Introduction,' p. 38.
85. The main exception to this timeline is the ongoing TV show *Homeland*, and here the analytical focus rests on the first two seasons.
86. White, 'Heaven Knows We're Digital Now', p. 5.
87. Although *Homeland* has been ongoing at time of writing and therefore challenges the outlined timeline, the analysis will focus on the title sequence of the early seasons as representative 'narrative images' of themes relevant to the entire show.
88. Pisters, 'Logistics of Perception 2.0', p. 237.
89. Cf. Chapter 7, note 30.
90. Cited in Williams, 'Mirrors without Memories', p. 10.
91. Olick et al., *The Collective Memory Reader*, p. 196.

CHAPTER 1

Visible Torture: The Case of *Zero Dark Thirty*

Kathryn Bigelow's *Zero Dark Thirty* (*Zero*) was released into a public space already flooded with narratives and images of the historical events it references: the 9/11 terror attacks, the detention camp in Guantánamo Bay, the torture at Abu Ghraib. The film was thoroughly cross-examined in relation to its historical (in)accuracy and the graphic visibility of its torture scenes, while its aesthetic and formal strategies *in relation to* this visual pool of knowledge received considerably less attention, to the extent that its alleged politics was turned into ammunition for contradicting stances on US policy. Yet close textual analysis of key moments in the film demonstrate that there is a significant amount of ambivalence built into the cinematic text. The systematic layering of *Zero* with such conceptual ambiguities creates what Elsaesser called conceptual 'double binds', which help to explain the contradictory readings of the film.

Zero Dark Thirty (*Zero*) condenses the decade-long manhunt for Osama bin Laden into two and a half hours made up of investigative work, the interrogation and torture of prisoners, sifting through wrong leads and dead ends, and the eventual discovery of the al Qaida leader's compound in Pakistan. The film culminates with a Navy SEAL team's nighttime raid and the killing of bin Laden in May 2011. In interviews, the makers of *Zero* have described their film as 'journalistic' and as a 'reported film'. Following journalist terminology, the film's epigraph asserts: 'The following motion picture is based on first hand accounts of actual events'. Bigelow claims to have taken pains to depict the events leading to the capture of bin Laden 'truthfully', a word she frequently employs in interviews, and which is echoed by protagonist Maya in *Zero*.

While Bigelow points out that 'depiction is not endorsement', she has been echoing the CIA's line of defence: that we cannot know whether the US would have captured bin Laden without using what she described as 'harsh interrogation techniques'.[1] Likewise, screenwriter Mark Boal insists that *Zero* is 'a movie, not a documentary'. Yet both Boal and Bigelow *do* advance a claim on the historical real. As Alex Gibney points out, 'Fictionalised "movies" purporting to be based on historical events are not exempt from questions of "truthfulness"'.[2]

This touted fidelity to historical facts provided fodder for the debate following the film's release and the makers' focus on historical accuracy. But what do we mean by historical truthfulness? The 'boots on the ground experience'?[3] The 'maniacal' fidelity to indexical place, which 'extended to building a perfect replica of bin Laden's huge compound, brick for brick'?[4] The truth about the alleged utility of torture? To lean on Rosenstone, 'what truth? The factual truth, the narrative truth, the emotional truth, the psychological truth, the symbolic truth?'[5]

Following Rosenstone and Žižek, we can look at what films say about the history they depict or what they say about the present moment of their production, and also what they say about themselves and their role in this process. Given the close temporal proximity between the film's release and the events it depicts, *Zero* is better understood as a political actor in itself, actively *shaping* not only the perception of the past, but the ongoing history of these events.

The Torture Debates

The debate that anticipated and succeeded *Zero*'s theatrical release in 2012 repeated the debate that followed the publication of the Abu Ghraib images in 2004; it was reprised when the Senate released parts of its investigation into the programme at the end of 2014. All these debates, as well as the so-called 'Torture report' itself, focused on the *utility* of torture: the question whether the torture programme had produced 'results' in the form of intelligence.

Apologists argued that it was enough if torture 'works' *sometimes* for it to be considered a legitimate tool – to be regulated and supervised, but acceptable nevertheless.[6] Opponents countered that even discussing utility was unethical: 'Torture – like murder – is categorically wrong no matter what benefits it produces'.[7] Several progressive journalists attempted to disprove torture's utility by volunteering to undergo waterboarding; predictably, they emerged to describe its horrors.[8] Of course, it is impossible to conduct experiments that would actually adhere to scientific standards (empirical, double-blind, peer-reviewed …). Such well-intentioned stunts do create some vaguely titillating footage but fail to redefine the agenda or convince proponents of torture, who are well aware of its painfulness.

Finally, the official CIA line of defence suggests that the efficacy of the torture programme has been, at best, 'unknowable'. The CIA issued a statement that both disputes a pro-torture interpretation of the film and leaves the question of torture's potential utility wide open.

> The film creates the strong impression that the enhanced interrogation techniques that were part of our former detention and interrogation program were the key to finding Bin Ladin. [sic] That impression is false ... whether enhanced interrogation techniques were the only timely and effective way to obtain information from those detainees, as the film suggests, is a matter of debate *that cannot and never will be definitively resolved*.[9]

This insinuation – that the programme may somehow have helped in tracking down Osama bin Laden – has been contested in no uncertain terms by the Senate Report. Moreover, among seasoned interrogators, there is consensus that the testimony obtained by torture is notoriously unreliable. The tortured might be ignorant, lie or confess to what they believe the torturers want to hear. Why then do we not only keep torturing but also keep pretending that the objective of torture is intelligence-gathering?

In her seminal *The Body in Pain*, Elaine Scarry describes how we 'misdescribe' violent activities such as war and torture. Torture affirms something beyond its alleged purpose: its goal is not to gain information but to win the contest over the social imagination by reinforcing power relations through the production of certain bodies as 'torturable'.[10] Torture targets a social body, an audience beyond those immediately hurt.

And yet, as Darius Rejali points out, both opponents and supporters of torture remain invested in maintaining 'convenient truths' about torture.[11] One of these central falsities is the notion that the prime purpose of torture is to 'make people talk', whether torture is framed as a tool able to break biological defences (the torturers in *Zero* claim that 'everybody talks – it's biology') or one that produces unreliable information (opponents of torture in *Rendition* fear that 'people will say anything on the rack'). In fact, the tortured person's words do not matter for the torture to be 'productive'. As a rhetorical tool, its truth is performative, not factual. The performance of torture creates its own reality where lies, confession or silence each play a part. It is not the actual reliability of torture that matters but rather the display of power and installation of fear in the targeted social body.

The debates' focus on discussing the claim that torture produces intelligence is not only a short-circuited intellectual fallacy but also works to cement torture's 'political fiction',[12] namely the claim that producing intelligence is in fact the purpose of torture. This conceptual dead end also explains the conundrum circled in the 'torture debates': how torture can be both a tool that makes people say anything – and one that fails, as some people never 'crack'.

If what matters is not actual evidence, but 'the *perception* that evidence was obtained through the use of torture',[13] insights on the phenomenology of perception should be but rarely are acknowledged in wider public debates. 'War and security analysts attribute the results and limits of perception to the lack of a clear view of the terrains of battle ... [they] impute the fog of war to external conditions rather than collectively engendered mentalities'.[14]

Mirroring these failures of perception in the broader public debate, initial discussions of *Zero* largely focused on the disputed utility of torture, as well as the depiction of the torturers and the torture as spectacle. The attacks levelled against the film were fierce, caused precisely by the aesthetic decisions in handling the incendiary subject matter, and concluded that the film condoned or provided an apology for real political torture,[15] as 'many critics fixat[ed] on the dramatic and/or ideological impact of the images of torture'.[16]

This complex piece of cinema, however, warrants detailed critical attention as a historical and political actor in its own right. To the extent that *Zero* has created a recognisable visual iconography, it has become part of a transnational pool of screen images, the film has become part of the event 'US torture in Iraq'.[17] I argue that *Zero* provides less an explanatory or justifying narrative than an aesthetic experience of ambiguity through the inscription of strategic double binds, which invite a Western audience to explore their feelings, especially through the emotional Rorschach test provided in the figure of Maya.

Double Binds

Zero opens with audio footage of the 9/11 terrorist attacks on the World Trade Center in New York, which is immediately followed by a long torture sequence. Through this chronological juxtaposition, the 9/11 attacks are positioned as the starting point and torture as defensive reaction. Four more terrorist attacks will punctuate the narrative trajectory, and briefer torture sequences are sandwiched in between. No external or additional information on these acts of terrorism is presented, but their presence sustains the impression of threat as well as the imperative to kill bin Laden. Framing terrorism as cause of and justification for torture suggests that if you eradicate one, the other will go away – a closure not backed by political reality. Through this 'neat chapter-like structure', Westwell argues, the film offers fictitious transparency and reduces historical complexity.[18] To tell of torture this way helps to perpetuate a historical amnesia and ignores the long US history of using, exporting and funding torture.[19] Omitted are also dissenting voices *within* the government and its agencies, and the fights about the (il)legality of the practice at the time that the real CIA torture programme was implemented.

After the epigraph, the film opens with a black screen and actual audio recordings of distress calls of people trapped in the World Trade Center towers. The original footage moves from criss-cross static to intelligible sound material as 'September 11, 2001' is blended onto the black screen, situating the spectator temporally, and unmistakably evoking the iconic 9/11 visuals in the spectator's mind. This strategy avoids, perhaps, a retraumatisation,[20] the fatigue which the much-repeated footage might have provoked, while preserving the legitimising power of the index on the less familiar sound footage.

As Eric Sundquist points out with regards to the attempted 'non-mediation' of holocaust narrative, the 'unknowability' of the event can in itself become a trope.[21] The 'unrepresentable' of 9/11 is frequently expressed with a cut or fade to black, an absent image paired with archive sound – for instance in *Fahrenheit 9/11* (Michael Moore, 2004) and *United 93* (Paul Greengrass, 2006). Apart from the danger of becoming clichéd, this aesthetic codification works only on an audience familiar with the original images, and implies a shared reading of the events as consensual mass trauma for all of the Western world.[22]

In the colour of mourning, the black screen creates a sense of foreboding or doom, evoking also the ending and beginning of a film, or of a 'dead' camera, whose 'eye' is broken. The 9/11 soundscape evokes a different level of traumatic indexicality, which points to a specific moment in the past.[23] While the attacks had been choreographed specifically for visual media, the experience itself was shaped at least as much by other senses, such as sound, smell and taste. By evoking these sense memories, the audio footage induces viewers to recall the first time of seeing and experiencing these images and creates a personal, affective entry into the film. With the usually privileged visual sense blocked, our awareness of and attention to other senses is enhanced. At the same time, this strategy draws attention to the aspect that is missing and thereby creates 'presence by absence'.

The progression of terror in the footage functions like an auditory long take, as the callers' comprehension of their situation increases, culminating with a female caller locked in the burning towers, moments before her death. The sequence ends on that call being disconnected, and the emergency call worker whispering, aghast: 'Oh my God …' We hear the voice of the woman trapped in the burning towers, moments before – as an auditory *futur antérieur* – she *will have died*. The audio tapes can be comprehended as the perspective of those locked in the tower, who have no knowledge – no clear vision – of what has happened. The audience is put in experiential alignment with those 'trapped in the dark', but we know what has and what will happen, and they do not – a disparity in knowledge that is a classic staple of the tragedy. We know, but like a backward-facing Cassandra, are sentenced to helplessly experience it all over again.

This two-minute-long footage is followed by the first and longest torture sequence of the film, which stretches to slightly over twenty minutes. As this sequence begins, two graphic titles – '2 years later' and 'The Saudi Group' – orientate the viewer temporally, but not spatially. The condensation of two years in real time into two seconds of screen time 'establishes a direct correlation between terrorist atrocity and the unbridled CIA response, lending urgency to the investigation and legitimacy to torture'.[24]

The first image shows a hole in the ceiling of a dark space, a short shot that is reminiscent of the haptic 'easing in' of opening shots, symbolic in its connotations of heaven, a yearning for freedom, from a point of view that can be associated with that of the (still unknown) prisoner. Off-screen sounds of footsteps and a metal door opening are audible. In the next shot, the camera rapidly pans along a row of blurred, camouflaged faces to focus on an unmasked man entering, followed by another figure whose face is concealed with a balaclava, who is later revealed to be protagonist Maya. A short close-up of her masked face centres the spectator's attention on her eyes. In a quietly edited sequence, the unmasked man approaches the prisoner and says: 'I own you, Ammar. You belong to me'. An over-the-shoulder shot shows the prisoner's bruised face, then medium shots alternate between Ammar and the man, who begins a monologue that escalates into a shouting rant, during which Ammar is pushed from side to side, while the agent, talking nonstop, circles him, establishing his freedom of movement. In a fast-paced montage, images flash by, fragments of Ammar's body – his hands, his legs and feet – as he is dragged along the floor, then strung up by the arms. As Ammar is being tied up, his captors are seen leaving in the background. The camera lingers for a moment, the frame of the image crowded by the guards' blurred outlines in the foreground, while the exiting agents are sharply silhouetted against the light pouring in from outside.

Only in the next scene does the audience receive an expository reading on the situation. Standing in a sunny area outside a white edifice, the shouting man is introduced as CIA agent Dan, who explains the situation to the now-unmasked character, the novice Maya, who has 'just arrived from Washington in her best suit'. We see a surveillance screen depicting the interior of the prison cell. Already, watching and access to vision are configured as absolutely central: when Dan suggests that Maya should stay outside and watch the process in mediated form on the surveillance screen, she refuses. Control over the prisoner's body includes control of his vision: he is hooded or told where to look. 'Look at me!' Dan shouts repeatedly, and his prisoner's refusal to obey seems to imply infuriating remnants of a free will. In the next shot, the intertitle 'Black Site: Undisclosed Location' is blended in over a nondescript image of the building from an elevated angle, offering spatial information that is in equal measures informative and obscure.

These torture sequences seem physical and intimate in nature, archaic in their brutality. The film creates a tension between visual physicality and verbally expressed rationale. Torturer Dan offers quasi-scientific rationalisations, professionalism and intellectual purpose.[25] Dan's pronounced physical proximity to Ammar is emphasised in a number of shots, such as close-ups of Dan taking his prisoner's hands, which would seem intimate, even loving, were the context different. But Ammar's hands are bound, and Dan is peeling away his prisoner's fingers from a juice bottle he is clutching. In another scene Dan holds Ammar from behind, to release his overstretched bound arms – before putting a dog-collar on him. At play is a perversion of the codes of social relations, what Scarry describes as torture's 'unmaking' of civilisation: the function of objects, physical intimacy and the act of helping, are corrupted and turned into instruments of torture.

Initially, Dan and Ammar are filmed from the same medium-level distance in over-the-shoulder framings. During and after the physical torture, Ammar is increasingly framed in extreme close-up: his bruised face, gasping for air or hidden under a towel. Interspersed are medium shots and close-ups of Maya watching in the background, often 'neutrally' positioned between Dan and Ammar. Objects in shallow focus frame and centre Maya's face.

Over the course of this sequence, the viewer's point of view correlates with various perspectives. Initially, the audience shares the disorientated experience of the prisoner. Next, we are told information *about* him: his name, Ammar. The following images, fragments of Ammar's body as well as the shots of Maya's face, could again be read as Ammar's point of view and his attempts at gauging the situation. Mostly though, the camera seems to show the perspective of an unknown first person, unidentified with any character in the film. For instance, the camera swivels in increasingly hectic fashion between Dan and Ammar, as if attempting to follow their exchange, then it attempts to follow Ammar's body being pushed around, 'crouches down' to be on a level with the torturing action, and finally tilts up to peer into Maya's face.

As painful as it is to watch the torture sequence, worse images of violence are available on screens every day. Much violence and humiliation in *Zero* remains off-screen. For example, the characters remark that the prisoner 'soiled' himself, and his pants are being pulled down; as this happens outside the frame of the image, the audience is not made to participate visually in these sexually charged humiliations. The victim does not become a visual spectacle, but the ghosts of Abu Ghraib, Bagram, Guantánamo, black sites and rendition practices hover in the audience's consciousness. The haunting quality of these scenes does not originate in any indexical power of the images but is derived from the *knowledge* of the relationship between the depicted scene and the real world. This explains both the acrimonious battle over historical veracity and the oppositional interpretations of the film, as the audience's 'pre-existing (political) condition' shape their interpretation of the scenes. More than the graphically realist mode of the depicted violence itself, it was the relation of the 'imaginary re-enactments' to the then-recent photographs of Abu Ghraib that fuelled the discussion on *Zero*. For instance, Ammar is subjected to waterboarding, a practice around which much of the torture debate clustered. The increasing thematic reduction of the issue of torture on waterboarding, as witnessed during Haspel's confirmation hearing, neglects other activities conducted under the programme and covers for other techniques, such as sleep deprivation, which are still allowed in Appendix M of the US Army Field Manual.[26]

Set at the interstice of real and fictional, between 'factual evidence, enactment and hypothesis or fictionalisation',[27] re-enactments always carry de-stabilising potential regarding their 'truthfulness'.[28] This ontological instability affects also their ethical appeal, and any emotional impact is effectively dampened by pairing those scenes with the indexical claim stipulated by the 9/11 audio material. This audio footage evokes sense memories, and thereby a physically experienced sense of certainty and an emotionally loaded atmosphere as entry to the film. In contrast to the 9/11 tapes, the torture scenes are more loosely tethered to historical evidence, and located firmly in the diegetic present. More suspenseful, they invite a different form of looking, a visceral, perhaps repulsed sense of affective claim.

Archive material is used again to precisely reference other terrorist attacks. Inserted into the diegetic world of *Zero* is footage from attacks on Khobar in Saudi Arabia, the 7/7 attacks in London, the 2008 bomb attack at the Islamabad Marriott hotel and a suicide attack on the CIA's Aghan

Forward Operating Base Chapman in December 2009. This combination creates fundamental epistemological instability: 9/11 and other terror attacks *uncontestably* and *irrevocably* happened, whereas the aesthetic presentation characterises torture more ambivalently: torture happened – perhaps in this way, or another.

* * *

The film's oppositional pulls, such as those created by juxtaposition of footage and fiction, are usefully illuminated with Elsaesser's description of 'conceptual double binds'. In an article on post-Hollywood cinema, Elsaesser argues that these double binds operate in addition to classical strategies of creating ambiguity. A film like *Avatar* (James Cameron, 2009) strategically inscribes such ambiguities into its very structure, as part of a strategy to provide 'access for all'.

If the undecidability of a film's premise motivates the spectator cognitively, it would explain these 'strong readings' that *Avatar* has given rise to: since the message is fundamentally self-contradictory, unravelling its meaning results in a higher 'ontological commitment' on the part of the viewer to his or her particular interpretation – a commitment that works in favour of the affective bond formed with a given film.[29]

In *Zero*, we also encounter many such strategically ambivalent or even self-contradictory messages, which necessitate high cognitive investment and result in 'strong readings'. For instance, a visual double bind is encountered in the image of Ammar, strung up in the position of a man being crucified, evoking *the* Western archetypal image of torture, Jesus on the cross. His symbolic counterpoint is CIA agent Maya's countenance and her 'exquisitely beautiful suffering … form[ing] a pieta'.[30]

In the torture scenes, the double bind results from the 'ontological doubt' created by their status as re-enactments, juxtaposed with the 'real' of the 9/11 footage, as analysed above. The torture scenes are clearly coded as constructed and performative: Dan's speech, in its over-familiar address and swaggering delivery, evokes the clichéd bravura of action films; the dramatic lighting suggests a theatre stage or film set, which, together with ropes dangling from the ceiling like gallows, evokes the medieval idea of torture as a punishment and spectacle.

The visual presence or absence of US presidents provides another example of a double bind. No footage is shown of George W. Bush, whose administration, after all, initiated the programme, while an archive snippet of Barack Obama, announcing the end of the programme, is decontextualised in such a way that he appears to deny rather than condemn his predecessor's programme. Considering that we have just seen extensive torture

Figure 1.1 *Zero Dark Thirty*.

scenes, seeing Obama say, 'The United States does not torture', sounds not aspirational or rectifying but hypocritical. Depending on the viewer, one may also interpret this shot as side-lining Obama's role in killing bin Laden, or as deflecting Bush's guilt in initiating the programme.

Reactions to the film were diverse and often strongly worded. Many reviewers concluded that the film was essentially 'pernicious propaganda', an apology for real torture by showing it as a necessary and effective measure after 9/11,[31] 'military orientalism', which allowed 'USA audiences [to] relive over and over again the triumphalist moments associated with the death of bin Laden'.[32] Aesthetic interventions are offered by Westwell and Shohini Chaudhuri, although she collapses together films as different as *Zero* and *V for Vendetta* (James McTeigue, 2005) plus the television show *24*:

> Although they often show the tortured writhing in agony ... these fictional representations do not tend to linger on the phenomenon. They deploy a conventional cinematic iconography of torture ... As Chuck Kleinhans suggests, action drama's kinetic pace 'allows the audience to *recognize, experience, and quickly move on past* the torture event'.[33]

This argument is difficult to maintain for the twenty-minute-long torture sequence in *Zero* (and the fundamental ambivalences in *V for Vendetta*).[34] Neither is the film particularly suspenseful; it is more a police procedural than an action film. Other reviewers had more ambivalent views, with some attempting to partition the film's politics from its aesthetic qualities.[35] A few could even discern a clear anti-torture message in the film.[36]

While it is true that, as Rancière argued, we must already be predisposed to a feeling for the film to successfully target us,[37] such 'pre-existing' subjectivities must find sustenance in the film. Later commentators and scholars also commented on the film's ambivalences. Only because of its strategic double binds and ambivalences could *Zero* function like a 'litmus test'[38] in which viewers of different political persuasions discerned different messages.

Zero Dark Thirty has become a projection screen for the audience's perceptions and sympathies, taking on different colours and contours depending on what the viewer brings to it.[39]

With regard to the torture sequences, the film creates oppositional pulls with the tension between visual brutality and verbal rationalisation. While looking at the results of torture, the images of Ammar's bruised face, is so appalling that the spectators' moral and emotional alliance with the victim would be a given, the interrogation pulls the focus of attention towards accommodating and crediting the torturers. Both within and outside the interrogation, the dialogue in *Zero* invites an oppositional way of reading the images of the hurt body.

Haptic close-ups of Ammar's sweating, bleeding, beaten-up body, and the equally uncomfortable sounds of him choking, pleading and crying out in pain, invite an intensifying somatic recognition that is sustained over long moments of screen time. The wish to withdraw from these vividly depicted sights and sounds of physical pain is strong, and it is a wish that the film purposely declines to meet.[40]

Initially, both Dan and Ammar speak, with an equally clichéd voice: Ammar spouts ideological vitriol, Dan responds with hackneyed phrases and jingoistic swagger. This verbal duel of irreconcilable positions is filmed in shot-reverse shot format. With the torture, Ammar's voice is extinguished – literally, as he is being waterboarded, and afterwards, gasping for air, his capacity for speech is reduced to pure sound – while Dan continues speaking without pause. Scarry describes how the goal of torture is 'to make ... the [victim's] body, emphatically and crushingly *present* by destroying it, and ... the voice, *absent* by destroying it'.[41]

The interrogation extinguishes Ammar's voice, and monopolises language for the torturer. Ammar becomes largely an image of pain, with Dan's voice as a caption read aloud. Dan's narration – how the CIA got hold of Ammar, why they keep him and what they want to know – demonstrates that he knows more than Ammar and offers a belated exposition to the audience. We are informed that Ammar is definitely a terrorist *before* the torture begins. The prisoner is presented to us as a priori guilty, to a degree that pushes him outside the zone of those owning human rights.[42]

When Maya has come to accept torture, the same structure is used: she narrates her deep knowledge and certainty about and to the (silent) detainee, as well as to the audience. Torture is envisioned as a controlled, targeted procedure, contrary to the frequently chaotic imprisonment and random torturing of the factual cases. Dan's narration follows the 'Omniscient Narrator Fallacy',[43] wherein the torturers have almost all relevant information: absolute certainty their prisoner is a terrorist, that he possesses actionable intelligence on a planned attack. Frequently combined with the 'Ticking Bomb Myth', this script creates a hyperbolic framework in order to undermine the absolute prohibition of torture.[44] The torturers are missing only a small piece of information, which must be extracted by the reliable tool of torture, as time is pressing.

As Scarry emphasises, the continuous display of the interrogation is hugely significant within the political fiction of torture, as it credits torturers with a justification and motive, confirming the idea that the purpose of torture is to obtain intelligence. The interrogation discredits the prisoner, who 'cracks', 'betrays', 'confesses', and thereby confirms that it was really about 'the question'.[45] Repeatedly, the discourse of the interrogators in *Zero* asserts that the victim is inflicting the pain on himself through his sheer obstinacy. Dan asks his prisoner, 'Why are you doing this *to yourself?*' (emphasis added); Maya tells her captive, 'You determine how you're treated'. The pretence that the prisoner, who is obviously *not* hurting or torturing himself, is in fact the one in control, is a staple of the interrogation in fiction about torture. Their choice of words – 'Give me one email and I will stop this'; 'Why are you doing this? You wanna have the water again? Have it your way' – pretends that the prisoner has the power to stop the torture by complying with demands. This alleges an amount of free will, recalcitrance and deliberate concealment, that is contested by both theory and testimonies on torture, and contradicted by the visuals of the scene, which show Ammar's power to speak extinguished. More importantly, the notion of compliance is predicated on the assumption that the victim does indeed possess and refuses to give up the desired information. Accordingly, silence is automatically interpreted as unwillingness to cooperate: 'Regardless of who is correct, a simple countermeasure that can be used by the subject to avoid this ordeal [of torture] is to fully and *truthfully* answer each of the interrogator's questions'.[46]

Compare this with the reality of Khalid Sheikh Mohammed, who was waterboarded 183 times, and gave only false information, or Abu Zubaydah, who was waterboarded eighty-three times (eventually over the objections of the interrogators on the ground, who emphasised that Zubaydah was completely compliant but had nothing to give up. Zubaydah died from the torture and had to be resuscitated).[47] While operating in blatant disregard of all the advances of due process and rule of law, the discourse around the interrogation frames the situation as one of cooperation versus reticence, a binary of truth and lie. Maya responds to the victim's plea for help by telling him, 'You can help yourself by being *truthful*'. The omniscient torturers also know when a captive is lying: Dan reiterates that 'partial information will be treated as a lie', and, 'When you lie to me, I hurt you'. The torturer controls the narrative – what the torture means, what silence means, who is doing what to whom.

Zero confirms both torture as truth-producing tool and the torturers' omniscience. When Ammar is allowed to speak again, he corroborates Dan's definition of him as guilty, indoctrinated and hateful: 'We wanted to kill Americans', and 'Jihad will go on for a hundred years'. The film also corroborates that Ammar knows the information they are after. A key piece of information ostensibly gained through Ammar's torture – the tip that leads to bin Laden's hiding place – is later shown to have been in the CIA files all along. So, in a convoluted way, the film does cast doubt on the utility of this particular torture but never on the practice in total. As the *general* utility of torture is not discredited, the implication is less of regret for the pain inflicted upon victims than chagrin over the futility of the torturers' efforts and an indictment of the inefficiency of (bureaucratic) agencies.

The brief scene revealing the presence of duplicated intelligence takes place late in the film, far distanced from the emotional impact of the torture sequence, and it is embedded in a larger sequence in which Maya's CIA colleague dies in a terrorist suicide attack, after having shown naïve goodwill to negotiate.[48] This economy of delayed revelation allows the visual and visceral impact of the torture scenes to subside. The admission that the data gained by torture was not instrumental to the capture of bin Laden appears almost as buried in the film structure as the crucial piece of information that was lost in the files.

While the torture does not produce immediate results, the *option* to use it is depicted as a critical tool. After having been extensively tortured, Ammar is offered some food and threatened with further torture should he continue to withhold information. Ammar surrenders the desired information. The fact that the prisoner *had* been tortured establishes the credentials of his adversaries. In a later scene, when Maya threatens a prisoner with torture, he immediately asserts his willingness to comply.

Torture even serves an educational purpose, akin to punishment as deterrence, for the prisoner mentions that he *has been* tortured and does not wish to suffer again.

Privileging the interrogation legitimises torture as a meaningful strategic tool of counterterrorism and intelligence gathering. Even when torture is not used, *having used it* and having the *option* of using it are shown as blatantly effective. There is no admission of even the possibility of alternative ways of perceiving the events of the world. As long as we subscribe to that political fiction of torture being perpetrated for the sake of information gathering, we are positioned with the torturing side. For this reason, the question of how the film steers the viewers' emotional, cognitive and formal alignment with the perpetrators of the torture is the subject of the next section.

The Torturers and Us

In framing torture within the world of bureaucracy and regulation, and depicting it as a professional activity, critics like Faisal Devji and Žižek argue that *Zero* banalises and normalises torture.[49] Yet showing torture in this way disables the convenient narrative of a few aberrant 'bad apples'. As Nicholas Lemann suggests about terrorism, neither practice belongs 'to an entirely separate and containable realm of human experience'.[50] Those who commit violent acts are not usually sadists, but motivated to tend to social-relational functions, often operating with moral imperatives.[51] Could it not be the 'normal' quality of the perpetrators in *Zero* that feels so terribly uncomfortable to the audience? To what extent are these torturers 'like us'?

For instance, in his research on torturers in Argentina's Dirty War, a campaign of state-sponsored terrorism against political opponents between 1976 and 1983, Mark Osiel points out that torturers did reveal awareness of facing a moral conflict, but they came to different conclusions.

> [Their] sense of moral obligation surpasses the 'role morality' of the unreflective clerk, that is, the highly limited sense of moral duty that Arendt ascribed to Eichmann ... it would be a mistake to overestimate the gap between the moral universes of officers and civilians[52]

Hannah Arendt had famously described how Eichmann positioned himself as victim, shifting the focus towards the torturer, his personal burden and ethical dilemma:

Instead of saying: What horrible things I did to people!, the murderers would be able to say: What horrible things I had to watch in the pursuance of my duties, how heavily the task weighed upon my shoulders!'[53]

Zero's cinematic torturers are neither psychopathic monsters, conveniently distanced from ourselves, nor bureaucrats who simply follow orders. But to what extent is their resolve to torture presented as the result of an inner struggle, as a moral decision?

Regarding Dan, there are few indications of moral conflict. Near the end of the film he refuses to torture the latest detainee. Depressed that his pet monkeys have been killed, he tells Maya he is quitting. As a result of the minimal information available, we may either imagine Dan as a morally questionable person who cares more about monkeys than the people he tortures, or read this attachment symbolically, where the monkeys function as a 'legitimate' emotional outlet of male vulnerability. Maya on the other hand changes her behaviour, a shift which seems all the weightier as it appears to be her only character development, and her use of torture has been read as a form of teaching the spectator to approve as well. Described as America's 'Joan of Arc',[54] Maya 'stands for American virtue' in ways that make it 'easier for us to identify with the SEALs who take out Osama',[55] and 'by the end of the movie her successes become national successes'.[56] Due to this alleged identification, her apparent conversion merits closer attention. If Maya represents America – beautiful, exceptional, obsessed – what do we know and feel about this America?

In the first torture sequence, Maya seems nauseated and occasionally averts her eyes: like the audience, she is abruptly thrown into the scene. Forty-three minutes later, in Maya's own torture scene, the *mise-en-scène*, framing and shot length are similar to the first sequence, alternating between close-ups of her face, master shots of the scene and close-ups of the prisoner's face. The opposition between the darkness and light of the settings also remains. Torture takes place in dungeons, where people are locked up in ever smaller cages, while the outside is brightly lit: natural light in the first torture, the over-lit neon light of a bathroom in the second. These symmetries highlight Maya's changed behaviour. Where she conveyed her discomfort in the first torture sequence with movements of physical discomfort and by looking away, she now coldly stares at her prisoners. With a slap, she orders a guard to hit her prisoner and watches the beating. Afterwards, there is a short shot of her putting water on her face in a bathroom, then gripping the lavatory as if for support. The scene is juxtaposed with images of people locked up in cages. The bathroom scene demonstrates the toll the work takes on her, a fact also mentioned in the dialogue. The graphic messiness of the torture scenes would then only reinforce this 'Eichmann Syndrome', in which the perpetrators consider themselves as the true victims. This is why Westwell suggests that Maya's 'exquisitely beautiful suffering ... seeks to elicit sympathy for the traumatic experience suffered by those working within [the CIA]'.[57]

Yet such interpretations assume that the film's ideological position is identical to Maya's and overestimates our emotional engagement with her. Towards the end of *Zero*, Maya does not look away from the torture, but while *she* watches the torture, *we* are watching *her*. There is alignment in the act of watching, but no collapse, for we see very different things.

Maya is almost a visual constant throughout the film; she is more closely framed than other characters and she is very beautiful, which would tend to guide us favourably towards her, and after the first torture sequence, our spatio-temporal alignment is mostly with her. At the same time, with the certainty of hindsight, the audience knows more than Maya, and with aerial shots, we often see more than she does. She is excluded from the raid on bin Laden's compound, while we share the SEAL team's view of Osama bin Laden's compound. (The exception is Maya's final look at the killed Osama bin Laden: here, she sees more than we do.)

Yet we learn almost nothing about Maya as a person: no personal network, no backstory, no interiority. Compare Murray Smith's account of the limits of emotional engagement in *United 93* (Paul Greengrass, 2006):

> [*United 93*] gives ample screen space to the facial expressions of the hijackers – mostly expressions of anger and fear. And I think we do feel their fear by mimicry and contagion. But the film doesn't nurture a deeper imaginative engagement with the hijackers; no attempt is made to contextualise their immediate affective states in terms of their life stories.[58]

In a similar way, Maya's inner life remains opaque,[59] and the audience is offered little incentive to feel emotionally close to her: Lisa Purse speaks of a 'Kuleshovian structuring absence at the heart of Maya's characterisation'.[60] This complicates the argument that the film is *teaching* approval of torture. Because we do not have privileged access to her interiority, we do not even know if her position on torture has really shifted that much. While the close-up of Maya's response in the first torture scene might be read as Carl Plantinga's 'scene of empathy', not only do we know nothing about her at this point, but her dislike could have more to do with a disapproval of the messiness of it all rather than with genuine compassion, as 'base ... revulsion' rather than 'moral discomfort'.[61]

More importantly, perhaps, our immediate emotional response to the first torture scene is *not* channelled through Maya, who is initially camouflaged with a balaclava and introduced only later. In that first scene, we are left alone with the affective side of our reception, without a protagonist as emotional guide.

Nevertheless, one must note that the audience is mostly in spatio-temporal alignment with the CIA perspective. Like the torturers and unlike the prisoners, the spectator is allowed to see both the inside and the outside of the prison compounds. Besides this physical closeness in space, screen time and perspective, we are linked to the agents through the common work of decoding, of searching for clear vision within an onslaught of contradictory, potentially unreliable information that buries the most important pieces of the puzzle. This imaginative detective work on behalf of the audience illustrates what Murray Pomerance characterised as 'indicative' contemporary cinema, obsessed with signs and counting.[62] As already indicated by the film's title, *Zero* is a world of signs and codes; much of the dialogue is conducted in military jargon; information is disclosed in such a way that the viewer is one step behind the narrative, except for the ending and the information on the prisoners.

This way, the film's narrative becomes a *mise-en-abyme* – duplicating a component of the textual whole – of its own relation to its audience. Mirroring the narrative, the audience has to decode; like the agents, we rather suffer from too much information. The film here 'articulate[s] the conditions of possibility for the characters' understanding of what they and the world are about'[63] while the spectator is drawn into the story through the act of having to piece the message together. This kind of shared activity can result in an alliance between the character and the audience, as V. F. Perkins argues in his analysis of *Marnie*: 'By restricting his heroine to an activity which the audience can share on completely equal terms, Hitchcock involves us more closely with her. We enter into her situation and become to some extent accomplices to her theft'.[64]

Like Marnie, Maya is a singularly focused but oddly blank mask. The characters are completely confined to their work-world, held in an almost claustrophobic present. No scene that presents a social relation between characters is unrelated to the manhunt; all narrative material is integral to zoning in on finding and killing bin Laden, the 'needle in the haystack'. By trimming off all the thematic fat (no secondary or subplots, no life before or after), the film's narrative mirrors the set-up of Maya's mind, while its glacial aesthetics mirror her beauty. It seems legitimate then to wonder to what extent we resemble her, and to what extent she really is a heroine.

'We can see that there's something monstrous in the zealotry that sustains [Maya's] belief ... but ... American viewers understand her because "she's our monster"'.[65]

Maya's obsession with capturing bin Laden occasionally features undertones of providence, exceptionalism, an almost religious zealotry: she believes she has been 'spared' for this mission and asks the SEAL team to kill bin Laden 'for her'. She articulates (and ultimately satisfies) a widespread desire for revenge: 'I'm going to smoke everybody involved in this op, and then I'm going to kill bin Laden'. Then there is the question of how Maya's beauty interacts with her pathology, specifically how, in the film's problematic colour policy, her whiteness is juxtaposed with the darkness of the detainees. Robert Burgoyne comments that '[Maya's] striking "whiteness" ... creates a disturbing and dramatic contrast of skin tones and textures during the interrogation scenes ... At the same time, her beauty challenges the easy notion that violence is deforming and dehumanising'.[66]

One may also recall Roland Barthes's portrayal of Greta Garbo's face as both beautiful and somehow removed – ethereal, divine, solitary in its perfection.[67] Chastain's porcelain skin seems to subscribe to the colour scheme that codes whiteness as purity and innocence, in contrast to active torturer Dan's tanned face and the darker hues of the prisoners' skins. On the other hand, the glacial coldness also recalls *whiteness* as ideological, cultural and historical category that signifies the uncanny and the deathly.[68]

Maya's beauty, enhanced in frequent close-ups, also clearly codes her as *to-be-looked-at*. Maya is frequently described or discussed by unknown male voices. A sceptic remarks that she is young, another person retorts that 'in Washington, she is known as a killer ... recruited right out of high school' and the pilot at the end of the film says, 'you must be pretty important, you got the whole plane to yourself'. She remains a surface, more a slate than a rounded character, an *image* of great beauty, which provides the viewer with a visual counterpoint and aesthetic respite from the torture. Maya has a delicate, fragile, slender frame, '[p]re-Raphaelite looks, bone china complexion and watery gaze',[69] and long red *Gilda*-esque hair. These physical attributes make her stand out visually, enhanced by spatial separation from other characters in the frame. Often framed in enclosed spaces, imprisoned by her surroundings, Maya is narratively and spatially isolated in emotional moments. When the SEAL team horse around after their mission, she leaves to stand alone in the silent desert; she is alone when she recovers briefly in the bathroom; and she is alone in the carrier taking her away at the end of the film.

Like a hunter entering a magical alliance with her prey, Maya possesses instinctive knowledge that a certain lead is important. Though unsubstantiated within the information available in the diegetic world, the audience knows with retrospective certainty that she is right. At one point, Maya seems to corroborate the truthfulness of a prisoner's account with a probing, scrutinising gaze. As if this were a duel between her and the al-Qaida leader, Maya's devotion to her cause mirrors the single-minded focus of her target. Both are driven at the expense of everything else. The way in which Maya devotes her life to this quest, overruling any other interests, resembles the consent of men who go to war, agreeing to hand over their lives and their bodies. She comes in personal danger – she is shot at in her car, and she survives the Marriott attack – which, like the soldier's willingness to sacrifice his own life, establishes permission for her to step over the ethical boundary and to kill or torture. Yet rather than being a role model, in her obsessive drive and proclivity to use violence – even to 'drop a bomb' on a hunch – she appears monomaniacal, pathological, even slightly unhinged.

Such an unusual heroine is in line with previous films by Bigelow, and her 'feminist reconfigurations of action genres' featuring 'assertive, active, and even violent female protagonists'.[70] Speaking about *Point Break* and *Strange Days*, Shaviro suggests that Bigelow's camerawork produces a new, 'free-floating' regime of vision, which implies affect but is not linked to a particular subjectivity. This camera elicits 'a visceral, emotive response from its viewers as well as an intellectual one'.[71] In *Zero*, too, at crucial moments the camerawork takes the perspective of an unidentified first person. During the raid and in the torture scenes, the perspective of the camera is independent of a particular character, though the pace and direction mark this point of view as distinctly *human*. These images are clearly presented as coming *from* a particular point of view, in contrast to the self-effacing, invisible camerawork and narration usually identified with classic Hollywood. Shot in an extremely visceral manner, where the hand-held camera 'jerks and rolls with the punches', this first-person point of view combines an 'immediacy [that] is strangely divorced from presence'.[72] The rapid panning back and forth between action and witness resemble eye-movements; the camera also frequently tilts to the floor and up, as if looking down and peering into a character's face; the unsteady handheld camera seems embodied, resulting in images as 'faulty' as human perception. The increase in tempo and fluid movement of this visceral camerawork correspond to the kind of vision that Shaviro described as an 'authorial signature' for Bigelow. We are drawn into the affective dynamics of the scene but not into the mind of a particular character. Moreover,

Bigelow's signature camera here condenses *various* affects: the stress and disorientation of the prisoner, the hectic and anxious movements of an anonymous witness trying to grasp what is happening, the adrenaline rush of the torturers.

Similar camerawork emerges from the final raid scene, which is visually structured similarly to the torture sequence, moving from an introductory overhead shot to close-range action from a 'fluid' camera, mediated via screens and through the night vision goggles of the SEAL team. They visually translate the lack of clear vision, and symbolically, of definite knowledge. Once inside, the camera stays too close to the action for us to make out bin Laden or his murder; all we hear is the shot. The camera then holds back and lingers; as the soldiers leave, the camera tilts down to a bloodstain on the floor, showing the chaos and destruction they leave behind. These images eschew first-person shooter suspense, gung-ho dialogue and action film heroics. *Zero*'s final violence is 'sobering, rather than transformative [and] the effect of violence on both character and history is left open, unresolved'.[73]

Nicholas Rombes reproaches *Zero* for depicting an empty version of history, leaving out any larger meta-narratives or 'deep history': precisely because there is no interiority to Maya, and personalised psychological explanations are discarded, '*history itself* becomes psychotic'.[74] I would modify this reading of *Zero*'s history as an absence by suggesting that *Zero* is less a film aimed at educating or setting the record straight than one that attempts to offer (Western) audiences a way of participating in, of experiencing, 'their' history. This experience is often translated through an intense visual style, where the camera expresses a largely unattributed affect. Additionally, the temporal proximity between original events and their fictionalisation – *Zero* appeared only eighteen months after the killing of bin Laden – likely factored in the decision to leave out more detailed historical background information.

The film is about process rather than narrative, aiming not to explain history but to offer a *feeling*. When Maya confirms the corpse as the body of bin Laden, she is clearly acting as surrogate for the audience. She channels an approximate, a visual *habeas corpus*: she sees him, whereas our final image of (this fictional) bin Laden's corpse remains a fragment, a distant, oddly angled shot. Compare Jason Horowitz's reading on the famous 'Situation Room' image as some kind of *ersatz* visual: 'With so much to see, and with the government withholding the bloody bin Laden images, it's no wonder that the photo is on track to become the most-viewed image on Flickr'.[75]

Similarly, Amy Davidson has suggested that the debate on the film's merits became virulent because the filmmakers claimed privileged access while everyone else remained in a vacuum, surrounded by classified information: 'So much about our recent history as torturers has been left unexamined, with no accountability ... left open to the imagination'.[76]

It was logical then that the proximity between CIA personnel, Bigelow and her scriptwriter Boal would come under scrutiny, extending even to a senatorial inquiry. It has since been revealed that the character of Maya is partly based on CIA officer Alfreda Bikowsky, who headed the Bin Laden Issue Station and the Global Jihad unit. Bikowsky has been named as one of the chief apologists of torture, who told congressional overseers that the torture worked.[77]

Considering the lack of apology, admission of wrongdoing or punishment of those responsible, the lack of clear culprits in *Zero* resonated bitterly for some. Jane Mayer, for instance, argues that *Zero* missed the point: 'If [Bigelow] were making a film about slavery in antebellum America, it seems, the story would focus on whether the cotton crops were successful'.[78]

Yet rather than creating an incorrect understanding of torture, the film reflects the limited circumference of the public debates, with their narrow focus on the political fiction of torture, the utility fallacy and the fixation on waterboarding.

Moreover, the film does raise some important questions, and these do not dissipate with its formal closure. The death of bin Laden, while closing this particular narrative, obviously did not end terrorism. The repeated terror attacks in the film have reminded viewers for over two hours of the ongoing threat. And if terrorism necessitated and justified the torture, how could the torture have ended? Where did this expertise in and readiness to use torture come from? Who gave the order, and who is, ultimately, accountable? What will happen to the prisoners held in a setting that visually evokes Guantánamo and who, we are informed early in the film, will 'never get out'? What will be the wider consequences of America's response to the 9/11 attacks?

Zero ends with Maya embarking alone on a cargo plane, crying. '[While *Zero*] ends with victory — as most American war movies have — it also ends in tears'.[79]

This ending is modestly cathartic but also profoundly ambivalent, especially if read in terms borrowed from Linda Williams's analysis of the body genres. We know the ending of *Zero*, we know what will happen, but we do not know precisely when the film will offer us a visceral release.

Figure 1.2 *Zero Dark Thirty*.

These strategically inscribed ambivalences are in fact the film's strength: not because the use of torture can be ethically justified – it cannot – but because the film offers the viewer a space to encounter their own pre-existing notions on torture, rather than seeking to convince or convert the audience. Rather than demonstrating an ideological persuasion on the politics of torture, *Zero* offers itself as an art work meditating on the role of audiovisual media, and cinema as art in particular, in politics, clearly locating that audience as actor within an existing pool of visual knowledge.

Regarding Bigelow's 'witnessing' camerawork in *Strange Days*, Shaviro argues that it indicates her awareness both of cinematic and audience complicity, creating a new point of view, that is 'neither precisely objective nor conventionally subjective, but transpersonal and social'.[80] In *Zero*, too, Bigelow's fluid camerawork does not shy away from where the medium and the spectator might be implicated, shooting in a viscerally impactful but unattributed manner. The fluid camerawork does not align the audience so much with Bigelow's point of view as with that of an abstract third witness: the camera, the film, the audience.

Beginning with Maya's insistence on going back into the torture room, Burgoyne suggests that in *Zero*, 'the intimate witnessing of torture becomes inseparable from the act itself ... witnessing becomes enmeshed with violence'.[81]

The next chapter follows up on this notion of witnessing, exploring which actors – the camera, the audience and the diegetic characters – can serve as witnesses, and the notion of witnessing itself, in a number of recent Iraq War films.

Notes

1. Schultz, 'Interview with Kathryn Bigelow'; cf. Filkins, 'Bin Laden, the Movie'; Coll, '"Disturbing" & "Misleading"'.
2. Alex Gibney in Chaudhuri, 'Documenting the Dark Side'.
3. Filkins, 'Bin Laden, the Movie'.
4. Hoby, 'Zero Dark Thirty'.
5. Rosenstone, *History on Film / Film on History*, p. 32.
6. Cf. Dershovitz on 'torture warrants'. Dershovitz, 'Should the Ticking Bomb Terrorist Be Tortured?'.
7. Greenwald, 'CIA hagiography'; *Economist*, 'Terrorism and civil liberty'.
8. Christopher Hitchens let himself be waterboarded in 2008, writing about the experience for *Vanity Fair*, and Hilary Andersson experienced several torture techniques for an edition of the BBC1 current affairs show, *Fighting Terror with Torture* in 2015.
9. Morell, 'Message from the Acting Director', emphasis added.
10. Scarry, *The Body in Pain*. Compare the assertion that former Iraqi dictator Saddam Hussein was not tortured because he was deemed not to be 'the kind of person' who would be responsive. Gordon and Fleisher, *Effective interviewing and interrogation techniques*.
11. Rejali, 'Convenient Truths'.
12. Scarry, *The Body in Pain*, p. 47.
13. Farrell, *The Prohibition of Torture*, p. 133, emphasis added.
14. Shapiro, *Cinematic Geopolitics*, p. 65.
15. For instance, Hasian, 'Military Orientalism'; Greenwald, 'CIA hagiography'; Bruni, 'Bin Laden, Torture and Hollywood'.
16. van Raalte, p. 23.
17. For instance, the BBC documentary *Fighting Terror with Torture* (see note 8) mimics *Zero*'s visuals in *mise-en-scène*, actor Chastain's demeanour and attire. As the link is never mentioned, audience familiarity with the source text must have been assumed.
18. Westwell, 'Zero Dark Thirty'.
19. Cf. Bass, 'Counterinsurgency and Torture'.
20. Cf. Kaplan, 'Empathy and Trauma Culture'.
21. Sundquist, 'Witness without End?'.
22. Cf. Meek, *Trauma and Media*.
23. In her sensitive reading, van Raalte not only contrasts the 'spectacle of authenticity' and 'documentary aesthetic' of the opening scenes with the fictionalised coverage and 'perverse intimacy' of the torture scenes, but she also points out that the recordings – remixed, enhanced with Foley – are already blurring the line between fiction and documentary, a strategy the audience is not yet aware of at this point. Van Raalte, pp. 24–30.
24. Westwell, 'Zero Dark Thirty', p. 86.

25. Westwell complains that this depiction is in stark contrast to the real torturers at Abu Ghraib; but as the orders for the programme as well as its particular techniques were indeed concocted by people with a high educational degree, such an assessment is too reductive. Westwell, 'Zero Dark Thirty'.
26. Riechmann, 'The issue of Appendix M'.
27. Bruzzi, 'Restaging History'.
28. Cf. Bill Nichols' (contested) claim that certain, generalised re-enactments such as these 'typical particulars' forfeit the '*heightened sense of viewer responsibility* that attends to the historical instead of a fictive world, contributing an affective function', which he opposes to the ethical appeal of footage. Nichols, 'Documentary Reenactment', pp. 85–8, emphasis added.
29. Elsaesser, Access for all', p. 260.
30. Westwell, 'Zero Dark Thirty'.
31. Cf. Wolf, 'A letter to Kathryn Bigelow'; Bruni, 'Bin Laden, Torture and Hollywood'; Wolff, 'This torture fantasy degrades us all'; Žižek, 'Hollywood's Gift'. Winter and Rothman, 'Art of Darkness'.
32. Hasian, 'Military Orientalism', p. 466.
33. Chaudhuri, 'Documenting The Dark Side'.
34. Jung, *Narrating Post-9/11 Action Cinema*.
35. Greenwald, 'CIA hagiography'; Westwell, 'Zero Dark Thirty'.
36. 'Moore Launches Defence of *Zero Dark Thirty*'.
37. Rancière, *The Emancipated Spectator*.
38. Brody, 'The Deceptive Emptiness of *Zero Dark Thirty*'.
39. Winter and Rothman, 'Art of Darkness', p. 25.
40. Purse, 'Ambiguity, ambivalence and absence', p, 141.
41. Scarry, *The Body in Pain*, p. 35.
42. Cf. Schillings, *Enemy of All Humankind*.
43. Marks, 'Logic and Language of Torture'.
44. For the rhetorical and artistic tradition of the ticking time bomb, cf. Rejali, *Torture and Democracy*; Farrell, *The Prohibition of Torture*.
45. Scarry, *The Body in Pain*. Scarry largely sets violence, body and language in opposition. In crimes such as torture, however, language often acts as perpetrator, corrupting and colluding, while the physical 'disappearance' of the torturer's body does not work in the case of rape and sexual violence. Butler, *Excitable Speech*; Franco, *Cruel Modernity* and Eckstein, *The Language of Fiction in a World of Pain* regarding the need to attend to the cultural and historical specificity of pain.
46. Cf. Gordon and Fleisher, *Effective interviewing and interrogation techniques*, p. 231, emphasis added.
47. Danner and Eakin, 'Our New Politics of Torture'; Filkins, 'Black Site Past'.
48. This attack relies on the 2009 case of Jordanian physician Humam Khalil al-Balawi, who was thought to be a double agent with great intelligence about al-Qaeda. When he arrived at a CIA base near Khost, Afghanistan, he instead detonated an explosives vest, killing nine Americans and himself. The way

in which *Zero* portrays the attack – including details such as the baking of a 'goodwill cake' – confirms the unprecedented access enjoyed by Boal and Bigelow who appear to have gained detailed information not publicly known at that time. Cf. Taub, 'The spy who came home'.
49. For instance, Devji, 'Torture at the Limits of Politics'; Žižek, 'Hollywood's Gift'.
50. Lemann, 'Social scientists do counterinsurgency'.
51. Fiske and Rai, *Virtuous Violence*.
52. Osiel, *The Mental State of Torturers*, p. 135. Cf. Agnieszka Piotrowska's argument that Maya's behaviour is ethical if read through Lacan's notion of the ethical act in which, once a commitment is made, one is faithful to it 'beyond the limit'. Piotrowska, '"War Autism" or a Lacanian Ethical Act?'.
53. Quoted in Scarry, *The Body in Pain*, p. 58.
54. *Economist*, 'Terrorism and civil liberty'.
55. Thomson, 'All the Depth of a John Wayne Movie'.
56. Hasian, 'Military Orientalism', p. 472.
57. Westwell, 'Zero Dark Thirty'. For a different interpretation of Maya, cf. Westwell, *Parallel Lines*; Melley, *Covert Sphere*.
58. Smith, 'Empathy, Expansionism, and the Extended Mind', p. 101.
59. Burgoyne, 'The Violated Body', p. 254.
60. Purse, 'Ambiguity, ambivalence and absence'.
61. Plantinga, 'The Scene of Empathy'; Chaudhuri in Purse, 'Ambiguity, ambivalence and absence', p. 134.
62. Murray Pomerance, 'Talking Space in Vertigo'; cf. Bordwell, 'Intensified Continuity'.
63. Shapiro, *Cinematic Geopolitics*, p. 143.
64. Perkins, *Film as Film*, p. 142.
65. Hasian, 'Military Orientalism', p. 474.
66. Burgoyne, 'The Violated Body', p. 251.
67. Barthes, 'The Face of Garbo'.
68. Cf. Dyer, *White*. I thus disagree with van Raalte's claim that Maya's beauty is 'incidental' (p. 28).
69. Westwell, 'Zero Dark Thirty'.
70. Shaviro, 'Straight from the Cerebral Cortex', p. 174. Maya is subjected to a flippant, casual sexism; and her gender is used to (supposedly) humiliate the Arab prisoner.
71. Shaviro, 'Straight from the Cerebral Cortex', pp. 26–8.
72. Ibid., p. 163. Cf. Westwell, who describes similar shifts in point of view for Bigelow's *The Hurt Locker* as 'diegetically unanchored positions'. Westwell, 'In Country', p. 27.
73. Burgoyne, 'The Violated Body', p. 251.
74. Rombes, 'Zero Dark Thirty', emphasis in the original.
75. Horowitz, 'Breaking Down the Situation Room'. Melley makes the same argument in *The Covert Sphere*, i.e. that surveillance and the increasing secrecy

of a 'National Security State' transformed 'the cultural status of fiction' so that imaginary representations become a primary source of information about government action, even within news organisations. Melley, *Covert Sphere*, p. viii and p. 218. In that interpretation, some of the more obvious absences, for instance regarding precise location, could also be read as reflecting how the public is excluded from knowledge about black sites.

76. Davidson, 'Three Senators and *Zero Dark Thirty*'.
77. Information on the real 'torture queen' Alfreda Bikowsky was leaked long after the release of *Zero*, but considering the cooperation between Boal and the CIA, could well be counted as a reality effect 'invisible' to the audience at this point. Bruck, 'The Inside War'; Mayer, 'Queen of Torture'.
78. Mayer, 'Zero Conscience in *Zero Dark Thirty*'.
79. Dargis and Scott, 'Movies in the Age of Obama'.
80. Shaviro, *The Cinematic Body*, p. 172.
81. Burgoyne, 'The Violated Body', p. 249. Burgoyne suggests that *Zero* offers a new, violent imagery that draws on and appropriates the close connection between aesthetic form and the history of violence, but eventually refuses to 'enchant' its violence with symbolic and cultural potency.

CHAPTER 2

Witnessing Torture, and Mediated Witnessing in War-on-Terror Films

The traditional definition of the witness carries an element of embodied presence. A witness is someone who is present at the time and place of an event, who literally *sees* something happen – a crime, a marriage – and can therefore attest or testify to it.[1] The testimony of historical eyewitnesses has been framed as a duty, a political, sometimes empowering act that works against the attempted erasure of historical crimes, the silencing of lives and voices.

Yet there exist also atrocities that lack documentation or witnesses, where recorded and fictionalised stories may step in. A witness certainly does not have to be alive, able or willing to speak, otherwise we would exclude the dead, the mute, the mentally disabled, those who have been small, who have not yet been born,[2] who have forgotten or repressed the memories, or those who may choose to remain silent. They all nevertheless *embody* a witnessing capacity. Moreover, memory studies, adjunct with neurological experiments, have complicated our understanding of the vicissitudes of memory, confirming that even those present at an event cannot speak with absolute authority. This dilemma of the eyewitness, the malleability of memory and the always 'insurmountable impasse in communication'[3] is exacerbated with additional screens of mediation.

Who – or what – can be a witness then? In an attempt to distinguish between the historical eyewitness and screened mediation, various terms have emerged, such as 'secondary witnessing, co-witnessing, proxy witnessing, and witnessing through imagination'.[4] These terms have been criticised as inviting appropriation, attempts to acquire a 'privileged position in relation to the event'.[5] Some scholars insist that only a person can be a witness, not a thing like a machine, while others point out that 'every act of witnessing implies some kind of mediation'.[6]

Mediated witnessing stands in a different epistemological tradition than the historical eyewitness. Mechanical or 'scientific' witnessing is considered authentic because of the presumed objectivity of the machine.[7] Scientific instruments – and by extension media and film – gain their privileged position by excluding subjectivity. This is why, traditionally, documentary footage and live news media were considered providers of this mediated form of witnessing. Yet, as John Durham Peters suggests, this boundary between fact and fiction is ultimately ethical before it is epistemological. There is a moral dimension to witnessing, too:

> imagine a Nazi who published his memoirs of the war as a 'witness' ... to witness means to be on the right side ... [to witness] consists in having respect for the pain of victims, in being tied by simultaneity ... to someone else's story of how they hurt.[8]

The central premises for ethical witnessing are defined in *liveness* and *proximity* (or presence-at-distance). In mediation, these are in a precarious position because of the spatio-temporal distance between event and witness. For Peters, then, it is in the 'profane zone' of recording, where 'the attitude of witnessing is hardest to sustain' and 'our duty to action is unclear'.[9] Accordingly, the central question for mediated witnessing is whether a mediating screen can create an ethical appeal akin to the obligation created by a direct, face-to-face encounter. Today, the immediacy of real-time technologies alongside ever-increasing speed of transmission invite a re-exploration of our perception of presence, distance and proximity and their key place in witnessing.[10] For this reason, Leach suggests that even the terms of 'testimony' and 'witness' belong to 'a previous regime of epistemological concerns', unable to account for current 'human–machine reconfigurations'[11] which aim 'to make the recipients of scientific testimony [the presumed objectivity of the machine] into virtual witnesses: we can all say that we have seen by proxy'.[12] As the flip-side to potential appropriation of experience, this also means that 'we can no longer say that we didn't know'.[13]

Before delving into the cinematic experience as an option of 'public witnessing', another component must be added. Linking the witness, torture and cinema as configurations of truth is an element of *embodiment*. Following Michel Foucault, torture produces a 'different order of truth', manifested in the pain felt by the victim's body and certified by the embodied presence of the witnessing body. Witnessing and torture share an epistemological approach towards truth.

As Page DuBois shows, this idea of torture as truth-producing tool dates back to slave torture in ancient Greece. The Greek word for torture, *basanos*, originally referred to a touchstone that attested authenticity of a golden artefact. This identifiable legitimacy was extended to the notion of a truth hidden inside the slave's body, then on to the certainty *felt* by a witnessing body. In the public ritual of medieval torture,

Foucault explains, the main addressee of the extracted confessions, abdications and recantations was the witnessing audience, a core dynamic and function that did not change with the historical shift from penalty to correction: 'In the ceremonies of public execution, the main character was the people, whose real and immediate presence was required for the performance'.[14]

Moving on to the field of representation, Jennifer Ballengee suggests that the rhetorical meaning of torture is determined by an audience passing moral and aesthetic judgment. As a representation may produce a range of possible meanings, it is the certainty felt in the witnessing spectator's *body* which fixes the meaning and thereby the 'effectiveness' of torture: 'Torture's rhetorical intent, as it is represented before an audience, demands interpretation; it solicits a verdict'.[15]

At this point, the scholarship on the rhetorical function of torture can be productively intersected with scholarship on cinema spectatorship. The witness, central element in the torture constellation, may be located both within and outside the diegesis: the choir in the Greek play or the witnessing characters in a film versus the theatre or movie audience.[16] Watching a film may offer the collective, public, even communal aspect of witnessing, and through cinema the witness perceives herself to be *present* at the event.

Cinema enables an audience to be 'actually present' in other moments and other parts of the world. Cinema expands the subject's mobility virtually, while its presence extends that subject's sense of sovereignty over a range of events from which she was previously excluded.[17]

Both Ballengee and Dubois suggest that the spectacle of torture persists today, displaced to media relations: 'And it may be that the function of torture today, rather than the production of truth, is still one of spectacle, of the production of broken bodies and psyches, both for local and international consumption'.[18]

The cinematic experience here emerges as an option of 'public witnessing'. As the witness 'cannot not judge', spectators are by necessity implicated. When we witness a representation, we have a visceral reaction that *feels true*, and this bodily response stabilises the rhetorical potential of the representation. We become participants, part of the performance of torture, and our response and judgement determine its effectiveness and legitimacy.

Thus, in the figure of the witness – whether as embodied verifying presence or as material recording that substitutes temporal and/or spatial distance – categories central to theorisations of both torture and cinema intertwine: truth, embodiment, public spectacle. Building on these differentiations, close-readings of key moments of witnessing and the witness as narrative figure in recent US war films help determine their politics of torture.

Witness Politics and Failing Witnesses

In *Rendition* (Gavin Hood, 2007), Anwar el-Ibrahimi, an Egyptian living in Chicago with his pregnant wife and young son, is abducted from his flight home, flown to an undefined North African country and tortured at the behest of the CIA. Present as observer, CIA analyst Douglas Freeman grows increasingly critical of the proceedings and ends up freeing Anwar at his own discretion. Douglas then publicises the story, which causes public outrage.

The film has been criticised for situating its moral focus with US positions, which are expressed through Douglas's choices and his struggle, effectively appropriating the pain of the torture victim and rendering his experience non-political.

> [The victim's] moral status ... [is] being transferred to the torturer, who is seen as the only one with the luxury of choice ... A free moral agent, [the hero] must take on weighty moral responsibility, to the extent of putting his own life and career on the line.[19]

This conforms to the conventional narrative, where torture is a mere supplement to politics. From his reactions to watching scenes of suffering to his alcohol abuse and momentary inability to perform sexually, Douglas's struggles claim 'the very suffering of this tortured victims for himself. [The] moral dimension of pain, both inflicted and endured, belongs to the torturer'.[20]

While Anwar's physical pain is 'made feelable' to the audience through the moral pain of Douglas, the emotional pain is channelled through Anwar's US-American wife Isabella. In a neatly gendered division, beautiful, young, white, and pregnant Isabella functions overtly as emotional catalyst. Similarly to Maya in *Zero*, Isabella's beauty is used as a respite from the visual terror of gruesome torture scenes. Where Anwar's innocence is in doubt during most of the film, unequivocal blamelessness is located with Isabella, who remains in the homeland, where she is frequently framed before national monuments in Washington or in suburbia.

Rendition seems to assume a Western audience incapable of imagining suffering unless channelled through a (white) Western person. As a result, the real violence and the real pain – *Rendition* is based on factual cases of mistaken identity[21] – recede into little more than a background foil for the moral conundrums of the Western heroes. This obliteration of the other's suffering constitutes what Elizabeth Goldberg aptly termed the 'political instability' and 'representational violence' at the heart of such 'supposedly politically liberal' films.[22]

The actual torturing in *Rendition* is displaced to Fawal, the local head of security; like Maya in *Zero*, the main protagonist does not apply torture himself. Even though it is obvious that the US ordered the rendition, and the act is clearly criticised in the film, the 'dirty fingers' remain elsewhere and the homeland remains free of contamination. As a visual experience, we remain with the image of Fawal as torturer. Crucially, feelings of shame, guilt and self-loathing are also pinned onto these 'other', dark bodies (in a narrative twist, Fawal realises his acts led to the death of his daughter), while Douglas expresses emotions in the range of moral conflict and nausea, rather than guilt. At no point does Douglas apologise to Anwar, neither acknowledging Anwar's wounded human dignity nor conceding Douglas's role and responsibility in his ordeal.

Walsh argues that for a (Western and white) audience, the cathartic ending of *Rendition* provides the possibility of assuaging shame that arose after the release of the Abu Ghraib prison photographs. Culminating in his eventual decision to free Anwar, Douglas redeems himself through bearing witness. As the audience is aligned with his perspective, of a 'good white citizen ... of the world', we, too, are vicariously reconstituted as 'ethically aware spectators'.[23] As Lauren Berlant explains, these narratives offer 'a form of compassion which assumes the other's pain ... while simultaneously maintaining a barrier between the one who witnesses and the one who suffers'.[24]

The witnessing sequences – cutting between close-ups of the eyes and face of the prisoner to those of the witness, between images of torture and of the onlooker, and the camera following Douglas's gaze – establish an analogy between the physical pain of the prisoner and the moral pain of the witnessing protagonist. Karl Schoonover criticises such visual strategies as 'uninterrogated witness politics': '[*Rendition*] appears to be unable to condemn state-sanctioned violence without structuring its climatic scene of gruesome torture around the gaze of the white Hollywood star'.[25]

Additionally, it is uncertain that Douglas's position has evolved. Recognising the futility of this particular torture, he might be motivated by a cost – benefit calculation. Douglas's characterisation in the film as 'a number cruncher' who 'loves pie charts', and his insistence on statistical analysis of the programme's efficiency, implies less a regret for the pain inflicted upon the victims than chagrin over the inefficiency of (bureaucratic) agencies. Previously, Douglas's superior had contrasted a single sacrificed person with the many potentially saved (implicitly Western) lives. Douglas's arguments

Figure 2.1 Crucified prisoner in *Rendition*.

against the torture resemble hers, limited to questions of efficiency, blowback and quantitative comparisons. At one point, the CIA superior is petitioned by a Senate aide and she replies, 'What are you taking issue with? The disappearance of a particular man – or national security policy?' As in *Zero*, the film does not answer this poignant question, but leaves it open, directed at us.

The most forceful moment of questioning the use of torture takes place at the home of Saeed, Douglas's local colleague. The sumptuous setting references cinematic orientalism and denotes affluence, even decadence: a large, dark, slightly cluttered room filled with comfortable sofas, low-lit lamps, a lit fireplace – perhaps a sign of prestige or postcolonial mimicry

Figure 2.2 Western witnesses in *Rendition*.

in what appears to be a rather warm country. A bath-robed Saeed tells Douglas, 'We have a saying: beat your woman every morning. If you don't know why, she does.' The statement crystallises that it might not be knowledge (or information) that is at stake, but the upholding of power relations and punishment. However, framing this as an Arab tradition in direct contrast to the Western paradigm of 'innocent until proven guilty' displaces Western guilt and responsibility. Douglas's facial expression (and actor Gyllenhall's comic timing) in his response – 'I don't know what that means' – turn this problematic instance of misogyny and indirect racism into a moment of comic relief. The statement complies with the right-wing narrative that this is the appropriate and only language 'they' (women, slaves, terrorists) will understand, and it also maintains Saeed as an 'other', in spite of his wealth, education and British accent.

As Egyptian, Muslim and engineer with potential bomb-building knowledge, Anwar raises red flags. (His being married to the 'apple pie American' Isabella only adds to this sleeper-agent potential.) The film intertwines suspense and moral focus by strategically and repeatedly withholding crucial information about Anwar, thereby exposing the viewers' readiness to believe in these racialised codes and naturalised red flags.

For instance, in the second or third torture scene, Anwar suddenly 'breaks' and offers names of alleged terrorists. So far, the viewer has been encouraged to believe in Anwar's innocence. Like Douglas, who had just called for the torture to stop, we are dumbfounded. Yet this dramatic turn of events is closely followed by a second twist, when Douglas reveals to Saeed, and to the audience, that Anwar has given out the names of the Egyptian football team of the year he left the country. His intelligence was bogus. In the time that elapses between such pieces of information, the spectator may waver between doubt and belief.

The film's final twist demonstrates not only the futility of torture, but also its part in perpetuating a vicious circle of violence. The ending reveals that the audience has been purposefully misled with regard to the different temporal levels of *Rendition*'s intersecting storylines. There is no information to be gained in the interrogation – not only because Anwar knows nothing, but also because the person he is supposed to name has already blown himself up in the initial terror event. Moreover, this suicide attack had been blowback, motivated by a desire to avenge a relative's death through previous torture. The ending thus exposes the hubris of being too certain of even having enough correct information to ask the appropriate questions. By making this realisation experientially available to the spectator, the effect is magnified: 'we, like the characters, are [tricked] into mistaking "replay" as play'.[26]

The standard account of torture in fiction film sees the audience in a position of control. In *Rendition*, the audience does initially enjoy superior knowledge, especially in relation to the blindfolded Anwar and his misinformed family. The eventual revelation of disparate narrative timelines disrupts this fictitious sense of control. To make sense of the film's plot, we must acknowledge that we always had only access to partial and preselected information. Considering such effects, Elsaesser notes that this kind of intervention exposes 'epistemological problems (how do we know what we know) and ontological doubts (about other worlds, other minds)'.[27] The 'mindgame film' creates an experiential moment that unsettles our relationship to the images – the film *Rendition* itself and the video shown within it – which were presented to us in an inadequate framework, yet we did not even suspect that information was missing. *Rendition* momentarily destabilises our epistemological trust in the certainty of our senses and thereby destabilises the truth of torture which, as discussed above, is founded on the audience's bodily certainty.

Tricking the viewer is also a way of acknowledging their presence – as a witness to the act or a witness to the witnessing done by somebody else. Rather than considering the diegetic witness as a stand-in for the spectator, we might say that the *spectator* corroborates the performative act of witnessing: we are watching them watching. This idea is usefully illustrated by the widely circulated image capturing President Obama and his inner circle gathered in the Situation Room on 1 May 2011 to monitor the nighttime raid on Osama bin Laden's compound in Pakistan from a live feed from a drone. Here, the viewer of the photograph cannot even see the broadcast. Clearly, the message is the 'live witnessing' of others, and the viewer of the photograph is witness to their witnessing, via the photographer and his camera. When a film provides images which 'ask to be witnessed', or when we are watching a diegetic witness, we are confirming their 'fictional' witnessing with our 'real' (albeit mediated) witnessing. We are also provided a way to be or feel in the cinepresence-at-distance of torture. These regimes of visibility are therefore key to understanding the politics of the films discussed here.

* * *

In *Body of Lies* (*Body*), brilliant CIA agent Ferris, played by Leonardo di Caprio, fights against both terrorists and corrupt superiors at home. Increasingly disgusted with his handler's lack of ethics, Ferris goes rogue. He must outwit his opponents, both the Islamists and his own superiors, along with their devices, until he is finally released from 'protective' satellite surveillance.

Figure 2.3 'The Situation Room' (Peter Souza © public domain).

The film begins with a voiceover, spoken by Ferris's superior, Hoffman. In a hawkish narrative he articulates a deep sense of vulnerability due to the US reliance on technology:

> Our enemy has realised that they are fighting guys from the future ... If you live like it's the past, and you behave like it's the past, then guys from the future *find it very hard to see you*. [Emphasis added]

Western high-tech modernity is contrasted with a cultural and religious otherness that is equated with backwardness and archaic forms of conflict resolution. All the films discussed here switch between aerial and distant shots – taken from drones, satellites or helicopters, often silent, mediated through a screen, suggestive of the sublime and demonstrating/establishing superior control – towards scenes in close proximity, often filmed with hectic, frequently handheld camera movements and edited into a fast-paced montage of closely framed bodies, suggesting confusion and latent danger. The movement is thus not only from air to earth and from large-scale to close-up, but also from machine to physical body. Where 'the aerial view of surveillance transforms places into space, [and moves] from concrete to abstraction, and distancing',[28] the opposite vision, up close and chaotic, is more human: inhabited, tangible, sensual.

This division of gazes corresponds to the separation of spaces and the bodies that inhabit them.[29] Western fetishisation of speed, mobility and connectivity, where characters are constantly on the phone, are contrasted with a low-tech, pre-modern Middle East. The film's formal language initially seems to corroborate Hoffman's discourse: an immobile Middle East is associated with the past, and a hyper-connected West with the future. However, the film more and more problematises the politics of disembodied warfare, exposing an increasingly ambivalent relationship with technology.

For instance, Ferris and Hoffman stage a terrorist attack – by transforming 'unclaimed' local bodies into victim-props, using technology to distort truth on a massive scale. In one of the film's many ploys, Ferris is captured, tortured and, about to be executed on video, saved at the very last minute. Even before the terrorists attempt to live-stream murder, they prevent a surveillance drone from registering a crucial moment by raising a sandstorm, exploiting technological weaknesses. At the very beginning of the film, Ferris's Iraqi friend and colleague Bassam asks him to promise that if he is killed, Ferris will not allow his death to be filmed and distributed. Bassam does not want to be turned into entertainment or a message, to be used as a tool. Similarly, when Ferris is saved from being executed on video, the first thing his rescuers do is to switch off the camera. This interruption of visual documentation via live stream is part of the rescue, as the camera is not a separate process of subsequent documentation but an integral part of the event itself. Circumventing the creation and dissemination of a beheading video, to be broadcast over the internet, functions not only as individual recovery but also as circumvention of a terrorist act.[30]

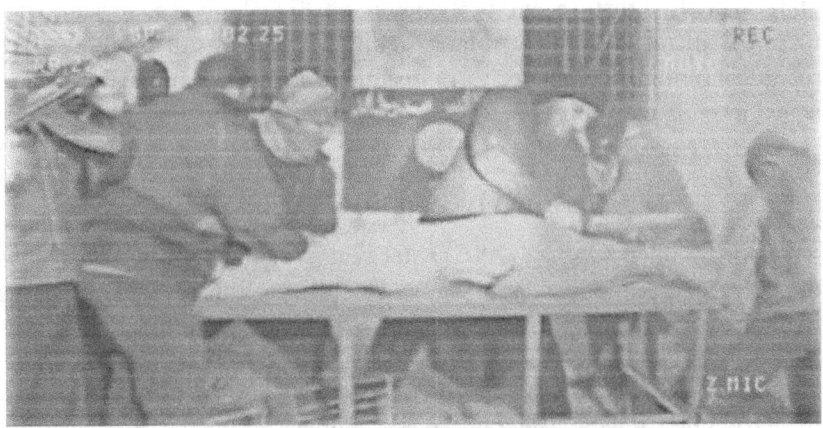

Figure 2.4 *Body of Lies*.

When Ferris forms a fragile bond with Hani, head of the Jordanian Intelligence Service, his cooperation attempts are foiled by his unscrupulous handler Hoffman. Like his local counterparts, Ferris is watched via live drone feed; like them, he has been deceived, manipulated, double-crossed and tortured by forces beyond his control. This false equivalency and division of blame allows the film to have its cake and eat it too. Decisions are made by abstract bureaucracies, or unscrupulous men like Hoffman who give cruel orders with, to paraphrase Pink Floyd frontman Roger Waters, 'the bravery of being out of range'.

After a failed double play, Ferris is taken by Hani to see a room in which a man – a local agent working for the CIA – is being whipped. Emphasising his awareness of Western practices and of Ferris's past, Hani sweetly comments to Ferris that he trusts him to have had 'experience' with torture. Upset, Ferris remarks, 'I thought you didn't believe in torture' to which Hani retorts, 'This is punishment, my dear. It's a very different thing.' What the audience sees, of course, is a man being tortured, and the contradiction between visual and spoken information exposes the linguistic manoeuvre as hypocritical.

Later, when Ferris is tortured, no interrogation precedes the smashing of his fingers. One might interpret this as an attempt to erect a difference between US torture (interrogative, righteous) and Middle Eastern torture (archaic, punishing). However, Hani's smug and finely ironic demeanour in the exchange suggests that he is consciously copying (and thus exposing) a Western rhetorical strategy of double-speak, of hypocritical renaming performances, such as the terminology of 'enhanced interrogation techniques'. A similar farce appears in *Rendition*, when a shaken Douglas is asked whether he is 'new to this'. He replies, taken aback but also annoyed, 'This is my first torture' and is reprimanded: 'The United States does not torture, Douglas.' While the rhetorical dimension points to different codes for interpreting the violence as punishment or interrogation, the images signal interchangeability.

Crossing Over to 'the Dark Side'

Syriana (Stephen Gaghan, 2005) interweaves the complicated storylines of several father – son relationships, which 'form the basis of the film's humanism which suggests that, regardless of location on the globe, bonds between fathers and sons are universal'.[31] Roger Ebert borrows Alissa Quart's term when he described *Syriana* as a 'hyperlink film ... in which the characters inhabit separate stories, but we gradually discover how those in one story are connected to those in another'.[32] Complex to the point of unintelligibility, its plot 'surrounds' the audience, aligning us with its characters, who do not receive the whole picture either.[33] While *Syriana* provides context for the origins of extremism, this narrative confusion and the film's pessimistic ending result in a kind of moral equivalency, in an 'amoral complexity' which finds 'all of the players in the oil game corrupt and compromised'.[34]

Similarly to the previously discussed films, the personal awakening of a former CIA agent Bob Barnes (George Clooney) leaves him dissatisfied and disillusioned with the organisation, but in contrast to *Body*, Barnes's 'middle-aged, slightly overweight and unkempt body'[35] is eventually killed by a CIA-led, remote-controlled drone strike. There is no more escaping, no safe homeland to return to, confirming Jyotsna Kapur's argument that modern war and terrorism have 'eroded the boundaries between the military and civilian life. Both state terrorism and its opposition employ secrecy, stealth, and surveillance as core tactics'.[36]

And yet: at one point, Barnes is tortured by an Iranian intelligence officer, who lectures his prisoner on 'ancient Chinese' torture methods – displacing his acts through this 'foreign' genealogy, just as the film itself associates the origins of torture with a barbaric premodern 'other', upholding the political fiction of torture coming to 'us' from 'them', who are coded as not responsive to other forms of conflict resolution.

Where is torture happening? Diegetically, while the Western settings are specific, a visually interchangeable Middle Eastern locale functions as the place of torture: Jordan (*Body*), Iran and Lebanon (*Syriana*). In *Rendition*, the Western places are named or clearly coded by visual landmarks, whereas even a diegetic television report rather irritatingly subtitles its images with a vague 'suicide bombing in north Africa'. Visually, narratively, symbolically, the torture is located with an 'othered' place, even if the films admit – and criticise – that the torture is enacted with the support, tacit approval or even on the behalf of the USA.

Postcolonial criticism has legitimately criticised the cultural discourse that frames the US as visually and metaphorically open and enlightened, contrasted with Middle Eastern locales as backward, chaotic and teeming with indistinct, threatening masses, 'visually configured as a degenerate nation' or else 'as spaces and places that provide mere backdrops for geopolitical conflict'.[37] These settings then demarcate danger zones, which a white hero may navigate in order to ultimately emerge safely, superior, separate and perhaps regenerated. Thus, even films that have been critically understood as clearly opposed to torture and supportive of liberal politics contain a political instability at their core that seems to reveal imperial anxieties by literalising former US Vice President Dick Cheney's infamous declaration that America needs to work 'the dark side' to fight her enemies.

> Soldiers of the West must somehow cross over the borders that separate Self and Other ... in order to gain access to the deadly and amoral practices that the Other commands. Bounded by the moral and ontological restraints of Western civilisation, the Western champion cannot effectively combat the gothic Other ... [Imperial gothic] narratives describe an often sacrificial transformation of the Western body and psyche to allow for a less restricted engagement with evil.[38]

The conventional torture narrative codes those who resort to violence as manly, often revolving around a theme where 'real men will have the courage to torture ... [it is] a rite of manhood, a test of moral character'.[39] In *Rendition*, when Douglas, a self-described 'pencil-pusher', voices doubts regarding Anwar's guilt, Saeed turns his interventions into a test of Douglas's manly stamina: 'If you don't have the stomach for it, let someone else do it.'

Similarly, being able to resist torture is linked to manhood and even heroism in problematic ways. This tendency to lionise those who remain silent and condemn those who 'break' under torture is present even in films clearly opposed to torture.[40] Not only does this dichotomy implicitly support the political fiction of the interrogation, but it also maintains the 'moral fiction' of ancient Greece, where 'torturability' delineated the slippery boundary to separate 'free, truth-telling creatures' from barbarians.[41] Silence under torture was associated with aristocratic virtues and nobility, whereas the slave was thought to have no resources with which to resist.

In *Body*, a male triangle offers three types of masculinity. Hoffman is decadent, gluttonous, ignorant and seemingly deliberately offensive. His lack of ethics is linked to a failed masculinity – he works the phone rather than 'in the field', while driving his kids to school and tending to their games – and childish impertinence: when Ferris voices legitimate criticism in an agitated phone call, Hoffman's petulant response – 'Whatever' – is parroted back to him by his pre-teen daughter in the subsequent scene, matched in pitch and tone. Educated, elegant, ruthless and menacing, Hani's character seems also strangely dated, as if he were the elite of a vanishing world, from his code of honour, suave behaviour and his impeccable tailored 1990s Savile Row clothes, to his habit of calling Ferris 'my dear'.[42] Finally, a confident traveller between two worlds, Ferris is able to 'pass' as physically and culturally mobile: he speaks Arabic and moves with ease back and forth between US and Arab cultures and forms of negotiation, communication and technology, demonstrating a cultural awareness derided by his superior, Hoffman.

'[These imperial gothic] narratives describe an often sacrificial transformation of the Western body and psyche to allow for a less restricted engagement with evil'.[43]

Ferris's transformation and redemption bears echoes of the frontier narrative, the trope of 'going native', the white American discovering 'the savage' in himself and also recovering or regenerating a kind of manhood lost to the comforts of modernity, technology and automation, which 'threaten to render obsolete the men who push and pull things'.[44] Initially characterised as being ruthless and cynical like Hoffman, by the end of the film a disillusioned Ferris seeks to escape the grasp – and the panoptic surveillance – of his callous superiors. Ferris's eventual transformation entails no reckoning for any of his actions that have hurt others – his betrayals, his killings, his role in previous torture.

Ferris's eventual rejection of his superiors' hypocrisy is foreshadowed when he finds in his own wounds bone fragments of his Arab friend Bassam, who was shredded in an attack that Ferris barely survived. His scarred body becomes a vessel for memory, physically incorporating his friend. This friend served as little more than a means to give Ferris emotional depth; his torn body literally serves to mark Ferris. Similarly, in the torture-as-punishment scene, the Arab victim serves as a tool, a violation of the Kantian principle that no person may be used only as a means, as a demonstration for Hani towards Ferris, who sees him through a window, and for the cinematic narrator towards us, who see him through our screens. That victim remains unnamed, representative and disposable.

The question 'where is torture happening?' also refers then to its staging, the exchange between foreground and background which in these films renders the true subject of the torture if not invisible then not quite perceivable. As Judith Butler has pointed out with regard to news media representations and political discourse, visual and narrative norms – or media 'frames' – determine a 'field of perceptible reality'. These frames a priori exclude certain groups of people as expendable, and hence, building on her previous work in *Precarious Life*, as not quite grievable.[45]

The visual setting and the relegation of the victim to a plot device, motivating the narrative of the main US characters, contrast with the highly individualised plight of the US characters when they are subjected to torture. Embodied by Hollywood stars DiCaprio in *Body*, Clooney in *Syriana*, Witherspoon and Gyllenhaal in *Rendition*, the Western characters are the emotional placeholders. Film critic Dana Stevens describes this as a shift 'from the political to the personal, from "Never again" to "No! Not Leo's fingers!"'[46] In a similar scene in *Syriana*, when Clooney's fingernails are about to be pulled off, the camera appears to avert its gaze,

Figure 2.5 *Syriana*.

focusing instead on the man's trembling feet: like us, the camera would rather not see. These are instances of a visualised politics of the squirm, expressions of anticipated spectatorial discomfort channelled through the camera. When the prisoner loses consciousness, the camera image falls along with him to the ground, as a blinking lens and black blend mimic his loss of vision, claiming the discretion and modesty of 'good taste' that Susan Sontag has detected when it comes to the news showing pain of our own:

> The more remote or exotic the place, the more likely we are to have full frontal views of the dead and dying ... oblivious to the considerations that deter such displays of our own victims of violence; for the other, even when not an enemy, is regarded only as someone to be seen, not someone (like us) who also sees.[47]

In recent US fiction productions featuring the human impact of the war in Iraq, including the torture events, the focus on Western characters results in victimisation, trial and redemption narratives, or, conversely, in condemnation of specific actors, but pushes the victims aside, narratively, spatially, sonically and affectively. For instance, films such as *Boys of Abu Ghraib* (Luke Moran, 2014) and *Camp X-Ray* (Peter Sattler, 2014) play on the trope of the 'white saviour film', in which a sole white figure engaged in a civilising or redeeming project, saves a non-white individual.[48] In both films, the focus is squarely on the soldiers, their boredom, their challenging circumstances, adding an improbable friendship between the protagonist and a detainee. In *X-Ray*, Kristen Stewart serves as identificatory figure, a well-meaning private who is put in a bad situation. *Boys* focuses on the impact of the torture, which remains in the background, on the affective state of handsome Moran and ends on his victimisation through media circulation of an image that does not 'say it all', as the film has just shown the genesis of its production. The opportunity to tackle perpetrator stories in way that gathers deep insight – by including contingent and specific factors but also cultural pathologies and intended cruelty, instigated by the military as institution – is wasted in these victimisation narratives.

Conversely, a film like *Vice* (Adam McKay, 2018) which entirely focuses on a perpetrator figure, also relegates torture and its victims to the background. A dark comedy centring around former Vice President Dick Cheney, the film explains dry topics such as the interpretation of constitutional law which formed the premise for the infamous torture memos.[49] The torture cases appear in these films as image fragments: they appear and disappear suddenly, slipped in as visual shock, in the same way as images of an operation on an open heart and the jolting audiovisual texture of bombings. In both the ostensibly more ideologically 'liberal' and in the more 'conservative' of these films, torture becomes a tool, marking a narrative turning point in the lives of the US protagonists, characterising the Western protagonist, adding flavour to the *mise-en-scène*.

Visual Regimes

As elaborated in influential models on the dynamics of the look and the gaze by film, critical race, feminist, cultural and postcolonial studies, watching can be an exercise of power. Most pervasive when translated into social structures, certain gazes become invisible and normalised. At the same time, not only looking but also choosing *not* to look can be a right and a privilege – just as invisibility can denote both vulnerability and control or agency.

Beyond the notion of a general structural complicity of cinema with warfare, particular gazes carry more historical baggage.[50] A prime example of a cinematic gaze of dominance is the aerial shot, typical of war films and newsreel footage. This disembodied gaze conflates military and media apparatus. It objectifies the target and makes 'mass destruction psychologically viable'.[51] Viewers can share this 'imperialist gaze' so that 'by viewing we are bombing, identified with both bomber and bomb'.[52] The all-seeing panoptic vantage point connotes military might and technological superiority. It is also associated with the CIA, which is introduced in *Body* and *Rendition* with just such an aerial shot of its headquarters and a legend spelling out 'Langley, Virginia'.

The panoptic vision which turns the whole world into a target emerged as a standard shot of the coverage of the second Gulf War. In *Zero*, the raid on bin Laden's hide-out is also initiated with a 'possessive' aerial and panoramic gaze before shifting to a different aesthetics, the fragmented, multi-screened chaotic plurality of gazes which visually reproduces changes in modern warfare. Filmed through night-vision goggles, the raid sequence in *Zero*, with its images of chaos and confusion, reflects the prevalent optical forms and aesthetics of remediated modern warfare. As we move from a distanced helicopter shot to greater and greater proximity to the target, the closer we get, the less we seem to comprehend, and at the end of the raid, we never even see bin Laden. This shift from panoptic to fragmented vision reflects also more broadly that the politics of visibility have changed dramatically and concurrently, and so the ethics of looking relations must be adjusted.

Both in cinema and in warfare, the ocular metaphor suggested a worldview in which seeing equalled agency and possessive power. But more and more, watching is occurring all the time – surveillance footage and CCTV promise total visibility but also information overload and endless repetition, prompting Patricia Pisters to argue that Jean Baudrillard's diagnosis of an 'aesthetics of disappearance' should be revised to accommodate today's 'radically changed logistics of perception that includes many more types of images'.[53]

Considering that 'our new media wars [...] are themselves executed, not just disseminated, in new media',[54] it seems fitting that these films reflect contemporary violence in both aesthetic and formal construction. Chaotic proximity and excess of visual information translates this experience optically, along with what Bordwell has called 'intensified continuity' – a decrease of average shot length, close framing, a narrowed focus on actors, and a free-ranging camera[55] – and Shaviro expands to 'Post-Continuity' – when 'preoccupation with immediate effects trumps any concern for broader continuity'.[56] The 'hypermediated optics of War on Terror films'[57] reorganise how power and knowledge are constructed through the gaze. As Rob White suggests, contemporary war films double as media studies and deal with 'a regime change in media as well as military control'.[58] Contrasting 'decorporealised' warfare, war as technological, mediated experience and the trauma of embodied violence in a 'battle of the screens',[59] Burgoyne reads such films as having picked up the aesthetics of those pictures of war that were circulated online, and which promised to show what was missing on the TV news, i.e maimed bodies of wounded survivors or the corpses of those who did not survive.

Like terrorism and modern warfare, modern torture, too, is frequently linked to remediated and distorted images on multiplied screens in public and private spaces, often via images of surveillance. In his 2001–3 installation *Eye/Machine*, Harun Farocki had called these images 'operational':

Figure 2.6 *Body of Lies.*

made and meant to be 'viewed' by machines. Trevor Paglen built on this work when he suggests that 'We've long known that images can kill. What's new is that nowadays, they have their fingers on the trigger'.[60]

The films frequently express related anxieties around the presumed objectivity of technology: the computer, the lie detector, the documentary image. Yet their feared failure is mostly linked to human error or manipulation. In *Rendition*, the case against Anwar is built on the flimsy evidence of a suspicious phone call placed to the phone registered in his name;[61] after his abduction, Anwar's name is digitally 'disappeared' by erasing him from the passenger list of his flight home. Cell phones trigger bombings in *Body*, and they help to track, police and visually 'possess' people.

Who sees, and who understands, the barrage of surveillance footage and the multiplied screens of modern warfare? Neither of these images allow for an ideal viewing position: clearly, the expert needed to read and select among the suffocating quantity of data[62] cannot be the spectator, who needs additional information – hence the superimposed titles in *Zero* ('Black Site', 'Samara, Iraq' and so on). As a solution, the films indicate an expert reader, typically CIA or FBI, who receives and interprets this scientifically mediated data. These analysts are characterised as 'knowledge worker[s] whose work depends upon [their] control of surveillance equipment and [their] ... ability to interpret images and signs ... What empowers the FBI is not their technology but their interpretative skills'.[63]

Catherine Zimmer even suggests an intrinsic link between surveillance and torture, as 'the ambiguous narrative formation around surveillance asks for torture, hailing it in order to turn the zones of indistinction into resolved deployments of power'.[64]

Shots of diegetic experts decoding such screens, data that is incomprehensible to the viewer, negotiate the problem of intelligibility. Their

Figure 2.7 *Zero Dark Thirty*.

study of these images is contemplative: they repeat, rewind, dissect, compare, while the audience watches them: images of experts watching images, bearing witness to the performance of expertise. Excluded from understanding the investigating process, we are also absolved from feeling responsible to act.

Without this expertise, the images can be misleading. In *Rendition*, the images' significance eludes the (Arab) investigators. Torturer Fawal is given a tourist's accidental footage of the explosion, evoking many famous cases where footage is used in the attempt to reconstruct a crime. The footage does not provide Fawal with the information he was looking for – the identity of the bomber – but more crucially, he fails to read the image for the information he was *not* looking for but would have needed in order to understand the events. Contrast this with *Zero*'s Maya and her successful scrutiny of the torture footage. When the camera mimics her behaviour, zooming in on a close-up of the footage, the image dissolves into pixels, unintelligible to the viewer: *we* cannot comprehend the image, but *she* does. The ability to discover a crucial detail hidden from view for ordinary humans, is related to Foucault's medical gaze, equally elusive to the uninitiated. This expertise to find truth hidden inside a (visual) body not only pairs surveillance and policing with healing, but also links the expert torturer and the CIA knowledge worker. Thus, the films articulate anxieties about the role of the human in a world of machines, the disappearance of specifically male-coded skills, including, apparently, the 'craftsmanship' of the torturer.

***

With the notable difference of *Camp X-Ray* and *Boys of Abu Ghraib*, whose protagonists are upstanding but naïve grunts, the figure of the expert 'knowledge worker' as protagonist links these films to *Zero*, discussed in the previous chapter, and *Homeland*, which will be a topic in the next one. But in contrast to *Zero*, the Western protagonists in *Rendition*, *Body* and *Syriana* are the affective centre of the film, channelling the sympathies of an imagined Western audience through the pain of their own body and suffering the moral weight of witnessing torture. These redeemed heroes, alongside a visuality that separates healthy from conflicted spaces in such a way that different gazes and types of images – regimes of vision – correspond to different mobilities and temporalities geopolitically, create a political instability at the core of films which have been critically understood as clearly opposed to torture. Close encounters of human bodies are distinguished from technological apparatuses of surveillance and remote drones, which are reflected in various 'new' kinds of images, articulating anxieties especially about the role of human men in a world of machines.

Where 9/11 is positioned as the original sin and 'time zero' in *Zero*'s neat narrative structure, *Syriana* in particular sketches a global interconnectedness and mutual vulnerability. Likewise, in *Body*, when Ferris is tortured and about to be killed, his flashbacks include a torture scene from the film's beginning, in which he witnessed – and perhaps instigated? – a man being tortured to death. The montage suggests equivalence: I have tortured, you torture me; I kill, you kill. The events are explained as a cycle of violence, further supported by the film's opening line, a W. H. Auden quote, 'Those to whom evil is done/Do evil in return'. Yet this strategy also conveniently relieves the US of specific guilt by describing violence as cyclical and somewhat universally human in nature.

Notes

1. Peters, 'Witnessing', p. 708.
2. Epigenetic research suggests that trauma can be transmitted even before the child is born, as genes are influenced by changes in environment and behaviour. For instance, Yehuda et al., 'Transgenerational effects of posttraumatic stress'.
3. Bronfen, *Specters of War*, p. 145.
4. Sundquist in Schoonover, *Brutal Vision*, pp. 222–3.
5. Sundquist, 'Witness without End?' pp. 68–9.
6. Frosh and Pinchevski, *Media Witnessing*, p. 1.
7. Leach, 'Scientific Witness', p. 190.
8. Peters, 'Witnessing', pp. 714 and 721.
9. Ibid., pp. 720–2.

10. Cf. Manovich, 'To Lie and to Act'; Bolter and Grusin, *Remediation*.
11. Leach, 'Scientific Witness', p. 194. Cf. Blondheim and Liebes, 'Archaic Witnessing and Contemporary News Media', pp. 120 and 115.
12. Shapin quoted in Leach, 'Scientific Witness', p. 194.
13. Ellis and Boltansky quoted in Blondheim and Liebes, 'Archaic Witnessing', p. 125.
14. Foucault, *Discipline and Punish*, p. 268.
15. Ballengee, *Wound and Witness*, p.144.
16. Cf. Ballengee, *Wound and Witness*.
17. Schoonover, *Brutal Vision*, p. 39.
18. DuBois, *Torture and Truth*, pp. 154–5.
19. Devji, 'Torture at the Limits of Politics', p. 248 and p. 253.
20. Ibid., p. 250.
21. *Rendition* is based on the kidnapping of Khaled el-Masri, a German citizen mistaken for a terrorist in 2003. In December 2012, the European Court of Human Rights ruled that el Masri's treatment amounted to torture. He was never charged with a crime or given access to a lawyer. Cf. 'About those black sites'.
22. Goldberg, 'Splitting difference', p. 267 and p. 264.
23. Walsh, 'What Stories We Tell', p. 159 and p. 155.
24. Berlant in Walsh, 'What stories we tell', p. 154.
25. Schoonover, *Brutal Vision*, p. 223.
26. Elsaesser and Hagener, *Film Theory*, p. 149.
27. Elsaesser 'The Mind-Game Film', pp. 15–16.
28. Butler, *Frames of War*, p. 77.
29. Cf. Jean Franco's discussion of the link between modernity and the victimisation of indigenous populations in Peru, who were presented as pre-modern and an obstacle to modernity and progress. Franco, *Cruel Modernity*.
30. Cf. Cettl, *Terrorism in American Cinema*.
31. Kapur, 'Childhood', p. 45.
32. Ebert, 'Syriana'. Quart's intervention appeared in *Film Comment*. Cf. Kerr, 'Network Narrative' and Cameron, *Modular Narratives*.
33. Ibid.
34. Ibid.
35. Kapur, 'Childhood', p. 45.
36. Kapur, 'Childhood', p. 47.
37. Hasian, 'Military Orientalism', p. 475. Cf. Goldberg, 'Splitting Difference'.
38. Höglund, *American Gothic*, p. 122.
39. Devji, 'Torture at the Limits of Politics', p. 228.
40. Compare how torture in the seminal *Battle of Algiers* (Gillo Pontecorvo, 1966) produces intelligence, or the proud assurance in *Rome, Open City* (Roberto Rossellini, 1945) that the victim, tortured to death, did not breathe a word.
41. DuBois, *Torture and Truth*, p. 62.
42. Cf. Laverty, 'Body of Lies' on Mark Strong's wardrobe in the film.

43. Höglund, *American Gothic*, p. 122.
44. Mishra, 'Crisis in modern masculinity'; cf. Richard Slotkin's analysis on the role of 'regenerating' violence in US-American imagination and identity. Slotkin, *Gunfighter Nation*.
45. Butler, *Frames of War*, p. 64.
46. Stevens, 'Glossy Torture'.
47. Sontag, 'Regarding the Pain', pp. 70–2.
48. Cf. Hughey, *White Savior*.
49. The 'unitary executive theory' asserts that the president's authority over the executive is so complete and unlimited, that he may ignore laws that infringe on this power.
50. On the historical 'osmosis between industrialized warfare and cinema' see Virilio, *War and Cinema*, p. 58.
51. Karen Frome in Guerin and Hallas, *Image and Witness*, p. 67.
52. Butler, *Frames of War*, p. 29.
53. Pisters, 'Logistics of Perception 2.0', p. 237.
54. Stewart, 'War Pictures', p. 112.
55. Bordwell, 'Intensified Continuity'.
56. Shaviro, 'Post-Continuity', p. 51.
57. Stewart, 'War Pictures', p. 127.
58. White, 'Heaven Knows We're Digital Now', p. 5.
59. Burgoyne, 'Embodiment in the War Film', p. 11; cf. Burgoyne, 'The Violated Body'.
60. Paglen, 'Invisible Images'.
61. Peter Bradshaw took this as a fudging 'the question of whether the CIA's phone-record evidence against Anwar is sound or not'. Bradshaw, 'Rendition'. But the point of the film is rather to make the viewer reflect upon torture *regardless* of the victim's presumed guilt or innocence.
62. Cf. Lyon, 'Surveillance, Power, and Everyday Life'.
63. Gooch, 'Beyond Panopticism', pp. 164–7.
64. Zimmer, 'Caught on Tape?' p. 92. Zimmer's analysis focuses on 'torture porn', a genre (if it is one) that is deliberately excluded here as it does not negotiate cases of factual torture.

CHAPTER 3

Television Torture, Made in the USA

Both in the US and in Chile, television shows have emerged which speak to critical political events, able to reflect on their moment of production in perhaps more immediate ways than cinema. The following two chapters move from the US series *24*, a television show where torture functions as central and much discussed set piece, towards *Homeland*, which engages with the impact of the 'War on Terror' including torture, on to the Chilean series *Los Archivos del Cardenal*, where the relation of the dictatorial past to visual evidence comes into clear focus, and ending on *Los 80*, about an 'ordinary' Chilean family during the 1980s, where the presence of torture is rarely made visually explicit but its shadows are clearly felt.

Television series stand in a generic tradition that prioritises affectivity and melodrama, and the shows explored here encourage complex emotional audience involvement, opening links between spectators' subjective and collective memory. Additionally, their serial rhetoric lends itself particularly well to the examination of collective structures and systemic problems. The format therefore offers a microcosm of the research questions explored and methodology used throughout this book, providing a structural fulcrum linking US and Chilean audiovisual output. Leading from the visible towards the invisible and back, from the visual dominance and repetition of relatively few images, which clutter and cover others, to images negotiating the absence or presence of visual evidence of factual historical events, and ending on the activation of nonvisual modes of perception through the 'presence of absence', these chapters mirror the structure of this book.

* * *

Long before the touted 'second golden age of television' beginning in the 2,000s, television scholars have pushed back against the tendency to associate television with the commercially standardised, ideologically conservative and aesthetically impoverished,[1] highlighting instead its unique possibilities. Television drama, with its 'rhetoric of discussion', could work as a 'cultural forum', argue Horace Newcomb and Paul Hirsch, and influence 'public thought': 'Television does not present firm ideological conclusions – despite its formal conclusions – so much as it comments on ideological problems ... Conflicting viewpoints of social issues are, in fact, the elements that structure most television programs'.[2]

Contrary to the lament that television trivialises history and acts as 'death to memory',[3] television and (collective) memory are not mutually exclusive. As the medium of television historically brought its reproductions into the domestic sphere, television is comparatively intimate, emotional and vernacular. The format offers even potential advantages for the depiction of history. For instance, the narrative formulas and aesthetic strategies associated with classical Hollywood cinema have been criticised for privatising collective pain and historical stories, and for reconciling ideological–political issues by projecting them onto the level of individuals. Serial television on the other hand 'give[s] voice to an increasing number of perspectives and points of view'.[4] The length and form of the serial, its subplots and digressions, Glen Creeber argues, help to understand history as

> a shared social experience ... [which] reveals the complexity and not the simplicity of historical 'truth' ... The very length and 'soapiness' of the serial's form ... makes it an ideal vehicle through which politics and history can be understood; not as mere 'fact' or 'polemic', but as *memory* and *experience*.[5]

The temporal structures of a television serial allow for extended psychology and development of characters and situations, which makes room for the audience's emotional relationship to the characters and situations to mature and change over a longer period of time. Additionally, within episodes or for different seasons, television dramas can offer variations on endings, resolving some storylines and leaving others undeveloped or open, achieving partial and temporary closure.

> [The serial's increasingly] 'flexi-narrative structure' ... mixes a number of narrative levels together (frequently without offering any neat resolutions), [it] is arguably better able to reflect and respond to the increasing uncertainties and social ambiguities of the contemporary world.[6]

Many contemporary television drama series employ both such narrative complexity and the personalised preoccupation of soap opera techniques to re-examine historical matter. As a result, these shows manage to achieve both emotional intimacy and 'paradigmatic narrative complexity',[7] producing a peculiar relationship with its engaged and dedicated audience. Precisely this quality of decades-spanning longevity posed a challenge to this research.

After providing a contextual reading to determine the shows' cultural significance and rather than attempting an exhaustive survey, the analysis is focused in particular on the title sequences of each show. As Karen Lury suggests, these introductions not only serve a 'heralding' function, but also encapsulate the essence of a TV show, often as 'quite complex audio signifiers of the style, pace and structuring narrative of the programmes they identify'.[8] To convey the essence of a general plot that 'cannot be represented directly', Lawrence Kramer explains, the title sequences illuminate what is called the 'narrative image'[9] of a television show: a plot which belongs 'not just to the individual episode, but to the series as a whole',[10] giving both a general form and specific feeling. Following this line of argument, the title sequences will reflect and condense major themes and preoccupations of the show at large.

24: Torture on Repeat

Although its fictional, even fantastical, nature and lack of engagement with specific factual torture cases might seem to position the television show *24* outside the perimeters of this research, the show must be addressed for its long-lasting impact.[11] *24* has become shorthand for 'torture on USA television', and subsequent productions featuring torture necessarily position themselves in relation to *24*'s style and iconography. The show's terminology has seeped into public and even political language to a disturbing extent.[12]

The show picked up on a *zeitgeist* of collective paranoia in post-9/11 America,[13] as demonstrated by the considerable change to its narrative paradigm in the aftermath of 9/11. In season 1, filmed before the attacks, the protagonist threatened but never actually resorted to torture; from season two onwards, torture became a central and recurring spectacle of the programme. In fact, the show was most strongly criticised for its incessant depiction of torture as productive. Many critics argued that the show normalised, promoted and institutionalised a 'torture culture',[14] shaping the attitude of the general US public and military recruits by normalising and promoting 'the acceptance of policies of surveillance, detention, and interrogation'.[15]

> Guantánamo torturers developing their 'enhanced interrogation techniques' looked no further than prime-time television for inspiration: Jack Bauer offered a treasure trove of techniques in his weekly torture of terrorists.[16]

Yet this approach veers close to a media effects model, without sufficiently interrogating its hidden assumptions and problematic causalities.

Following Stephen Prince's critique of that approach, beyond the clear evidence that there is an increase of certain themes, it is far less clear how viewers read these and react to them, and whether such themes are a symptom of engagement with existing policies or an ideological preparation for even harsher policies. Worse, blaming popular culture for creating amateur torturers indirectly absolves a chain of command from responsibility. As Prince remarks, 'the emergence of a surveillance society, a condition of perpetual war overseas, and the militarisation of domestic life ... may owe more to political decisions and sociological factors than to television'.[17]

The worry about and focus on the influence of *24* (or violent audiovisual content in general) is not limited to media analysts. In 2006, the Dean of West Point came in protest to talk to *24* producers and writers, claiming that too many new recruits took its depiction of torture literally,[18] and the sidelined leader of an élite (and rapport-based) interagency Criminal Investigation Task Force at Guantánamo, Mark Fallon, also referred to the imaginary of *24* when explaining the ignorance, lack of expertise and abundance of power handed over to Guantánamo guards:

> Most of the interrogators were 'basically conscripts' who would 'walk into a room for the first time thinking the detainee was just waiting to be cracked open and they were the next Jack Bauer ... impervious to nuance, or to the notion that some detainees may have been sent there in error ... each failed interrogation 'was taken as proof that the detainees were both Al Qaeda and trained to resist these methods'.[19]

Yet James Mitchell and Bruce Jessen, the two psychologists hired by the CIA to develop the interrogation programme (despite their lack of expertise in interrogation or knowledge of the cultural region), seem to have based their recommendations for coercive techniques not on television, but on what a former section chief of the FBI's International Terrorism Operations described as 'voodoo science',[20] a form of 'reverse-engineered SERE tactics',[21] outsourcing torture in the process. The military training programme SERE – Survival, Evasion, Resistance, and Escape – originated in World War Two and was further developed during various wars and covert operations in Korea, Vietnam, Iran and Central America.

To be clear: *24* certainly contributed to the cultural imaginary and a visual presence of preemptive violence, including torture, on our screens. But the criticism that such shows act as 'political socialisation', or that 'prime time television ... is "adult education"',[22] needs qualification. Rather than contributing to the media effects debate, my focus here is on outlining the crucial difference, which I assume to be key to audiences' perception, between what is encoded as pure fantasy, and what is continuously referenced as 'based on real events'. What I want to maintain is the – in my eyes crucial – difference between the sheer 'acting out' in the fantasy land of *24*, and the supposedly referential nature of a film like *Zero* or the TV show *Homeland*, discussed in the next section. In a tone of supposedly clear-eyed realism that can only be read in response to and rejection of the enemy cliché of tree-hugging, naïve liberals, these latter products depart from an implicit acceptance that Western democracies torture.

In *24*, even though opposition to the use of torture is either converted or proven wrong, the *prohibition* of torture is never dissolved; it remains an extra-legal method. *24* does not propose so much a pro-torture world *tout court* than to promote a pro-Jack-Bauer world, 'a gun in the hands of the right man'.[23] Reading *24* with Richard Hofstadter's seminal work on paranoia, Jacobus Verheul usefully clarifies that 'paranoia is first and foremost a style' of presentation.[24] Embedded in *24*'s paranoid narrative style – apocalyptic battles with absolute evil as enemy – are all kinds of questionable assumptions, from toxic masculinity to torture as productive tool. The template for Bauer is the figure of the vigilante who combats both the enemy and an inept bureaucratic apparatus, and its 'weak' masculinity and/or liberal values. The show is embedded in a historical tradition of a narcissistic fantasy, of fairytales or superhero films, where 'things [tend to] happen to other people … because Jack has, or has not, acted'.[25] Rejali's descriptions of the 'conventional cinematic iconography of torture' or a 'torture folklore'[26] could double as a description of *24*: extraordinary circumstances, usually evoking the *ticking bomb scenario*, became the show's formal structuring device, and were embedded in *24*'s narrative structure.[27] In *24*, an agent of a fictional agency, the Counter Terrorist Unit (CTU), Jack Bauer, races against a (visually present) clock in order to stop various terrorist plots. Each season is made of twenty-four episodes, spanning the twenty-four hours of one day. The trademark temporality of 'real time' communicates a 'world of the permanent emergency, the permanent exception, the absence or exceptional suspense of law'.[28]

But this treatment of temporality and repetitive seriality, including its 'real time' set-up, also serves to stabilise its location within the realm of fantasy. To begin with, the sheer quantity of torture in this show is remarkable. Over *24*'s eight seasons, there is a torture scene in almost every episode; torture is applied compulsively, and infallibly produces results. Its writers and producers describe their use of torture as 'just a convenient dramatic device [which] moves the plot along quickly'.[29] Precisely its function as quick dramatic fixer and narrative shortcut demonstrates that the use of torture as magic wand situates the show in a dreamworld of omnipotence and wish-fulfilment:'[*24* is a] fantasy about national, economic, and communication systems free of drag, whether it be the drag of subversive activity, the drag of wasted time, or the drag of "obstacles and opacities" ... inherent in mediation'.[30]

In *24*, cause and effect clearly correlate; there are no language barriers, no complications, no uncertainties. A reasonably intelligent audience understands the unreality of this set-up, where precisely the fantasy structure of *24* is a fundamental part of its enjoyment. Compare Lisa Coulthard's argument regarding the similarly aestheticising framing of violence in Quentin Tarantino's films: 'The framing, artifice, referentiality, and clear parameters of violence give the spectator a permission to enjoy – an authorisation that domesticates the audiovisual violence, renders it isolated, controllable, and slightly unreal'.[31]

This incessant repetition also highlights where the fragility and strenuousness of the ideological performance calls attention to itself. The very slipperiness of hegemonic ideological constructs, requiring continuous display and performance, becomes visible through excessive emphasis and hyperbolic repetition. Repetitions become a way to revisit emotionally charged imaginative scenarios, to be explored as a potentially productive navigation tool that points to the cracks in ideology.

In interpreting the fantastically fictitious world of *24* as collective release of psychic shock of 9/11, these repetitions can be read not only as operating on the past but also as orientated towards the future, as Richard Grusin outlines in the concept of 'premediation'. Premediation involves the mediation of anticipated future threats, to become 'affectively accustomed' to and to prevent a renewed experience of shocks, and a particular temporal formation: 'Premediation imagines multiple futures which are alive in the present, which always exist as not quite fully formed potentialities or possibilities'.[32]

Expanding on Niklas Luhmann's analysis of the temporality of modern mass media, Grusin argues that

> It is now not only the case that 'what has just gone into the past is still present', [as with Luhmann] but that what is about to go on in the future is also depicted as occurring in the present. The aim of this double presenting is ... to produce a sense of potential surprise ... [but] also to try to protect against a catastrophic or disruptive surprise.[33]

Within its outlandish set-up, the show maintains a sense of stability through a comforting temporal rigidity. In other words, the world of *24* is released from the normal, yet contained by the formal ritual.[34] Time, in the sense of constant urgency, is built into its formal structure, from the title and narrative premise to the exact time denoted by a literally ticking clock, an on-screen countdown and a digital display at the beginning and end of each segment. The show takes place in 'real time': each episode takes place over the course of one hour; time continues to elapse during the commercial breaks.

The title sequence eloquently displays this focus on time. Over nine seasons, the sequence remains identical: synchronised to the sound of accelerating electronic beeping, a pulsing pixel expands to a blinking digital clock, which flickers faster and faster and finally settles on the number '24', followed by an intertitle outlining the time frame of the episode, such as 'The following takes place between 11:00 a.m. and 12:00 p.m.'

To intensify suspense, the show made extensive use of the split screen, a technique which conveys the 'sense of time passing as simultaneity'[35] and creates an aggressively artificial image, within the otherwise 'excessively intimate and atmospheric'[36] visual style of *24*. The viewer is allowed to enjoy an all-seeing vantage point and the illusion of following several narrative strands at the same time (de facto sound usually focalises attention towards the primary plotline). While the split screen collapses various places into screen space, it does not cross temporal lines: spatial omnipotence never extends to time travel. This means, on a temporal level, there is precisely *no* possibility of repetition in *24*, only a relentless and inescapable thrust forward. Whatever happens and will have happened cannot be undone. This relation to time is where the show speaks most clearly to (post-9/11) memory, to both a (traumatic) past and (feared and desired) future.

24's appeal derives at least in part from this tension between the rigidity of its formal structure – 'real time' and the repeated ritual of torture as narrative element – and the fantasy of control –spatial omnipotence and 'magic' wands.

Homeland

Created by two veteran writer-producers of *24*, *Homeland* (Showtime, 2011–20)[37] which began as an adaptation of the Israeli TV show *Hatufim/Prisoners of War*, was widely perceived as a re-negotiation with, even an apology for *24*.[38] Both shows clearly speak to the moment of their production: the terror attacks of 9/11 in *24*, and the moral reckoning with the ensuing 'War on Terror' and increased domestic surveillance in *Homeland*.

In *24*, enemies divulge relevant information under torture; in *Homeland*, all attempts to secure such knowledge yield only partial results. Suspense in *24* is created by racing against time to hunt down the guilty; suspense in *Homeland* arises precisely from the partiality and unreliability of any given information, moment, or characters.[39] Where *24*'s plot line is twisted but ultimately reliably teleological, *Homeland* emphasises uncertainty and doubt. While *24* allows simultaneity of events, it does not provide the thick web of what Shaviro describes as an emerging quality of contemporary serial drama: the 'periodicity ... when one dramatic conflict recalls past relationships, themes, or plot development'.[40] This web-like, associative and cross-temporal structure, crossing inner and outer worlds, is in fact encapsulated in *Homeland*'s title sequence.

Homeland's first season follows CIA officer Carrie Mathison in her attempt to prove that a recently released prisoner of war, Marine Sergeant Nicholas Brody, who had been held by al-Qaeda for eight years, 'turned' while in captivity. As the audience subsequently discovers, Brody's identity is multi-layered: suburban American father, prodigal husband, white convert to Islam, potential sleeper agent, ex-Marine and war hero.

Brody's similarly complex counterpart is CIA operative Carrie, his hunter and lover. The show emphasises the extent to which Carrie and Brody are almost the missing pieces to each other. Where Brody is introverted and frequently unable to express himself, Carrie reacts in 'excessively' emotional ways: 'Carrie's feelings are always on display, just as Brody's are always seen simmering just below the surface. Neither character's motivation is certain, whether to other characters or to the audience.'[41]

With her uncompromising behaviour, Carrie ties her career and sense of self-worth to the enigma of Brody's identity: conclusive evidence of his guilt or innocence would prove Carrie's clairvoyance or have her fired for insanity. As it happens, both results occur at different moments in the show, demonstrating again the show's signature play on certainties: 'viewers understand relatively early that Carrie is right to be suspicious of Brody, but the show withholds [and reverses] diegetic recognition'.[42]

When Brody makes a suicide video before attempting to blow himself up in the company of high-level politicians, the video emulates the style of the videos of Islamist fundamentalists, from the way in which he is framed in the image – speaking directly to the camera – to the military dress code. Clothed in US marine uniform, Brody fully embraces his hybrid identity as intermittent employee of a terrorist leader, the US vice-president and the CIA.

This ambivalence turns Brody into a difficult character, both to sustain and to kill off, as demonstrated by the show's various attempts to do either. After attempting suicide and being rescued twice, Brody is eventually hanged in Iran in the final episode of season 3, which for Negra and Lagerwey suggests that he 'sacrificed his life to redeem [Carrie] Mathison's love and his reputation as an American patriot'.[43] Yet the eventual formal closure of killing Brody cannot undo that the proverbial box has been opened. This is not to mistake the show as progressive or to disregard its ideologically problematic, even revisionist proclivities, but to insist on Newcomb and Hirsch's contention that 'in popular culture generally, in television specifically, the raising of questions is as important as the answering of them'.[44]

Homeland also features frequent – and unresolved – clashes of opinion, risk-evaluations and strategic preferences within the CIA. For instance, Carrie's mentor Saul, a key and at least initially sympathetic figure, opposes torture, while the CIA's chief torturer Quinn – who is also given sympathy, screen time, even love interests – increasingly comes to resemble a psychopath and killing machine. In these as in many other instances, *Homeland* presents a 'dense, polysemic text ... [which] has been analyzed as both a straightforward articulation of and a subversive critique of US foreign policy and the national security mind-set after [9/11]'.[45]

In this context, it is interesting to consider how the show deals with collective structures, the relation between individual and institutional accountability. The messiness of the decision-making process is much on display and often appears chaotic and random. Obedience is repeatedly demanded for decisions that appear opaque, mistaken or even motivated by personal political gain. The CIA of *Homeland*, like the fictional CTU of *24*, replaces the family relations of the traditional soap.[46] Unlike *24*, the institution appears more powerful than any of its individual members. Being fired from the fictional CTU does not stop Jack Bauer from doing his job, whereas a fired Carrie loses all access. Several times Carrie is forcefully, physically stopped – she is variously drugged, shot, institutionalised and publicly betrayed on television – when she acts in a maverick 'Jack Bauer' mode. Carrie's overreach – for instance, she puts Brody under illegal surveillance – can be read as *acting out*, rather than *working through*, her (read: the intelligence agencies') trauma of having missed the signs that might have prevented 9/11.

A Crisis of Epistemology

In spite of such ambivalent, even potentially progressive moments, and in spite of the show's narrative and psychological complexity, which maintains that 'the trauma of war does not disappear', James Castonguay argues that the series ultimately works as 'a "quality" propaganda arm for the

Obama administration', analogous to *24*, which he considers 'effective PR for the Bush administration'.[47] *Homeland* may open up possibilities for alternative and even subversive meanings in a US context of reception, but it closes them down by rearticulating, reinforcing and ultimately amplifying the familiar representation of the militant Muslim terrorist.[48]

Yet the show's fundamental structure is one of contained uncertainty (or conditional certainty), which extends, in a remarkable turnaround from *24*, to all key characters, and to the 'discourse of objectivity' itself, 'teasing out the questionable fidelity of surveillance footage with its blind spots and lacunae',[49] even highlighting US institutional fragility. The loss of certainty for the spectator is channelled through unreliable or restricted narration and the chronology of disclosure, which holds the spectator in doubt regarding Brody's allegiance throughout the first season. It is also embodied by and enacted as loss of control by the deceived protagonist Carrie, especially in her mental health, as well as the shift towards highlighting the unreliability of the mechanism meant to certify truthful information, such as the visual image, the lie detector, and the unreliable truth of the body that speaks against or in spite of the mind, through torture or a mental health condition.

Torture scenes occur at several moments in the series. As shown in brief flashbacks, Brody was tortured in captivity. The representation of this torture is unremarkable. What should be noted, however, is that he seems not to have been interrogated, and that his conversion to Islam seems to have happened unrelatedly. When CIA interrogator Quinn stabs Brody with a knife during questioning, this does not render (immediate) results: it is Carrie's rapport-building and intense emotional vulnerability that incites Brody to speak. And yet, at another point, Saul gathers intelligence by means of rapport building, but this information, too, ultimately turns out to be false. Thus, not only is 'knowledge ... depicted as problematic, but just what knowledge *is* is itself problematic'.[50] The problem and danger both for Carrie and Brody is within their heads. His trauma and post-traumatic stress, or PTSD, which includes a sexual dysfunction, is clearly linked to Carrie's mental illness: in terms of cultural metaphor, both shameful, even 'abject' conditions.[51] Films often depicts those suffering from mental conditions or illnesses as *genius savant*, whose bodies speak, occasionally in spite of or independent of the subjects' conscious minds, and *Homeland* 'participates in the contemporary habit of rewriting mental illness as specialness'.[52] In the show, Carrie's inherited bipolar disorder provides her with superior intuition. This notion of a sixth sense resembles the structuring paradigm of our concept of torture, where a higher truth

– an advanced capacity of knowing – is hidden in the body. (When Carrie is force-medicated, the justifications – 'You are not leaving us any choice!' – resemble those used to support torture: 'Why are you doing this to yourself?') Body knowledge is acknowledged, even trumps the objectivity of machine knowledge, yet it, too, is far from infallible, and eventually only serves to foster paranoia and epistemological uncertainty: who or what is knowing there (who is that I that observes myself thinking), and what is the connection between knowledge and self?

Alex Bevan links Carrie's body as expressive tool of 'invisible' matters to overarching themes within the series, such as state surveillance, security, digital-era warfare: 'Carrie's mind and body territorialise geopolitical struggles that elude representability ... drone warfare and surveillance ... rely on elusiveness, invisibility, and the porousness of national borders'.[53]

And yet, information generated through the CIA's surveillance apparatus is also demonstrated as partial and fallible, containing 'both literal and metaphorical blind spots'.[54] It is not just selective perception and mental problems which limit clairvoyance, but also the devices meant to convey certainty: the ruthless vice-president claims on television that images of killed children during a drone strike were propaganda fabrications (series 1, episode 9); Brody cunningly stages a fight in the blind spot of the surveillance cameras in order to smuggle contraband to a prisoner (series 1, episode 5); riots instigated by video footage of a drone attack wreaking havoc on a Pakistani wedding party (series 4, episode 1) were a premeditated fake aimed at covering the killing of a CIA agent (series 4, episode 3).

Images fail to provide sanctuary as impartial and objective, an epistemological vertigo that in *Homeland* extends to other machineries of truth, such as the repeated use of the polygraph. Lie detectors promise to penetrate to the truth by surpassing the autonomous will of the subject and tricking the body into betrayal through involuntary reflex. This idea of 'the body as the haven of truth' links the polygraph to the belief that in torture, bodily pain produces truth, and to torture as *24*'s infallible magic wand.[55] In *Homeland*, however, the machines fail. Several times, key figures have to take a polygraph test, and the results are inconclusive or wrong. The lie detector incriminates an innocent Saul, while Brody passes. (This is factual: polygraph tests are notoriously vulnerable to examiners' own personal prejudices, systematic biases and to producing false positives.[56]) In *Homeland*, it is Carrie's supreme intuition, rather than machine intelligence, which is her superpower. Carrie is characterised as an intelligence *savant*, her gift for espionage and counterterrorism fuelled by a genetic affective imbalance. But Carrie is not a fully realised example of what

Meghan Daum criticised as idealised dream-girl versions of CIA officers, who emerged as a result of the need in the 'American imagination ... to believe that it's not mere mortals who are keeping us safe from terrorists but, rather, superhumans who never exercise poor judgment or lose their moral compass in the fog of war'.[57]

Frequently unreasonably and overly confident, Carrie replaces the absolute certainty and authority of Jack Bauer with emotional instability. She literally embodies a paranoid-pathological response to the permanent threat scenario. Elsaesser hypothesises that paranoia is 'the appropriate – or even "productive" – pathology of our contemporary society, of being able to rely on bodily "intuition" as much as on ocular perception; or being able to "think laterally" and respond hyper-sensitively to changes in the environment'.[58] Carrie's mental and bodily health has been read as 'synecdoche for the current state of the post-9/11 American psyche, oscillating between aggressive offensive actions abroad and fear-filled defensive manoeuvres at home'.[59]

Homeland's title sequence clearly announces these central themes. Uncertainty, confusion, volatility of knowledge and truth are translated through the audiovisual texture of the sequence, which highlights the fragmented, necessarily selective nature of documentation, the unreliability of both human and mechanical perception, as well as accidental and purposeful media distortions and the danger and threat that comes from incomplete or false information. At the same time, in its aesthetic dialogue with preceding and current images and sounds, from verbal references and visual analogies to the employment of archival footage, the sequence manifests the show's ambition to speak to real events. For instance, when Sergeant Brody is found, he is 'pulled bearded and filthy from a "spider hole" à la Saddam Hussein';[60] this image appears in the title sequence. Repeatedly, there is generic mention of 9/11, Abu Ghraib and drone strikes; in season 3, several episodes circle around the CIA being 'punished', the 'leak' of a memorandum to Congress committee; before being 'sacrificed to protect the agency', Carrie is interrogated by a belligerent Congress Committee as if she were on trial ('we are going to put you all in jail ... you have done great harm to your country ... the president wants closure').

The title sequence visually and aurally sutures several narratives. A genealogy of terrorist attacks is traced through visual snippets and declarations of presidents in response, which, along with citizen footage from 9/11, grounds the show historically, offering both the continuity of terrorism and clearly dated attacks. This narrative strand is interspersed with moments from the diegetic world of the show, and of the character Carrie growing up. By using photos of a young Claire Danes, the actor who portrays Carrie, this narrative thread also criss-crosses the boundary between fictitious and factual.

A jazz score (a quintessentially US musical genre) provides the binding 'voice-over' of the title sequence. As the show's 'DNA', the theme of free jazz is reflected in the visual texture of disjunctions.[61] Interspersed with this jazz piece are auditory snapshots of sound footage, excerpts from the actual show, words from a Middle Eastern news reporter that are not translated, the sounds of helicopters and gunshots, a few words by presidents from Ronald Reagan to Barack Obama (with the notable exception of George W. Bush). A trumpet's haunting cadence leads through the auditory montage as if it were a grieving wail. According to its musical composer Sean Callery, the jazz motif is linked to Carrie, and the title sequence can be read as a 'stream of consciousness' of a sleeping Carrie.[62] The frequent use of the ghostly technique of superimposition enhances the dreamlike quality of the sequence, and the fast-paced rhythm of the montage mimics the eye movements in REM sleep. Carrie's fictional subjectivity is thus connected to instances of public memory.

The title sequence of *Homeland* encapsulates its central themes of a search for knowledge and a crisis of trust, which extends from distrust of the efficiency and ethics of the country's institutions and its representatives to fundamental distrust of traditional methods of visual and mechanical verification. The opening-credit sequence highlights both technological and human perceptual limitations. Emphasising the unreliability and even 'failure' both of vision and visual evidence, the sequence stages doubt in their respective epistemological capacities. For instance, shots of images upside down point to the usually hidden perceptual mechanics both of our eyes and of the cinematic apparatus. Other shots highlight limited or warped perspectives: the back of a head, prolonged close-ups of open eyes and of closed eyes, a maze, and a girl wearing a lion's mask, which evokes the notion of performance, camouflage, double-faced presentation. The motif of the maze introduces the cat-and-mouse game of the show. Carrie and Brody appear in the maze, alone or together, demonstrating nicely that it is not clear who is beast, hunter or target.

Linked to Carrie's dream-subjectivity, these repeated motifs indicate traumatic recurrence, repeated both within and *as* title sequence, recurring before every episode. We hear Carrie fretting about having 'missed something before', in a clear allusion to 9/11: 'I won't – I can't – let that happen again!' followed by the voice of her mentor Saul suggesting that 'It was ten years ago – Everybody missed something that day.' Carrie

Figure 3.1 *Homeland.*

retorts, 'Yeah, well, everybody's not me.' It is interesting to read this personalisation with the trauma studies-inflected interpretations of post-9/11 material, which emphasise the need to recover hardness and masculinity, to reassert a wounded 'USA national manhood',[63] or read such cultural dreams as 'terror management'.[64]

Even the *real* torture programme, argue Mark Danner and Hughes Eakin, was meant for an *internal* audience, as anxiety management for an agency that had failed to prevent or anticipate 9/11. The torture worked, because it allowed the CIA to 'alleviate their own anxiety': 'when it did not render information, it made absolutely certain that there was no information to be rendered ... We translated our ignorance into their pain'.[65]

In *Homeland*, this pain is appropriated and gendered. We often see Carrie as the object of a threatening, hunting camera-gaze, beginning with the title sequence's shots of Carrie-as-a-little-girl in front of the television set, always observed from behind, and a shot of her fleeing something, looking anxiously over her shoulder into the camera.

In a 1993 analysis of genre and the figure of the female investigator in Bigelow's *Blue Steel* (1990) and *The Silence of the Lambs* (Jonathan Demme, 1991), Linda Mizejewski uses the frame of genre to link the threat of a female intruder in traditionally male-dominated work environments (FBI, the police department) and the films' stretching of genre confines and self-reflexive moments. With reference to J. P. Telotte's remarks on *film noir*'s interrogation of epistemology, Mizejewski suggests that such self-reflexive gestures call attention to 'a deconstructive movement to problematise investigation itself as part of a larger cultural anxiety about ways of knowing'.[66] Despite its datedness, then, the analysis offers a useful vantage point to consider the linking of gender and a perceived threat to established ways of knowing. Both Carrie in *Homeland* and Maya in *Zero* are framed as 'out of place' and as 'transgressor in [a] male narrative', through visual isolation and narrative inscription as lone wolfs. Both can be read in reference to the real Alfreda Bikowsky,[67] and each woman's true partner is the target, the enemy she knows intimately. Moments of self-reflection for institutions as powerful as the CIA are channelled through a female body; and any ambivalence towards such institutions presents a backhanded reflection and they then also double, in Mizejewski's words, as the 'industry's own ambivalence concerning the success of ... the female dick'.[68]

The failure to anticipate 9/11 is personalised in *Homeland*, but it is also made experiential to the audience. For the rapid montage highlights the limits of the human audience's perceptual apparatus to compute this onslaught of images – we cannot see fast enough or well enough to 'get' it all. This experience is repeated throughout the show by strategically withholding and adding narrative information. On a more practical level, this strategy ensures that the sequence retains enough suspense and diversion to create a slight sensual overload, in spite of not being changed over the course of the first three seasons.

This difficulty of *seeing* or *hearing clearly* is also expressed on the level of the medium. Blurred and fraying images point to the limits of vision and the decay of visual evidence. Various media formats – stills, archival and diegetic footage – and image types – optics which mimic security camera images, or the photo-shopping of a home movie – are cut together and emphatically worked on, using (colour) inversion, superimposition, negative frames, images that are upside down or that seem to be filmed through a distorting glass. Sound and images create a mutually affirming tapestry of diegetic and factual material, interweaving various media sources and different languages. Non-English language snippets are not translated; what is mined, apparently, is not the content of the words but the texture or associative evocations of, for instance, veiled women shouting into a television camera.

Mirroring the visual material, aural effects foreground the materiality, and thus the artifice of the recording device: from the clicking noise of a slide projector, the sound of breakage or static, to aural interferences and deteriorations over time. If we shift towards examining *how* a medium says something, that is, how meaning is aesthetically expressed, this foregrounded materiality and self-awareness builds on and expands Ryan

Caldwell's notion of 'televisuality' as an excess of style towards calling the viewer's attention to the construction of the show.

These aesthetics point to the authenticating function of media, in particular archive footage, to orientate the viewer temporally. At the same time, the presence of mistakes and gaps in recordings, even possible tampering with the material, perpetually throws its reliability into doubt. The sequence also alludes to the mechanical changes that happen to media memory over time, by highlighting how footage material decays over time. It also emphasises that individual and public media memory are interwoven. Thus, central to the newer texts' renegotiation of these issues is how they were previously told and how they are remembered on *television*. The self-referential engagement with such questions links a US show like *Homeland* to a Chilean show like *Los Archivos del Cardenal*, which will be the topic of the next chapter.

Notes

1. Corner, 'Television Studies and the Idea of Criticism'.
2. Newcomb and Hirsch, 'Television as a Cultural Forum', pp. 565–6, emphasis in the original.
3. Fredric Jameson and Andreas Huyssen in Holdsworth, *Television, Memory and Nostalgia*, p. 192.
4. Creeber, *Serial Television*, p. 7.
5. Creeber, 'Taking Our Personal Lives Seriously', pp. 452–3, emphasis in the original.
6. Creeber, *Serial Television*, p. 7.
7. Allen in Creeber, *Serial Television*, p. 4.
8. Lury, *Interpreting Television*, pp. 74–5.
9. Kramer, 'Forensic Music', pp. 202–3.
10. Stanitzek, 'Reading the Title Sequence', p. 44.
11. *24: The Game*, *24*'s spin-off video game, effectively fulfilled Sontag's nightmare question, 'Can the video game "Interrogating the Terrorists" really be far behind?' Cf. Mark Sample's analysis of videogames that specifically employ interrogation and which go to great lengths to integrate torture as craft and as a repeatable, quantifiable action. Sontag, 'Regarding the Torture of Others"'. Sample, 'Virtual Torture: Videogames and the War on Terror'.
12. For instance, various public figures, including former US president Bill Clinton and the late US Supreme Court justice Antonio Scalia, have referred to Jack Bauer in their arguments.
13. Mayer, 'Whatever It Takes'.
14. McCoy, 'Beyond Susan Sontag', p. 127.
15. Takacs in Prince, pp. 179–80.
16. Ten Brink and Oppenheimer, *Killer Images*, p. 2.

17. Prince, p. 180. Prince also drily remarks that internal 'cultural imperialism' is a far more laborious and blunter tool for control than what current media developments offer in terms of microtargeting and surveillance.
18. Dunn, 'Torture, Terrorism, and *24*'.
19. Taub, 'Darkest Secret'.
20. Eban, 'Rorschach and Awe'. Cf. Hennelly, 'Evil Torturers Catch a Break' on the financial incentives to torture.
21. Mayer in Hutchings, 'Spectacularizing Crime', p. 12; cf. Hutchings, 'Entertaining Torture' on SERE, the 'torture memos' and the architects Mitchell and Jessen.
22. Nacos, 'The Image of Evil', p. 286. Cf. Bloch-Elkon and Nacos, 'News and Entertainment Media'.
23. Slotkin, *Gunfighter Nation*, p. 134.
24. Verheul, 'Paranoia and preemptive violence'.
25. Lury, *Interpreting Television*, p. 145.
26. Rejali, 'Convenient Truths', p. 228. The torture iconography includes an emphasis on immediate, stereotypical effects, such as convulsions from electroshocks.
27. Prince in Chaudhuri, 'Documenting the Dark Side'.
28. Hutchings, 'Entertaining Torture', p. 6.
29. Danzig, 'Countering the Jack Bauer Effect', p. 29.
30. Little, '*24*: Time, Terror, Television', p. 4.
31. Coulthard, 'Torture Tunes'.
32. Grusin, *Premediation*, p. 18.
33. Ibid., p. 53.
34. Cf. Newcomb, who links television to the formalism and repetition of ritual. Newcomb, *Critical View*, p. 47.
35. Lury, *Interpreting Television*, p. 172.
36. Ibid., p. 173. Cf. Talen, '*24*: Split Screen's Big Comeback'.
37. While the show is ongoing at the time of publication, the focus of the analysis, beyond the broader concept of the show, is on seasons 1–4.
38. Nussbaum, '*Homeland*: The Antidote for *24*'; Goffe, 'The Homeland Phenomenon'. The first season kept several narrative premises, such as trauma and mental illness, and visual motifs from *Hatufim/Prisoners of War*, whose writers and producers (Avi Nir, Ran Telem and Gideon Raff) are also credited on *Homeland*, next to writers of *24*.
39. Cf. Ossa, 'Sleeping Threats'.
40. Shapiro, 'Crisis of Middle-Class', p. 153.
41. Steenberg and Tasker, 'Pledge Allegiance', p.137.
42. Ibid. p. 134.
43. Negra and Lagerwey, 'Analyzing Homeland', p. 126.
44. Newcomb and Hirsch, 'Television as a Cultural Forum', p. 565.
45. Negra and Lagerwey, 'Analyzing Homeland', p. 126.
46. Bellafante, 'Family Is the Main Casualty'.

47. Castonguay, 'Fictions of Terror', pp. 140–1.
48. Ibid., p. 143.
49. With slightly different emphasis, Steenberg and Tasker describe the 'singularly intense' concern over 'the impossibility of fidelity' as a 'structuring concept' of the show. Steenberg and Tasker, 'Pledge Allegiance', p. 137, cf. Shapiro, 'Crisis of Middle-Class'.
50. West, 'Close Reading'.
51. Cf. Sontag, *Illness as Metaphor*.
52. Negra and Lagerwey 'Analyzing Homeland', p. 130. Compare Steenberg and Tasker's reading of *Homeland* as a gendered reversal of hard-boiled *noir* hero and *femme fatale*, where the portrayal of Carrie 'taps into the crime genre trope of the tortured investigative genius', Steenberg and Tasker, 'Pledge Allegiance', p. 134.
53. Bevan, 'National Body', p. 145 and p. 148.
54. Steenberg and Tasker, 'Pledge Allegiance', p. 134.
55. Peters, 'Witnessing', p. 712.
56. Harris, 'The Lie Generator'.
57. Daum, 'Hollywood's Idealized View of CIA Officers'.
58. Elsaesser, 'The Mind-Game Film', p. 26.
59. Edgerton and Edgerton, 'Pathologizing Post-9/11 America in *Homeland*', p. 91. Cf. Bevan, 'Mental Health in Homeland'.
60. Edgerton, 'Brody Must Die'.
61. These descriptions of the title sequence are from a YouTube clip featuring Sean Callery and produced by Film Music Reporter, 'Homeland – Creating the Opening Titles Music'.
62. Ibid. Shapiro suggests a connection between this kind of jazz and bipolar disorder as an attempt to 'think about simultaneous registers of history and to situate events as variations on a structuring theme'. Shapiro, 'Crisis of Middle-Class', p. 155.
63. Faludi, *The Terror Dream*. Cf. Kleinhans, 'Imagining Torture'.
64. Slowik, 'Controlling Terror'.
65. Danner and Eakin, 'Our New Politics of Torture'.
66. Mizejewski, 'Female Dick', p. 20. The analysis further strengthens the notion of Bigelow's auteurist touch mentioned in Chapter 1.
67. In series 4 episode 1 Carrie is presented with a birthday cake inscribed as eponymous 'The Drone Queen', cf. Chapter 1, note 77.
68. Mizejewski, 'Female Dick', p. 15.

CHAPTER 4

Television Torture, Made in Chile

In Latin America, the demand for a 'different depiction of reality' has been mostly answered by documentaries and by television, from soap operas to serious dramas or sit-coms.[1] Beginning with the bombing of the Chilean presidential palace La Moneda on 11 September 1974, the coup d'état was incessantly televised and rebroadcast. '[The] relentless repetition of the bombing in the media [is] a 'symptom' of this traumatic event for Chilean society'.[2]

As Chilean television played a major supporting role to the regime, the negotiation of such iconic archival material *on television* introduces an element of reflexivity. For this reason, the relation of television to public memory has to be analysed with attention to the country's media history. Applying Paul Ricœur's fractioning of questions around memory – 'At what time are events remembered or commemorated; which are forgotten, in which form, by whom and for whom?'[3] – to serial television, we may ask, how and when does this format help or prevent us from rememberingcertain events? How are public memory and our individual perception of events shaped by and filtered through media images? As Walescka Pino-Ojeda remarks, '[as] the future of the past [prefigures] the future ... memory has become the locus of epistemological debate and political dispute'.[4]

The country's 'memory question', or 'memory wars'[5] must be understood in the context of a sense of 'unfinished business' in terms of justice. The understanding and meaning of Chile's recent historical past and its effect on the present continue to be a site of contestation and dispute. This chapter examines how the contemporary and popularly successful Chilean television shows *Los Archivos del Cardenal* and *Los 80* engage with such public memory, from hinting at the memory of television's pro-government role to the show's approach towards (the absence of) visual archive material. Set in the dictatorship years, both shows are part of the current trend to return to the 1980s in Chilean documentary, fiction, film and television.[6] Many of these works employ, reconceptualise or extend the existing archive material.[7]

Figure 4.1 *Los Archivos del Cardenal.*

Los Archivos del Cardenal

The television drama *Los Archivos* (TVN, 2011–14) is based on the historical records documented by the so-called *Vicariate of Solidarity*, an institution founded by the Pope on request of Cardinal Raúl Silva Henríquez – hence the eponymous title, which translates as *The Archives of the Cardinal*.[8] The show recreates some of the most striking and symbolic cases of human rights violations committed or coming to light in the supposedly stable 1980s. The show combines a contemporary 'global CSI aesthetic' with a distinctly Chilean, nationally resonating topic, which taps into local knowledge of the work of the Vicariate. This hybridity in content is mirrored by the show's hybrid form, which uses both fiction and documentary forms.

The title sequence of *Los Archivos* already sets up this aesthetic and narrative alliance of the documentary and the fictional, the amorous and the political. An obligatory disclaimer confirms that the show is based on facts, but is nevertheless a piece of fiction. The sequence begins with the first bars of a rock song,[9] and an archive image of the historical cardinal. Onto this photograph, text is visibly and audibly 'typed', as if by typewriter, evoking the documentary basis of the show, and outlining the historical development of the vicariate.

Then ringing church bells are added to the rock intro. There is a sharp cut to the image of a projector, emanating a blazing light which expands onto and overexposes the whole image. The image effectively dissolves into a white screen. Now the vocals of the title song set in, and the rest of the title sequence is a fast-paced montage of diegetic snippets. Apart from these initial photographs in the title sequence, the show does not use archive material again – until the very last episode of the last season, which ends on a montage of documentary photographs. All images, diegetic and archival, are framed as if they were emanating from a television screen. The images thus emphasise the role of media in transporting, conserving or distorting visual evidence. The sequence's second part, which consists of diegetic snippets, sets up a way to relate to the past and its political positions via an emotional link, for instance taking moments from the storylines that focus on the Vicariate's daughter having to choose between two men who embody oppositional political and social positions.

As in this title sequence, the show employs a fictional present tense with a narrative base in the documentary realm, visually and narratively combining fiction, documentary and dramatisation of iconic images and cases. The advantages of this docudramatic mode of representation consist in combining documentary's authenticating effect and its 'promise of privileged access to information' with drama's narrative immersion, which tends to increase emotional involvement.[10] As suggested by Álvaro Bisama, fiction is a mode of remembering which helps us to return to something already known, to relate past to present in different ways. Where *Homeland*'s emphasis on asking questions and distrusting answers was mirrored in the paradigmatically impermanent or partial closure of storylines, in *Los Archivos*, due to its bottom line being rooted in the documentary, the narrative begets closure. *Los Archivos* seeks to speak to a broad audience and to activate a different form of seeing, of looking *again*, from the vantage point of the present, at parts of the past that might have been left out.

What do such fictional works offer to the Chilean public space – in a way that, to paraphrase Miriam Haddu and Joanna Page, is perhaps not fulfilled by documentary?[11] For one, spectatorial immersion seems harder to achieve in a documentary, where historical veracity and neutrality – at least the shadow of Bill Nichols' favoured 'discourse of sobriety' and its contrast of rationality and 'matters of feeling' – are still the dominant norm.[12] More specifically, the prevalence of visual synergies and a 'hybrid' aesthetics in Latin American cinema, Haddu and Page suggest, has to do with a 'need that fiction fails to fulfil' while something about the real world 'escapes the documentary camera'.[13] Might a show such as *Los Archivos* fulfil an ex post facto 'archival function', by recreating – and creating – missing images for the collective pool of memory?

Perhaps because the 'forensic turn'[14] has created a specific and recognisable look, *Los Archivos* has been dubbed the 'Chilean *CSI*'.[15] The narratives of both shows happily mix politics, historical record and the vicissitudes of the heart in a racy style developed by this model for television drama. Though seductive, the comparison is ultimately inadequate. Shows like *CSI* and its spin-offs[16] provide a shortcut to experience 'death by proxy'. This obsession with the fictional cadaver as 'pop culture's new star'[17] is perhaps a collateral of the 'tastefully safe' treatment of actual (Western) corpses in Western media. Leach describes how on *CSI*, 'the truth-telling status of machinery and instrumentation [where] the data spewed from machines authorise a kind of moral discourse ... "The facts don't lie ... but people do"'.[18]

The codification that mechanical evidence 'cannot lie' taps into a desire for absolute certainty. The testimony obtained from machinery and instrumentation is understood to be superior to those of human witnesses, who might forget or embellish. In Chile, this aesthetic figure must be read differently. Forensic investigation featured strongly in documentaries and their focus on the recovery of the remains of the disappeared, the traumatic search for the traces left behind, from photographs to human bones. Yet the forensic logic that 'truth lodges in matter'[19] creates a tension between activist potential, which seeks to prove and to back up witness testimony, and a certain technological formalism and determinism, lured by the promise of scientific certainty. The possibility of skeletal identification, the scientific analysis of inanimate objects, may support prosecutions against the 'winners of history' who attempt to rewrite the past. But forensics, too, are subject to narrative, and to error. In Chile two impactful documentaries, about the mistaken identification of a disappeared, captured forensic investigations and exhumations. *Fernando ha vuelto* (Silvio Caiozzi, 1998) and *¿Fernando ha vuelto a desaparecer?* (Silvio Caiozzi, 2006) attested to how traumatic these processes of re-identification were for the family members seeking closure. In view of these historical experiences, constructing 'forensic science as superscience'[20] would not only be anachronistic but also ring decidedly false in the Chilean context.

The very first case that appears in *Los Archivos*, *Los Hornos de Lonquén*, focuses on the discovery in 1978 of fifteen bodies found in an abandoned mine in Lonquén, a transformative case that rebuked an official narrative that negated the sheer existence of the disappeared. The show clearly anticipated an audience aware of these historical events and of such images, which form part of Chile's 'concentrationary imaginary'.[21] In these episodes, visual evidence appears as puzzle pieces to solve crimes: family members bring photographs, and photographs are taken of the bodies in

Figure 4.2 *Los Hornos de Lonquén* (Fundación de Documentación y Archivo de la Vicaría de la Solidaridad).

Lonquen. At the same time, much of the work of the Vicariate consists in contesting the state media's fabrications and spread of false information.

This historical experience of deception, hoax and absence of images is also part of Chile's media history. Recognising media power, the junta at different points in time either prohibited images completely, in classic anti-pictorial fashion, or used them for spectacular social deceit.[22] For instance, an early episode shows how torturers force their victim to assert, on camera, that his confession was obtained without torture. As in previous examples, such visual evidence, the 'machine as witness' needs an expert reader to deconstruct the visual truth of a lie.

Like forensic science, the motif of *looking at corpses* functions differently in *Los Archivos* than in *CSI*. Ruth Penfold-Mounce argues that the glamorous corpses in *CSI* are subjected to various objectifying gazes: abject, erotic and clinical. The corpse becomes a prop that helps the science-as-detective narrative to unfold. By contrast, in *Los Archivos*, references to past and present political realities anchor the viewer in the historical real and disrupt any potential for an erotic gaze; spectatorial desire is restricted to the love triangles of the fictional protagonists. *CSI* shows feature uncannily sensitive central characters communing with the dead, speaking both *for* and *with* them.²³ In *Los Archivos*, there are no long, intimate talks over and with the dead bodies: the protagonists concentrate on talking to the living. These conversations with survivors and relatives are more central than exegetic close-readings of corpses. Channelled through the protagonists, the gaze upon the dead bodies in Lonquén, and their suffering relatives, is neither clinical nor voyeuristic but empathic. This humane stance continues throughout the show and may be read, ultimately, as a compassionate gaze on history itself. As José Miguel Palacios has argued, although *Los Archivos* can be considered a show *about* the value of documentation,²⁴ archival documentation is largely absent, as explained in the section above about the title sequence. The show uses production design to create a feel of 1970s and 1980s authenticity, and evokes the iconic images and footage associated with the resistance against the dictatorship, but abstains from using the material texture of original material. It thereby avoids the distinct sensibility associated with archival aesthetics and positions itself squarely within contemporary conventional television language.

How to interpret this aesthetic 'presentness' in the Chilean context? The past demands justice, argues Sergio Rojas, and art may tranquillise these demands. The increased attention given to forensics in artistic productions relates then also to what Rojas calls the current 'fetishization' of archive. He explains this trend with the 'exhaustion' of history in the neoliberal present, which is perhaps particularly true for the particularly neoliberal Chile.²⁵ The dictatorship installed not only an economic system but had deep and lasting impact on cultural production and aesthetic imagination. In Chile, the political coup was also a coup against representation: a broad and radical extirpation of cultural production, enforced by censorship, the destruction of films and closure of cinema studies departments, the exodus or forced exile of artists. This destruction resulted in a cultural blackout ('apagón cultural')²⁶ and the loss of historical and ideological sense-making narratives. Chilean cultural critic Nelly Richard has termed this loss a *cultural aphasia*:²⁷ the dispossession of discourse, of a form with which to speak of the dictatorship experiences.

Inundated with an excess of information, current culture is obsessed with memory, and at the same time accused of amnesia. Following Rojas, one might argue that it is not the past but the *present* that is neurotic, both lacking history and being choked by its demands. We need a past in which the present can recognise itself, argues Rojas; and I suggest that *Los Archivos* creates the foundation for such a recognition of the past in the present. While the show's aesthetic *form* adheres to a contemporary aesthetics and encourages emotional involvement, its hybrid format invites the viewer to look again at the familiar and recreates images and stories which have been invisible or 'missing' from the canon. Moreover, as the next section will explain, the show expands available 'memory options'.

Memory Formations

Clearly, the complexity of memory and its symbolic encodings are inadequately addressed with absolute categories of true and false. Trauma theory has been helpful in establishing the idea that certain events need a different kind of memory work, and its 'affective truth' can help unpack the 'vicissitudes of memory'[28] – but one should perhaps abstain from diagnosing whole nations with unconscious desires and trauma, given that 'nations do not have "psyches" or an "unconscious"; only people do'.[29] What kind of memory is made available then in this show, and for whom? Marianne Hirsch's concept of 'postmemory' and Alison Landsberg's notion of 'prosthetic memory' have found particular traction in this context. Both speak about the role of images in memory transmission and access to history.

Originally developed for memory processes in the families of holocaust survivors, postmemory refers to the transmission or inherited recollection of an authentic event over time and across generations, emphasising both the temporal gap and the affective connection. Postmemory is transmitted via absorbing, diffusing and filtering screens, which 'function analogously to the protective shield of trauma itself'.[30] By approximating memory in affective force, images are central in postmemory. As 'figures for memory and forgetting',[31] they have the power 'to address the spectator's own bodily memory; to *touch* the viewer who *feels* rather than simply sees the event'.[32] Mnemonic objects such as photographs may help memory transmission; hence cinema can provide a space to mediate affective states, to experience fictional encounters and the adjunct emotions through a screen which distances yet allows a mimetic encounter. Hirsch defines postmemory not as an *identity* position but a *generational* structure of memory transmission.

> Less-directly affected participants can become engaged in the generation of postmemory, which can thus persist *even after all participants and even their familial descendants are gone* ... Postmemorial work ... strives to *reactivate* and *reembody* more distant social/national and archival/cultural memorial structures.[33]

Thus, Hirsch herself implied that this connection perhaps needs no base in familial ties. Alison Landsberg's 'prosthetic memory' expands this argument that (post)memory can carry on a 'living connection' between the generations to a sweeping possibility of inclusion for a much larger collective. Created and disseminated by modern mass technologies – and therefore *prosthetic* – such 'privately felt public memories' may evoke affective solidarity across ethnic and group identifications, lines of gender, race and nationality. For Landsberg, prosthetic memories are the solution to a private memory culture that premises memory on authenticity, heritage and ownership and thereby creates obstacles to political alliances. Transferential spaces, such as films and experiential museums, can structure 'imagined communities' and teach empathy, by helping the visitor share vicariously in a 'bodily, mimetic encounter with a past that was not actually theirs'.[34] Here, rather than creating a mediating distance, images create visceral, mimetic-experiential and emotional experience and access to history.

This utopian reconfiguration grants impressive powers to media products but is deeply problematic in its insistence on using the term *memory*, which, granted all modifications to the concept and acknowledgements of memory's unreliability and malleability,[35] still carries the grain of an individual's experience in the past.

In Landsberg's conception, memory seems to be dislocated from its specific context, no longer grounded in lived experience. Many scholars have objected to such expansions, which potentially open the position of secondary witness to everyone, including perpetrators.[36] (For instance, Beatriz Sarlo cautions against the inflationary use of the term memory, Sundquist discusses 'memory envy' and Wendy Brown the 'injury-identity' in 'wounded attachments'.[37]) Landsberg also argues that Halbwachs's category of collective memory needs to be redefined as it is based on 'dissolving social categories' like family, religion or class, a Eurocentric perspective that needs to be historicised. Finally, it is not entirely evident precisely why the reception of mass-mediated memories would necessarily recognise 'the alterity of the other'.[38]

Nevertheless, both Hirsch's and Landsberg's models provide useful interventions to create a framework for discussing the role of images or cinema, to approach diverse audiences, and the relation between public and private memory(-ies). Important to retain then are Hirsch's emphasis on how mnemonic objects activate a spectator's *own* embodied memory in affective form, Landsberg's attention to the global dimension of memory questions, as well as the changing and expanding pools of possible audiences. Especially hybrid and layered audiovisual texts allow for different points of access for generationally, culturally or geographically diverse groups. These disparate audiences may be invited to access history, without collapsing the distinctions between different levels – memory of personal, lived experience, memory transmissions in the intimate setting of family or community, and global, public narratives of 'collective' memory. What emerges is a more *liquid* formation, a pool of cultural images and narratives which change with each retelling, overlap with cultural knowledge and facts and exist alongside individual or collectively asserted memories. As this reservoir of images and stories can be shared among groups of audiences, it will, along with its audiences, transform, shrink and expand.[39]

* * *

The emphasis on the affective *experience* mediated by images leads to an important point regarding the socially relevant memory work performed in *Los Archivos*, namely that the show offers a plurality of subject positions within a format that already entails a collective, public dimension. Chilean scholars have argued that the country's collective identity lacks the sense of a *shared* calamity and an acknowledgement of social pain, as a 'double distanciation' – ethical and emotional – separates contemporary Chilean society from its recent past. The privatisation of pain led to 'a questionable and convenient dissociation between "them", the "victims", and "us", those who were not directly affected by the climate of fear'.[40] Many cultural products, have sought to address and recover this sense of community. In Chile, the social function of remembering, informing and educating viewers has been taken up by its documentaries, historically shaped through a distinctive 'political vocation'.[41]

Yet one must ask who has the option, inclination and financial means to watch such documentaries. Lack of infrastructure, funding and sociocultural awareness means these documentaries suffer from limited distribution and exhibition. Until recently, domestic audiences have tended to shun Chilean cinema, including documentaries.[42] Television, on the other hand, reaches a larger pool of audiences, and it is able to offer space for a plurality of memory narratives. Emphasising television's relevance for public memory, Steve Anderson describes how 'part of the power and significance of televisual historiography lies in its flexibility and intangibility in comparison with "official histories" … [and] in opposition to historical discourse, which is propagated from the top down via cultural and governmental institutions'.[43]

A show such as *Los Archivos* allows a range of generations and audiences to imaginatively inhabit a plethora of subject positions – perpetrators and victims, but also, importantly, conformists and bystanders: those who saw themselves as apolitical. To discuss the approaches towards memory and the past enabled by *Los Archivos*, a framework is needed which extends the direction of thought offered by prosthetic and postmemory with regard to subject positions. Postmemory mainly describes the experience and relationship of children of survivors to the experiences of their parents. Prosthetic *memory* on the other hand, does not seem to provide much space for small stories, of those who did not act heroically, who did not become famous. The category of prosthetic memory is also inadequate as the show was mainly aimed at a Chilean audience – even though it developed a transnational appeal.[44] A broad variety of viewers can recognise themselves in the past offered by *Los Archivos*, beyond strongly ideological positions and beyond those immediately affected as survivor, relative or child of the victims and perpetrators.

The occasional narrative 'soapiness' of *Los Archivos* is then also a way of saying that this normality happened as well. People were laughing and crying, they fell in and out of love. Such a focus on the small, even banal, obviously counters the impact of the sublime, momentous event. The attention to the mundane and daily also appears in a different light if considered a reaction and potential remedy to the nationalist-authoritarian imaginary set into motion by the dictatorship and arguably carried forth in the hegemonic practices of a neoliberal state.[45] A broad variety of viewers can recognise themselves in this past, beyond the more extreme ideological positions, beyond being immediately affected as survivor or as relative or child of those more closely involved. Moreover, for the viewer, the quotidian can contain some of the narrative horror, when love entanglements and pleasurable aesthetics provide some respite from frequently gruesome stories. The partial, symbolic recovery of such 'small' stories and various subject positions are crucial to develop a sense of shared social pain. Inherently relational, television such as *Los Archivos* may be considered a counter to the trend towards atomisation and privatisation of pain.

Moreover, these positions can evolve. In *Los Archivos*, the political stance of the central young couple is meandering; several other characters also change their opinions and attitudes. The formal characteristics of serial television allow for such slowly developing shifts between subject positions, fostered by longevity of running time and the serial's rhetoric of open-endedness. As the audience comes to know the characters intimately, we follow as their political affiliations evolve and perhaps change our relationships to them.

A main narrative arc features the journey of upper-class lawyer Ramón towards political consciousness and responsibility, as he begins to work for the Vicariate. Ramón has his eye-opening moment from relative political unconsciousness when he witnesses a man being taken off the street; his interest in uncovering political realities is then nurtured by a budding love interest in Laura, the beautiful daughter of a lawyer at the Vicariate.

Recalling Pino-Ojeda's point of social 'double distanciation', Ramón's development may stand for various audience groups in various stages of ignorance, denial, of temporal or generational removal. At one point, due to his work for the Vicariate, Ramón is being tortured, which forces his family members to show their political colours. Again, several points of view and different reactions are expressed: Ramón's father uses his connections to ensure his son's release, his brother rejects him, his mother struggles to accept the realities of his torture.

The point about subject positions becomes most clear in the narrative of the 'prodigal torturer'. The defection of a CNI (Chilean internal secret service agency) agent, his confession, ultimate repentance and the varied, evolving reactions of the members of the Vicariate towards him stretch over several episodes. Torturer Mauro is introduced displaying physical symptoms of PTSD – nausea, insomnia, nightmares – and we see him with his wife and children, located securely within the human family. While the story of the defecting torturer is based in fact,[46] in the TV version, Mauro is shown as personally involved in some of the most striking cases of human rights violations:[47] he personally tortures several of the characters in the show, and he knows the fate of some of the protagonists' disappeared loved ones. Taking the liberty to condense various components into one character allows the show to play out various emotional responses when the Vicariate decides to hide the torturer and help him escape. Ramón initially plans to shoot Mauro. When the moment comes, he holds his former torturer at gunpoint. A flashback reminds us of the reversed dynamics during his torture. Ramón eventually refrains and he later describes Mauro to his girlfriend as 'a poor sad bastard [*weón*] who will never again sleep at night'. Also, Mauro is given time to fully realise what he has done and to repent his acts. It takes a painfully long time for him to reach that point; when he finally tells them all he knows, we are given ample shots of the pain visible in his face.

Aesthetically, the representation of torture follows the established style of translating the victim's loss of autonomy through image sequences that reflect a loss of control: distorted framing, blurred focus, shaky camera movements, jarring music. Yet what is remarkable about the representation of torture in *Los Archivos* is its recurrent appearance and the fact that its victims include most of the main characters at some point. Assisted by the serial format, the narrative emphasises also the aftermath of the torture, the reactions of family and friends. Ramón's traumatic flashbacks, represented in the same aesthetic fashion as the original torture scenes, interrupt the temporality of the main storylines. Aesthetically conservative, these repetitions nevertheless indicate how much torture was an institutionalised part of the regime's repression.

In this way, *Los Archivos* sets up a scaffolding for viewers to temporarily inhabit various subject positions and perspectives. This plurality of point of view is inherently political, for what is still mostly missing in mediated revisits of the national past are the perspectives of bystanders and *Mitläufer*, but also dissenting voices within the government and its agencies, in forms that are not a priori exculpatory or condemning. The show enlarges the collective pool of memory formations by dramatising the events around which key images and stories cluster. Following Newcomb and Hirsch's reflections on television as a 'cultural forum', its potential to trigger a public debate on the past is perhaps especially relevant in Chile, where the predominant socio-cultural public discourse is shaped by television anyway.[48] The show was widely watched, highly rated and successful in generating debates.[49] A book about the 'real stories' was published, a website maintained by the Universidad Diego Portales gives background information on the cases and the show itself at times condenses educational information.[50] The last episode of the first season was screened live at the Museum of Memory in the capital of Santiago, attended by over 2,000 people. *Los Archivos* is therefore an exemplary case of 'historical event television': frequently produced around memorial dates and official remembrance days, such television can constitute a social and media event that forms part of remembrance culture. Programmed alongside such extra-textual events, 'history can become a contemporary event through remembrance'.[51]

Los 80: Media Memories on Television

In Chilean narrative cinema, it is the *absence* of invitations to affectively relate or identify with protagonists that is remarked upon. Chilean television shows, however, are shaped by a transnational melodramatic current, which can be considered a method: 'the work of melodrama creates affective openings that facilitate potential connections cross-culturally'.[52] Inextricably intertwined with the political, this emotional component helps explore the personal cost of history.

A perfect example for this dynamic is provided by *Los 80* (Canal 13, 2008–14), a highly popular show, characterised by the Chilean film magazine *La Fuga* as companion piece to *Los Archivos*. Running for seven seasons and initially produced to commemorate the national holiday of independence, the Bicentennial (thus also linked to 'public event television'), the show features the Herrera family, a typical lower-middle-class Chilean family living in a village far from downtown Santiago. Once drawn into the story of an idyllic family life, helped by the nostalgic aesthetics of

1980s memorabilia, the audience is slowly introduced to more and more controversial topics, from economic problems, gender issues and class differences to, finally, politics. A main narrative arc in *Los 80* follows the initiation to political realities and the subsequent politicisation of the family's daughter, Claudia. The dinner-table rule of not speaking about politics (which also appears in Ramón's right-wing family in *Los Archivos*) can no longer be upheld when Claudia joins the protest movement. Her decision evolves slowly, as a drawn-out process, full of arguments with and interventions by friends and family. Eventually Claudia escapes to Argentina with her (more radical) partner Gabriel. Tortured by CNI agents, Gabriel's best friend gives up their whereabouts. As in *Los Archivos*, in formal and aesthetic terms, the torture scenes are unremarkable. Again, the show features the impact and long-term effects of torture: fear, repression, betrayal and threats to individuals, families and communities. The show's fourth season, in which Gabriel is betrayed and killed by a man who won the family's trust by pretending to be a long-lost uncle, was the most watched of the entire series and the most watched show of the year:[53] demonstrably, there is public interest in such narratives and formats.

The title sequence and first images of *Los 80* announce how the series will use historical documents and reflect on the role of the media in this history. Television archive material is interspersed with found footage or home movies, edited in a way that evokes the pre-digital snapping between channels. The sequence links public and private, or official history – footage of Pinochet, army tanks hosing demonstrators – with the small histories of home video footage. Eventually, these merge into documentary mimicry: an aesthetically corresponding 'fake footage' from the series itself. The title song *El tiempo en las bastillas* (originally by Fernando Ubiero, 1978) remains the same but the interpretation of the song changes with every season, performed by various groups and in various styles – rock, pop, punk, classic, electronic – as the show moves forward in time. The final season then reprises the original version and musically achieves closure by 'closing' the circle.

In the title sequence of *Los 80*, the television is the first 'protagonist' we see. In the first images of the show, the television image is identical to the first image we see, before receding into an *image of* the television, which appears now as a profilmic object on the screen. The television images are black and white and contained as emanating from the television set as an object within the series, which is shot in colour. After the title sequence, these two levels of temporality and reality do not overlap again.

The first episode opens on an image of a television set that shows a black-and-white image of a Chilean athlete doing crunches. The image

Figure 4.3 *Los 80*.

becomes static, then a fist is seen hitting the set. A reverse shot takes a perspective from behind and slightly above the television set, showing the family around the dinner table, mesmerised by the device and shouting excitedly about changes in the resolution of the image, as the father is seen knocking it carefully. The elder son joins him; both are whacking the television. Then the daughter intervenes and smartly hits the object from a different angle, clearing the image, which now displays General Pinochet making an announcement. The montage cuts back and forth between the television and the family, who resume eating. The sequence links small fictional history to momentous media history, emphasises the soapy family dynamics and hints at a social change regarding gender roles that are to come and to feature prominently in the show. The sequence establishes the point in time where the show begins: the first season extends from Chile's successful qualification for the 1982 FIFA World Cup to the first national protest against Augusto Pinochet in 1983.

In *Los 80*, archival footage as well as the medium of television itself, in the form of an analogue set, function as registers of public memory, communicating between different temporal levels. The foregrounded presence of television as *object* speaks to its historical relevance: then a modern and coveted, now an increasingly obsolete device, the television set was acquired as status object and centrally positioned in the home to be 'a domestic object watched within the space of the home'.[54] It carried political relevance not only as the primary communication tool for the dictatorship, but also as communicative tool generally, as the television images shown in *Los 80* often give cues for conversation or provide a pretext to initiate conversations within the diegetic world.

Television plays a central role as a powerful node of 'symbolic, autobiographical and generational reference'.[55] In the question 'where were you when (you watched...)?' public and private memory intertwine. The memories of television experience may feel quite intimate, for the ways in which the television set used to be 'embedded within the sensual aspects of the domestic environment'.[56] As an object, the television set transports nostalgia for today's convergence-trained audiences; and *Los 80* operates with the mode of nostalgia, evoked by attention to materiality. However, one must be attentive to different television memories here. In Western culture, nostalgic and archival impulses are often related to technological developments and an 'obsession' with collecting certain commodities, 'a reaction to the accelerated speed of modernization'.[57] For Chile, the role of state media, in particular television, during the dictatorship merits more critical appraisal. In contrast to other authoritarian regimes, the dictatorship did not seek to establish an official cinema; hostile to art and culture, the junta favoured only television among media,[58] a form of disciplining the populace aptly caught with the formulation of 'market, repression, television'.[59] Both *Los Archivos* and *Los 80* highlight how the state channels distorted or omitted the actual news, that what really happened had to be read between the lines of what the news was literally saying. For instance, when in *Los 80* the television news in the background is blaring about 'a group of armed extremists', the daughter Claudia says derisively, 'fine, let's stick with the government version then: they killed themselves amongst each other'. (This is based on an actual case of state propaganda.)

To conclude, their format allows each of the shows examined here to develop narrative complexity, explore long-term developments and provide multiple subject positions to the viewer. Their serial rhetoric in particular appears to be useful for the examination of collective structures, to tackle issues such as collective accountability and guilt. The double binds and ambivalences of *Zero* are here replaced by a 'rhetoric of discussion',[60] and partial closures.

Even though the shows allow an *experience* of history, of recognising oneself in the past, constitutively, television is present and future-oriented:[61] like emotions, television happens in the now. This emphasis on the affective *experience* is significant if one assumes – contrary to Susan Sontag – that memory is not photographic in nature, that we do not remember in still images, but that our memory is embedded in various sensations, in stories, songs and emotions.[62] Melodramatic structures provide an emotional access to historical events, even an emotional *public* space, as serial television generally reaches a broader audience and tends to feature more 'local' themes. The shows also combined fictional and documentary in ways that are responsive to their national (media) memory context.

Finally, as different as these shows are, they all formally and narratively engage with the reliability of visual documentation and with our epistemological strategies to access the past. This questioning, not only of original documentation, but also of how visual evidence reaches us, leads to the next chapter, which will discuss such changes in visual communication in relation to the images that emerged from Abu Ghraib and their exploration in film.

Notes

1. Elsaesser, 'Third Cinema between Hollywood and Art Cinema', p. 123.
2. Soto, (Un)Veiling Bodies, p. 33.
3. Ricoeur, Memory, History, Forgetting, p. 124.
4. Pino-Ojeda, 'Latent Image', p. 135.
5. Stern, Reckoning with Pinochet, Illanes, La batalla de la memoria.
6. Cf. Traverso, 'Conversations' on the recent 'boom' in second-generation personal-narration memory films, and Soto, especially on female documentary filmmakers.
7. Some other examples include the retro look of the biopic of Chile's important first pop band Los Prisioneros: Miguel, San Miguel (Matías Cruz, 2012), the television shows Los 80 (Canal 13, 2008–14) and Prófugos (HBO Latin America, 2011 – present,).
8. Despite its initial acceptance of the military regime against the threat of atheist communism, the Church then proceeded to persistently criticise the government's human rights record. The Vicariate denounced publicly the human rights abuses of the regime and provided legal assistance to 250,000 Chileans. The Church's powerful social standing and support provided it with some level of protection although the regime did seek to repress outspoken figures. Cf. 'Los casos de la vicaria'.
9. The title song is Santiago de Chile, by Silvio Rodríguez, composed in 1975. The song of the final episode of the last season is Déjame Pasar La Vida by Manuel Garcia and Camilo Salinas.
10. Paget in Ebbrecht, 'Docudramatizing History on TV', p. 40.
11. Haddu and Page, Visual Synergies, p. 23.
12. Nichols, Representing Reality.
13. Haddu and Page, Visual Synergies, pp. 21–3.
14. Cf. Steenberg, Forensic Science in Contemporary American Popular Culture.
15. Bisama, 'Los Archivos del Cardenal'.

16. The term 'CSI' is used as signifier for a type of TV series that encompasses the various *CSI*s as well as spin-offs such as *Without a Trace*. Cf. Kramer, 'Forensic Music', p. 203.
17. J. L. Foltyn cited in Penfold-Mounce, 'Corpses, Popular Culture and Forensic Science', p. 3. The top 10 most watched TV dramas, including *CSI*, now regularly employ 'corpse actors'.
18. Leach, 'Scientific Witness'.
19. Kramer, 'Forensic Music', p. 206.
20. Penfold-Mounce, 'Corpses, popular culture and forensic science', p. 8.
21. The term is modelled on 'concentrationary cinema' to speak about films such as *Night and Fog* (Alain Resnais, 1955) or the torture in *Battle of Algiers* (Gillo Pontecorvo, 1966) as 'concentrationary motif'. Brown and Rafter, 'Genocide Films'. In the Chilean context, Felipe Victoriano describes the 'concentrationary imagination' of the coup, quoted in Soto, *(Un)Veiling Bodies*, p. 160.
22. The peak of the mediatic involvement in public deceit might well be the so-called *Operación Colombo*, an international, DINA-orchestrated campaign to conceal the disappearance of 119 political prisoners.
23. Penfold-Mounce, 'Corpses, popular culture and forensic science'. For a political reading of *CSI*'s forensic narratives, cf. Kramer, 'Forensic Music'.
24. Palacios, 'Archivos Sin Archivo'.
25. Rojas, 'Profunda superficie'.
26. Cf. Errázuriz and Leyva, *El golpe estetico*; Traverso and Crowder-Taraborrelli, 'Political Documentary Cinema in the Southern Cone'; Bossay, 'Cineastas al rescate'.
27. Richard, 'Reconfigurations', p. 273. Cf. Richard, *Cultural Residues*; Avelar, *The Untimely Present*.
28. Janet Walker in Kaplan, *Trauma Culture*, pp. 42–3.
29. McClintock, 'Paranoid Empire', p. 91. See Wulf Kansteiner's methodological critique of Collective Memory Studies. Kansteiner, 'Finding Meaning in Memory'. Cf. Bennett and Kennedy, *World Memory*.
30. Hirsch, 'The Generation of Postmemory', p. 125.
31. Hirsch, 'Surviving Images', p. 12.
32. Jill Bennett in Hirsch, 'The Generation of Postmemory', p. 117.
33. Hirsch, 'The Generation of Postmemory', p. 111; emphasis added.
34. Landsberg, *Prosthetic Memory*, p.14
35. There is an original *event*, but the *experience* always only exists in relation to its (socially structured) mediation. As neuroscience has demonstrated, by telling or even only thinking of an event or a past action, we change our own memory of it. This is why it is possible to implant 'false memories' and why we can, to some extent, *choose* to remember and to forget. Broderick and Traverso, *Interrogating Trauma*, p. 5. See also examples of 'falsely remembered' memory, for instance from Holocaust survivors. Walker, *Trauma Cinema*.

36. In 'Surviving Images', Hirsch suggests that we can all become witnesses 'by adoption' and through repeated exposure, produce in ourselves 'the effects of traumatic repetition that plague the victims of trauma' (p. 29).
37. Sarlo, *Tiempo pasado*; Sundquist, 'Witness without End?', p. 79; Brown, 'States of Injury', p. 21.
38. Landsberg, *Prosthetic Memory*, p. 9.
39. The idea of 'liquid' memory is inspired by Anna Reading's keynote on 'Generative Memory'.
40. Pino-Ojeda, 'Latent Image', pp. 134–5.
41. Pick, 'Chilean Documentary Continuity and Disjunction'; Mouesca and Orellana, *Breve historia*, p. 209. Teshome Gabriel in Bossay, 'Cineastas al rescate'; Mouesca, *Plano secuencia*.
42. Soto, *(Un)veiling bodies*, p. 107.
43. Ebbrecht, 'Docudramatizing history on TV', p. 43.
44. *Los Archivos* was exhibited in Mexico and sold to Uruguay, Venezuela, and the United States. '*Los Archivos del Cardenal* llega a Uruguay, Venezuela y Estados Unidos'.
45. Quijada, 'El Golpe Estético'.
46. In 1984, Antonio Valenzuela 'Papudo' Morales searched for and found the journalist Mónica González, today director of the Chilean Center for Investigative Journalism and Information (*Centro de Investigación Periodística*), a nonprofit foundation dedicated to investigative journalism. González' interview with Morales was extensive and detailed, including names, methods, torture centres, the fate of the disappeared and the ways of making them disappear. Papudo was assassinated four months later. In *Los Archivos*, González' role is downplayed.
47. Cf. 'Los casos de la vicaria'.
48. Villarroel, *La voz*, pp. 161–6.
49. In this context of television memory and television as public space, it is interesting that the show was produced by TVN, a state-owned channel supposedly autonomous in its executive decisions. The institution was involved in some recent controversies: they botched the initial transmission of *Nostalgia de la luz* (Patricio Guzmán, 2010); and they bought but never screened *El diario de Agustín* (Ignacio Agüero, 2008). *El diario* presents a highly critical reckoning with the history and role of the powerful owner of the newspaper *El Mercurio*. Cf. Carter, 'Weapons of Disinformation'.
50. 'Más de dos mil personas en proyección de *Los archivos del cardenal*'; Insunza and Ortega, *Casos Reales*.
51. Ebbrecht, 'Docudramatizing history on TV', pp. 37–9.
52. Slifkin, 'Global Television Imaginary', p. 11.
53. Maira, '*Los 80* consigue 35 puntos de rating'; Ulloa, 'Final De *Los 80*'.
54. Holdsworth, *Television, Memory and Nostalgia*, p. 4.
55. Tim O'Sullivan in Holdsworth, *Television, Memory and Nostalgia*, pp. 13–14.
56. Holdsworth, *Television, Memory and Nostalgia*, p. 7.

57. Huyssen, *Present Pasts*, p. 23. Cf. Cook, *Screening the Past*.
58. Cavallo, Douzet and Rodríguez, *Huérfanos*, p. 32.
59. 'mercado, represión, television', Brunner in Richard, *Residuos y Metáforas*, p. 169.
60. Newcomb, *Critical View*, p. 49.
61. O'Regan, 'Television's Changing Aesthetic Norms'.
62. Sontag, *On Photography*.

CHAPTER 5

Negotiating Evidence

This chapter begins with an in-depth analysis of the infamous images taken in 2003 by US Military Police working in Abu Ghraib prison, followed by close-readings of two documentaries about these images and the war that produced them. In *Standard Operating Procedure* (2008), director Errol Morris, one of the best-known contemporary US documentary filmmakers, investigates how the Abu Ghraib images originated, how they have been read and mediated and how they have been used to deflect accountability. Where *Standard* seeks to expand and disrupt the dominant narrative of individual 'bad apples', transmitted through the ostensibly transparent visual narration of images, Morris's later *The Unknown Known* (2013) narrows down a specific culpable subject within the chain of command, former Secretary of State Donald Rumsfeld. The two films are here read in compendium: *Standard* begins with Rumsfeld's visit to Abu Ghraib, who, in *Unknown*, becomes the focal interviewee.

The Abu Ghraib Images

The photographs that emerged from the Abu Ghraib prison have come to stand as a shortcut to refer to the known (and the assumed) instances of torture in Iraq, Afghanistan, Guantánamo and various black site prisons. These images provoke questions centring around visual intelligibility, accountability and ethical responsibility. They implicate those present in the image, those taking and perhaps even those looking at the pictures. They also point towards a chain of command not visible in the image.

Stories on the mistreatment of American-held prisoners had been published as far back as 2002, but it took the pictures to turn the facts into a national scandal.[1] When efforts at containing or suppressing the publication of leaked images failed,[2] two master narratives quickly emerged. These blamed an overconsumption of violent media as well as pornography and identified a few 'bad apples' among a largely honourable and benevolent US military occupation.[3]

Countering such narrative spins, which deflected culpability onto individuals, six investigations unveiled systemic abuse in US Army detention centres, and the Senate Intelligence Committee's so-called 'Torture Report' confirmed that the CIA rendition and detention programme was ordered and sanctioned from the top. While there is indeed documentation of lack of oversight, a momentary lapse or breakdown in command and the programme perhaps *began* 'on the fly … under extraordinary pressure from the White House', as the product of rushed decisions made in the days after 9/11, it appeared to have quickly transformed into a sophisticated programme, which included, for instance, systematic training.[4]

The images' initial effect of a wake-up call increasingly turned into 'a form of camouflage',[5] that effectively blocked public understanding of how the events were related to US policy. For instance, the perpetrators present in the images were relatively low-ranking prison guards who had been charged by another group of interrogators with 'softening up' the prisoners. Those other agents, who have not been charged, do not appear in the infamous images and their work remained unknown to the lower-ranking guards. Moreover, some of the most egregious abuses at Abu Ghraib were either not photographed or not released to the public: 'even though the photographs that were made public were shocking enough, it is known that there are others, including video, that involved rape and even death and that were shown only to members of Congress'.[6] This is why McClintock describes the images as a 'redacted and redacting spectacle', which deflected our attention and 'resulted ultimately in an occlusion of war crimes'.[7]

As 'we often ask too much or too little of the image',[8] one must be careful to examine what exactly these images evidence and what they have *come to mean* through their subsequent use. The most infamous Abu Ghraib photographs are easy recognisable. As W. J. T. Mitchell points out, they provide the foil for numerous replications,

> [from] graphic secondary elaborations … early protest(s) … to fraudulent images of staged (usually pornographic) Abu Ghraib 'fakes' … a body of texts and images, recordings and remembrances that is centrally constituted by, but not limited to, the 279 photographs and nineteen video clips gathered by the Army's Criminal Investigation Command.[9]

And yet, the primary body of what Mitchell calls the 'Abu Ghraib Archive' remains centrally constituted by these still photographs: the so-called 'Hooded Man', the 'Human Pyramid', 'Leashed Man', images of dogs barking at a cowering prisoner, smiling privates with thumbs up next to a badly beaten corpse wrapped in plastic sheeting. They cut through much of the sanitising and censoring of the images of contemporary warfare and briefly arrested the notion of the 'disappearance' of reality. Here was irrefutable evidence that *something* appalling had been done to these bodies.

On a more abstract level, the Abu Ghraib images also demonstrated that in spite of what we know about the ease with which digital imaging technologies allow photographs to be manipulated, 'our belief in the documentary powers of digital capture is undiminished'.[10] Although technological innovations have disrupted the notion that reality is transferred from the object to its reproduction through the mechanical process of production, those images functioned as evidence of the real. To what extent does it matter, then, that they were digital?

Every image is inscribed with an intended audience and an authorial voice, reflecting 'the context of its production and a very specific embodied gaze of a photographer'.[11] In a *New York Times* interview, Errol Morris said that what is shocking about the Abu Ghraib images is that 'we want to smile back': that the images assume a benign, complicit spectator.[12] This is one reason why they have frequently been compared to what appear to be structurally similar images, such as the few pictures of the Holocaust taken by Nazi guards. Analysing these, Marianne Hirsch suggests that they contain structures in the images that seem to impede a non-violent gaze: when we confront such images, we cannot look independently of the gaze of the perpetrator, making ethical spectatorship impossible. Similarly, Dora Apel says, 'looking and seeing seem to implicate the viewer, however distanced and sympathetic, in the acts ... as if viewing itself were a form of aggression. Most of us would prefer not to look'.[13]

When looking relations are steered by the perpetrator, is it possible to escape from this inscribed point of view, other than by not looking? Disturbingly, the US soldiers present in the Abu Ghraib images mostly smile and often give the thumbs-up sign, in a perversion of a familiar spirit of play, distraction and fun.[14] This sentiment was mirrored, albeit under the reversed sign, by conservative talk-radio host Rush Limbaugh. By dismissing the events as 'guys blowing off steam', he turned torture into a recreational activity.[15] Butler argues that the images were 'clearly' taken without conscience that a crime was taking place, 'in plain view, in front of the camera, even for the camera'.[16] This claim is undermined however, by the testimony of Private Sabrina Harman, one of the main photographers. Harman seems aware of a moral failure and she credibly alleges that she started taking pictures to collect evidence.[17] What is clear, then, is rather that an image always shows more than what was intended by the photographer, that it may have audiences other than those originally intended and that one may be mistaken about these original intentions.

Lynching postcards, popular around the early twentieth century in the US, constitute another commonly discussed historical and aesthetic precursor.[18] Stylistic similarities range from the posing and attitude of the perpetrators to the handling of the victim's body as prop and background; shared also are the apparent enjoyment on the perpetrators' faces, their complete lack of sense of wrongdoing, the use of such images as commodity and souvenirs of pastime activities.

Both the act of *taking* the image and the act of *watching* the image have been considered as part of the mechanism of torture. Taking a picture of someone against or without the person's consent and to disseminate that record demonstrates a power differential, overriding the autonomy of the person turned into object and expanding the power of the one who decides to 'make a body do one's bidding'.[19]

Photographing the torture of prisoners in Abu Ghraib was clearly such a violation and has been experienced as such. At least some of the images, such as the 'Human Pyramid', also seem to indicate that they were staged *for* the camera. Nevertheless, the status of the circulated images themselves seems more inconclusive. Some theorists suggest reading the visual record *itself* as part of the torture:

> Almost all of the prisoners who testified about their experiences at Abu Ghraib specifically mentioned the use of photography and video [which] suggests that the shame and humiliation they experienced *extends to the visual record made of it* ... The visual record, in other words, is part of the torture.[20]

This argument is frequently based on Seymour Hersh's initial reporting. Hersh alleged that the orientalist and essentialist study, *The Arab Mind* (Raphael Patai, 1973) served as a manual for inspiration in the design of the torture techniques; that the torture and its visual record were designed in order to exploit specific (sexual) vulnerabilities of the targeted populations; and that the photographs were intended for blackmail.[21] The photos were also used to directly terrorise and humiliate the prisoners, to intimidate other prisoners, and, when shown outside the prison, to intimidate the prisoners' families and communities.[22]

Rejali considers this 'blackmail plan' as one of the 'convenient truths' or rather, convenient lies, about a case of torture that evolved much less strategically.[23] While the specific techniques employed here may have been influenced by misplaced ethnographic notions, such as Patai's, cultural anthropologist Laura McNamara finds no evidence that the *images* were used as leverage.

> None of the 13 detainees who testified ... mention photographic blackmail in their sworn statements, which are otherwise quite graphic [yet] the idea that Patai's book underpinned ethnographically-informed sexual humiliation at Abu Ghraib has permeated popular and academic culture.[24]

In addition, Hersh's assumptions of a particularly Arab sensibility sometimes border on the essentialist.[25] In any case, the emphasis on cultural specificities moves the focus away from what this behaviour says about the US army and the American GIs themselves, for, as Butler points out, the torture must be understood as 'the actions of a homophobic institution against a population that is both constructed and targeted for its own [that is the US military's] shame about homosexuality'.[26]

And if the presence of US faces in the photos implicates the viewer, projecting backwards 'that we are they, that torturers are us'[27] does that refer only to a US or a Western viewer, or to any viewer? To what extent can the codes present within the image truly cement the agency of viewer and object or lack thereof? Once the violation is done, do the images necessarily remain culpable, independent of potentially reframed contexts? The answer to these questions depends on whether looking at the pictures inevitably reproduces the 'torturable' subject, whether we continue the torture by looking at the pictures. Some scholars suggest that their exhibition prolongs and multiplies the effects of torture. Such readings are legitimately concerned that even the purest of intentions can transform 'the tortured bodies depicted in these photographs ... into things they never consented to be, including instruments of political enlightenment'.[28]

Viewed as extensions of looking relations based in racist notions of supremacy, the photographs 'not only represent and allude to [but also] reproduce and multiply the power dynamics that made these acts possible in the first place'.[29] A history of misogynist, homophobic, racist and colonial belief systems and the disavowed guilt over the US history of slavery enter in the selection of bodies that are forced to fuel these ideology systems; Hazel Carby draws a 'direct, but hidden, line connecting Abu Ghraib, the Rodney King video, the photographs and "postcards" of lynchings'.[30]

Going even further, Liz Philipose claims that the dissemination of the images continues ideological and supremacist positions '[r]egardless of the reasons for their circulation'. The images are part of a technology that produces a 'racialized body ... the servile, compliant, raced bodies of Muslim men', using and reproducing race as a 'practice of visibility'.[31] Similarly, McClintock interprets the images as 'personal trophies', a means of 'fixing as spectacle, in the photographs' promise of permanence' moments of 'borrowed and phantasmagoric' power for the soldiers, sustained by 'ritualistic' repetition: in the space of the web, modern state surveillance and private spectacle collide.[32]

Without a doubt, the images' staging evidences imperial, racist, homophobic and misogynist attitudes. Nevertheless, straightforwardly linking global circulation with 'a visual regime of domination', disregarding intent and context, is problematic and seems to automatically assume Western audiences. In contradistinction to previous photojournalistic documentation, these images were precisely not intended for public circulation. In Harman's case, they were meant, and ultimately served, as evidence, which complicates the argument that they intend to assure a home-front population of the racialised other.[33] Moreover, they have unintentionally turned into a form of unofficial embedded journalism, which clearly prompted an official investigation.

Part of the difficulty in separating violence as crime from violence as performance for the camera derives from the fact that the event and its partial visual record have become conflated. To some extent, it is true that the images *are* the event – part of it, its prolongation; only by documenting Abu Ghraib did it achieve 'existence' in the public consciousness.[34] The trophy argument is dissatisfying because there is much less 'promise of permanence' in digital images, a fact that is rather underlined by the proliferation capacities of the web as the images' platform and supporting medium. The changed modes of address and possibilities of dissemination in today's media environment mean that we document *everything* all the time.[35] Such images are indeed a form of curating the self on social media, perhaps even a form of self-surveillance, but they are also an affirmative way of *being* today, by being digitally present, a reassurance: 'I take pictures, therefore I am.'

Sontag's claim that 'the photographs are us'[36] expresses the fact that the particular iconography at work in these pictures is clearly recognisable as contemporary Western imaginary, from the evocation of a crucifixion and the KKK in the 'Hooded Man' picture, to the echoes of a particularly US-American (porn) culture: on the confiscated cameras, the torture images were interspersed with other private digital souvenirs, in particular amateur pornographic images.[37] Yet the fact that both amateur porn and torture proto-selfies were found on the soldiers' cameras has less to do with the erotic nature of (this) torture and more with the fact that digital technology is changing our ways of recording, hiding and sharing information. As Rodowick points out, 'digital photographs have become more social than personal.'[38] The behaviour of open posing in the pictures emphasises how the soldiers *performed* according to the rules of a larger collective and *for* a camera. Digital (self-)images are simply part of contemporary self-expression.[39] While the sexualised contents and the aspect of 'having fun' are deeply unsettling in their familiarity then, even more uncannily familiar, perhaps, is the use of digital media. Seeing the Abu Ghraib images, Grusin argues, the viewer is shocked to recognise that 'we use digital photos in the same way, to distribute our affective responses'.[40]

Such changes in media usage and reception matter, as they certainly influence our perception of their content. Digital images are made to be mobile, they are harder to confiscate, to censor pre-emptively, or to erase once they are alive online. Their accelerated proliferation and more interactive mode of address could influence our perception of proximity – a central factor in our capacity to feel for the suffering of another.[41]

A textual example for such changed codes of content and media usage is the thumbs-up sign which Private Harman makes in almost every image. Harman herself explains this gesture and her smile as a protective automatism, a performance for the camera; and her letters at the time corroborate this account. Elisabeth Bronfen reads these gestures as a form of embodied witness-recording, which signal, à la *pics or it didn't happen*: 'this happened. I was there to witness what we did'.[42] (Compare Richard Bégin's exploration of the semantic potential of 'picture postures' in portable phone footage produced in situations of extreme duress; this 'iconographie mobile' suggests the possibility – further explored in the last chapter – of accessing the reference in such images in another form, linked to the movements, gestures and postures of the one filming.[43])

Yet this particular gesture is also (or used to be) typical when *taking a photograph*. As a 'picture-gesture', it clearly indicates: 'this is a photograph'. The Abu Ghraib images speak directly to us because they are addressed to a *person* taking the pictures. In contrast to the disembodied panoptical gaze of modern warfare and the naturalised presence of surveillance, the viewer cannot hide in the illusion of invisibility: we are being smiled at.

While the Abu Ghraib images continue to exist online, the time span in which they actually harnessed attention proved rather short-lived. Yet it might be too early to dismiss their legacy, transformative power and 'memorative potency'.[44] The images have become enmeshed with the discourses on torture that accompanied and followed their release, layers which are peeled apart in *Standard*. These refigurations have expanded the dialectical relationship between image and viewer. Even a piece of archive begins to function differently over time, with repeated exposure and with our awareness of what followed, which is why Bronfen suggests to read such images 'preposterously': 'The resilient afterlife of images and narratives is conditioned on the fact that our critical reading of past representations can never be severed from the refigurations they have [subsequently] encountered'.[45]

Yet the 'narrativisability' of iconic material does not annihilate the veracity of their facts: it is not the *events* that are 'up for grabs', as Bill Nichols claims, but their interpretation.[46] At the end of *Standard*, each of the pictures is stamped, counting the depicted act either as torture or as normal 'standard operating procedure' for the military. Further illuminating this link between language, violence and image are the titles of both films. Where *Standard* concentrates on the spinning of *visual* evidence, *Unknown* focuses on how central figures in the Iraq War weaponised and distorted *language*. The following analysis will follow the film's lead and focus on the notorious rhetorical pirouettes used to deceive the public, before explaining the methods employed by Morris to cut through the obfuscation.

The Unknown Known

Illustrating the fact that today's 'alternative facts' are the logical extension of previous renaming operations, both *Standard* and *Unknown* address the notorious euphemisms employed under the George W. Bush administration: torturers became 'interrogation experts', torture a set of 'alternative measures', 'enhanced' or 'harsh interrogations', prisoners were 'softened up' or 'stressed out'.[47] Such efforts to obscure and distort language are part of a strategy aimed at dehumanising the opponent, gaslighting the public and eschewing legal responsibility. 'Abuse' signals a casual, unmotivated, even accidental behaviour, 'a private initiative, not an outcome of public policy'; and prisoners defined as 'detainees' were considered exempt from POW protection under the Geneva Convention. By describing what happened in Abu Ghraib as 'abuse', and by designating those captured as 'unlawful' combatants, the government could claim to be unaccountable to national and international law.[48]

Linking the semiological strategies of the War on Terror, 'at its core, a magnified case of state terrorism', to the state terror of Latin American dictators, Ernesto Semán points out that '[it] starts with language … the very idea that it was legal to torture detainees because they were not criminals or POWs is a proxy for the *desaparecido*'.[49]

This role of language in the political battle is key in *Unknown*. The film's title is taken from the infamous response that Rumsfeld gave at a news briefing on 12 February 2002, to a question regarding the lack of *evidence* that Iraq was supplying terrorists with weapons of mass destruction. In what seemed like a philosophical and contemplative meditation, Rumsfeld responded:

> There are known knowns. These are things we know that we know. There are known unknowns. That is to say, there are things that we know we don't know. But there are also unknown unknowns. There are things we don't know we don't know.[50]

These quips are seductive *because* they are reductive. As with other Rumsfeldian statements ('Weakness is provocative') it is less the normative abstraction itself than its inappropriate application to *concrete* atrocity that is offensive and infuriating. His diagnosis that 'absence of evidence is not evidence of absence' is legitimate and helpful when we think of the case of the *desaparecidos*. Imaginary scenarios, however, are not sufficient as justification for pre-emptive wars.

At a press briefing about the Abu Ghraib scandal on 4 May 2004, Rumsfeld offered another demonstration of his mastery at spinning, when responding to the question, 'Mr Secretary, a number of times … you said USA troops do not torture individuals … Is this one of those rare exceptions here that torture took place?':[51]

> I'm not a lawyer. My impression is that what has been charged thus far is abuse, which I believe technically is different from torture. I don't know if it is correct to say what you just said, that torture has taken place, or that there's been a conviction for torture. And therefore I'm not going to address the 'torture' word.[52]

Again, Rumsfeld uses rhetorical tools in order to refuse to answer the question, from qualifying language ('my impression is'), pedantry as diversion ('technically different'), a performance of modesty which conveniently clears him from giving a determinate response ('I'm not a lawyer'). He ends by distancing himself and locating the acts with his questioner ('what you just said, that torture has taken place'). Jared del Rosso describes this tactic, following Stanley Cohen, as 'interpretive denial'.[53] Through its redundant construction, Rumsfeld's 'torture word' turns the conversation into one about correct terminology. Is a 'torture word' even a word? Is it, as his formulation suggests, a dirty word? Expressions of affect, dirty words move from factual dirt to moral pollution, and from the actual practices, objects and people considered abject, to the words naming them. 'Consuming' such a word – taking it into one's mouth – threatens to contaminate one's body, by becoming, literally, part of it. By creating distance to the word/thing, Rumsfeld's political defence – shunning accountability or responsibility – is also an operation protective of his physical body.

As the use of language has long-term social and direct judicial implications, it was important that former President Obama used the 't-word', to rebut Dick Cheney in 2009: 'I believe that waterboarding was torture and, whatever legal rationales were used, it was a mistake'.[54] In 2014 – ten years after the images went viral – that became an explicit confirmation: 'We tortured some folks.'[55] The odd use of the term 'folks' evoked colloquial, unpretentious informality, but perhaps also a more humanising description of the victims, compared to 'detainees' or 'enemy combatants'.[56] Obama's most persistent quote on torture was the puzzling and paradoxical phrase 'this is not who we are' – which oddly echoes Rumsfeld, who, three days after the briefing quoted above, apologised to Congress for what he called 'fundamentally un-American' scenes at Abu Ghraib. Mark Danner deftly deconstructs this line of defence:

> What does it even mean? I guess it means, 'This is not what we would do, if we were who we said we are.' But we seem not to be who we said we are because this is what we have done.[57]

In Morris's films, visual material frequently appears on the screen as his interviewees talk, often illustrating, undermining or ironically commenting on something the interviewee has said.[58] In *Unknown*, this visual material consists chiefly of words taken from Rumsfeld's ample output of memos. Rumsfeld called these thousands of memos 'snowflakes'. Written on screen, twirling around Rumsfeld's head like blinding dust, these words create a peculiar kind of visualised voice. Symbolically, their elusive nature generates associations on the obfuscating role language played in these events. Their aesthetic organisation – they flash, endure or replicate – takes the images into a figural realm. They express visually the difficulty of holding him accountable and they define him; yet as words they belong to all of us and express also the viewer's responsibility and power.

Morris typically interviews his subjects with the help of devices he invented: the 'Interrotron', or its follow-up, the 'Megatron'.[59] By shooting through a two-way mirror with a video monitor mounted under the camera lens, Morris can film *and* simultaneously make virtual eye contact with the subject, which on the screen creates the impression of direct eye contact. '[The Interrotron] creates greater distance <u>and</u> greater intimacy. And it also creates the *true first person*. Now, when people make eye contact with me, it can be preserved on film'.[60]

Figure 5.1 *The Unknown Known.*

This means that the spectatorial gaze seems to become congruent with Morris's own; the viewer enters a position of virtual proximity, mirrored by Morris's own physical – and perhaps emotional – closeness. At the same time, as a form of direct address, the Interrotron offers 'a potentially rich metaphor for the problems of vision'.[61] The viewer is encouraged to struggle not only with the emotional responses created by the direct address but also to not 'mistake direct eye contact for direct access to the truth'.[62]

The perpetrators interviewed here stand in a long line of guilty subjects, beginning with Morris's first-ever taped interview, an uncompleted project as a postgraduate philosophy student, with a serial killer. Indeed, all of Morris's films concern judicial processes, 'the process of bearing witness to disputed facts', contested evidence and subjective testimony.[63] In his seminal *The Fog of War* (2003), Morris had interviewed Robert McNamara, another former US Secretary of Defense and a key figure in another war. After much obfuscation, Morris 'caught' McNamara in a moment of repentance. McNamara's face expressing regret is perhaps the most famous moment of the film. *Unknown* uses the same formal structure: patient long takes, visual and sonic close-ups which pick up minute changes in the interviewee's facial expression, hesitations and tonal shifts. But in *Unknown*, Rumsfeld's performance remains seamless, impervious, to all appearances untroubled by conscience. The closest to a response to Morris's initiating question, 'Why did we go to war in Iraq?' is a shockingly blasé 'Some things work out, some things don't. That one didn't.'

Perhaps in light of Rumsfeld's expertise at spinning information, Morris is uncharacteristically present as interviewer in *Unknown* and we hear many of his questions, follow-ups and contestations (in *Standard*, there are only three such moments.) As a result, Morris becomes much more vulnerable as a subject of his own film, getting lost in semantic battles. Instead of pinning down Rumsfeld's actions, the search for a seemingly indeterminable, final meaning of expressions such as 'unknown knowns' entangles the director and leaves the audience stranded.

Standard Operating Procedure

In his films and blog, Morris obsesses about how easy it is to misread an image, 'Photography can make us think we know more than we really know … what we see is determined by our beliefs. We see not what is there, but rather what we want to see or expect to see'.[64]

In *Standard*, Morris explores the creation, intelligibility and reception of the images that emerged from Abu Ghraib. While these present clear representational evidence of war crimes, these crimes were not necessarily or exclusively committed by the people posing in the photos or by those who took them. In the context of Abu Ghraib, this challenge to what images can actually tell us may feel uncomfortably close to exoneration. As a result, *Standard* was criticised for a lack of moral perspective. Prominently, Nichols wrote an open letter charging that the film was lacking a 'moral center'. Nichols had previously criticised Morris's interest in unreliable narration as relativist, encouraging 'controversy through the deliberate promotion of ambivalence', and suggested that conflicting re-enactments in Morris's earlier films led to a 'loss of voice'.[65]

Particularly condemned were the film's aesthetics, from the 'insinuating' musical score,[66] a 'conventional' and therefore obscene rhetoric which provided 'titillation through horror'[67] and 'familiar aesthetic thrills as a substitute for specificity of meaning'.[68] By contrast, Fallon suggested that the film expands its subject matter to an exploration of the medium that communicates and, to an extent, produces the horrors investigated by the film: the creation, transmission and reception of the event 'torture at Abu Ghraib' through its iconic images. In other words, the struggle over the meaning of these particular pictures is extended to an exploration of the nature of digital images.[69] The Abu Ghraib images are both a type of found object and a type of image *produced* by their mediation – selected among different versions, cropped and narratively embedded. The film makes us 'rethink photographs that, by virtue of their excessive and diverse media deployment, have been all but depleted of their meaning'.[70]

Yet rather than suggesting that only our initial response is legitimate and meaningful, Morris calls upon us to assess the accuracy of these first affective responses to the images. The film explores what can be gauged of the original event, its representations in various media formats, adding

Figure 5.2 *Standard Operating Procedure.*

its own layers through interviews, staging and re-enactments. Beginning with the title sequence and recurring at various moments in the film, Morris uses non-indexical approximations to animate abstract ideas and processes, such as the decoding of metadata. The title sequence visualises the images' journey in a spatially dynamic, combinatory structure: they appear as little squares, increase in scale as they approach, create formations and disappear, emphasising their fragmentary character, floating in what seems a three-dimensional black screen space resonant of the universe. At later moments in the film, the images from various cameras glide along horizontally until a double is found: an image from the same event but taken by a different camera. As if in a computer game, the images stop moving, a clicking sound indicates the double and as a 'reward', their metadata is superimposed.

By mining the metadata, the photographs' digital footprint, and by juxtaposing pictures taken from several cameras present at the scenes, it was possible to rectify a selective media narrative. Taken together, the title sequence visualises a graphic image for the hidden digital-genetic code, which enabled the detective work that led to the identity of the photographers.

The strategy of linguistic or visual dissection can be seen as problematic in its intellectual relation to an excessively self-absorbed poststructuralist hermeneutic. A favoured example of such misapplied 'intratextual narcissism'[71] was the 1992 Rodney King trial, in which George Holliday's video of the beating was dissected beyond recognition in a blow-by-blow freeze frame analysis, resulting in an initial acquittal of the attackers. In a similar way, the initial military investigation into the Abu Ghraib scandal enlisted the intricacies of digital analysis in order to close down political interpretation: by reducing torture to metadata, it attempted to redirect the thorny question of culpability.

In *Standard*, the struggle over the meaning of these particular pictures is extended to an exploration of the nature of digital images, expanding the subject matter to an exploration of the medium that communicates and to some extent produces these horrors. *Standard* is 'as much about digital ontology as it is about (photographed) detainee abuse', argues Caetlin Benson-Allott, claiming that the visual formations in *Standard* 'literally dissolve the Abu Ghraib photos into streams of binary code that finally render their contents invisible'.[72]

But Morris's epistemological scepticism does not succumb to relativism. Instead, a former private investigator, Morris aims the digital lens in the reverse direction; his examination becomes a form of hack. Digital images can be dissolved in code, but their footprint can also be used to reconstruct the timeline. Their large number allowed comparing pictures taken from several cameras, reversing the traditional media's selective editing and its resulting narratives. Adding metadata to the irrefutable presence of bodies performing 'picture poses' reveals the corporeal presence of the one taking the picture: the presence of absence. Through reframing and metadata analysis, *Standard* is able to determine who else was present at, and cropped from, the scene, to demonstrate both overlap and disconnection between photographers, actual abusers and those present in the images.

Moreover, highlighting that media must be 'read', and that viewers are always involved in this process of creating meaning, the film features various kinds of media, pairing old and new as if to emphasise the inherent restrictions of each. For instance, Harman reads aloud the letter she wrote to her partner; and in the title sequence, photographs appear in a four-square white frame, evoking pre-digital print photography. The interactive website for the film features a dynamic interface which lets viewers decide which image to privilege, while reflecting that these decisions are transient and subjective.

Home videos are featured as well, manipulated to resemble aged Super-8 films, and emerging, aesthetically defamiliarised, within a small window on an otherwise black screen. As home movies typically serve to create a 'warm, fuzzy feeling', Odorico reads their use in the film as a strategy to humanise the soldiers through 'normalcy footage'.[73] Of course, what makes the original images so shocking is at least in part exactly such an interspersion of violence with porn and banal souvenir footage and the resulting tension between brutality and the 'familiarity of spirit'. One of these home videos shows a hand playing with a kitten. The montage suggests the hand belongs to Charles Graner, who had emerged as ringleader at Abu

Ghraib. Odorico reads this kitten scene as a reminder 'that Graner was a human being, a man capable of moments of tenderness'.[74] However, in this clip, we see Grainer threatening the kitten with his hand, before grabbing it in play. The clip follows on Private Lynndie England's sobering account of her infatuation with Graner, a staff sergeant more than fifteen years her senior, and his manipulative behaviour towards her. England of course became one of the most public faces of the abusers; she is present in some of the most infamous pictures. Her account of their relationship is illustrated by amateur pornographic images featuring her in objectified, humiliating positions. Graner boasted of his ability 'to make her [England] do things'.[75] Rather than proof of Graner's humanity, the kitten scene associates England with the cat and Graner with abusive behaviour.

Thus, the film's moral voice emerges from this carefully constructed texture: the original digital images of Abu Ghraib; interviews with investigators and soldiers; re-enactments of some of the events; various intervisual commentary. The film's narrative agency speaks through the montage of these visual layers – and the invitation or request to the audience to participate in this cultural act of *reading* images. Where the stop-frame analysis in the King trial was premised on the idea that each individual image frame is telling an absolute truth, re-enactments definitely communicate their subjective and performative nature. They are clearly *a* version, they always perform – or re-perform – one history among several and thus reflect a different view on the nature of history. As Maria Flood points out, 'blurry images and blacked-out portions of the screen create a keyhole effect, pointing to the absence of the prisoners' perspectives and the role of higher military officials in sanctioning these acts'.[76] While there is a link between the re-enactments, the verbal accounts of the events and the contents shown in the Abu Ghraib photographs, Morris uses re-enactments specifically to make the spectator engage with the slipperiness of factual evidence, a gap made perceivable through the different modalities and temporalities of photography, film, home movie. Effects of defamiliarisation question the iconic autonomy the images have developed, the over-familiarity of certain narratives.[77] Unlike images, re-enactments are not coded as transparently intelligible; they are defined by a 'fantasmatic element',[78] partly fictional and imagined in nature. There is no pre-text at objectivity, no invitation to passive immersion here. Morris's aestheticised re-stagings are a reminder 'that we were not there'.[79] This inherent artificiality emphasises that '[all] attempts to recover [the events] – via photography, narration or re-enactment – are imperfect, removed from the so-called original moment'.[80]

A re-enactment also foregrounds the role of film as teller and audience as consumer of these images. Building on Barthes's *punctum* as the aspect that jumps out at the viewer within her study of a photograph, Laura Mulvey describes how a specific kind of delayed and interactive, 'pensive', spectatorship creates a cinematic punctum that belongs to the viewer.[81] The dreamy, temporally elongated re-enactments in *Standard*, by contrast, visualise a *directorial* punctum. As in *Unknown*, Morris examines people through the language they use, especially in memory narration. As the first receiver of the accounts, by selecting which elements to re-enact, and how, Morris manifests his authorial voice in a consciously subjective way. His re-enactments focus on distinctive, memorable, 'sticky' aspects within the verbal accounts of his interviewees. Devin and Marsha Orgeron call these moments first-person images or 'breakaway metaphoric moments':[82] scenes which often support but sometimes also undermine the utterances of the speaking characters.

The aesthetics of these re-enactments have been experienced and criticised as irritating, even repellent, and as gratuitously beautified.[83] Yet while not all re-enactments are beautiful, all do flaunt their artifice, with upside-down frames, overexposure, superimpositions. While re-enactments are often defined by their emotional pull, the richly stylised restagings here rather seek to disengage the audience from their initial affective reaction, as they aesthetically interrupt the clean *mise-en-scène* and constructed objectiveness of the interviews. This stylisation also comments on the content. In one scene, for instance, a soldier recounts how they would put on a 'dog-and-pony-show' when inspectors visited the facilities. Now, the film's re-enactments ironically create a 'show' for the cinema audience: a show we cannot watch without engaging with the question of our own possible complicity.

One scene in particular supports Morris's argument that re-enactments can help to 'burrow underneath the surface of reality in an attempt to uncover some hidden truth'.[84] Here, he 'spectralises' agents of 'Other Government Agencies': those intangible ghosts who, according to Morris's interviewees, did the 'real' interrogation and torture, but who neither appeared in the photographs nor faced prosecution. Though there are no images of these agents, they were clearly *there*. Rather than mimetic realism, these recreations, phantom figures made visible as transparent superimpositions, strive for a conceptual and emotional approach to the feelings and memories that are described.

In another example, writing to her partner, Harman describes a situation she witnessed of a sixteen-year-old prisoner trying to fend off an ant attack. Harman's letter reads,

Figure 5.3 *Standard Operating Procedure.*

The lights went out in the prison. So here we are in the dark. I hear *missus, missus*. I go downstairs and flash my light on a sixteen-year-old sitting down smacking ants. Now these ants are Iraqi ants. Large – so large they could carry the family dog while giving you the finger. All the ants in the prison came to this one boy's cell and decided to take over. All I could do was spray Lysol. The ants laughed at me and kept going. So here we were in the dark with one small flashlight, beating ants with their shoes.

The screen is plunged in (the cell's) darkness, then a small circle of illumination, like Harman's flashlight, glides over the pages of the letter, over images of sandals being smacked, before cutting to frantic movements of limbs to wipe off the ants, and several shots of seemingly giant ants, in close-up, crawling over the prisoner's skin. The scene is accompanied by an auditive close-up, a smacking sound clearly rendered and exaggerated in volume. A return to the distinctive qualities of still and moving images helps to determine the function of this re-enactment. While the very stillness of a photograph allows for a more distanced level of contemplation, *moving* images may more affectively *move* the viewer. Yet the limited narrative movement of the re-enactments in *Standard* invite contemplation. Their artificial aesthetic signals that the testimony might be unreliable, pointing to the elasticity of memory and remembering, the degree to which we rely upon the fictional in the process of re-creation that is remembering.[85] They offer a metaphor for the workings of our brain when we are *told* a story or a memory, illustrating the inherent fracturing that exists between the initial perception and its narrative in memory. Such re-enactments are then perhaps a better metaphor for memory than Sontag's claim that we remember in 'freeze-framed', single images.[86]

The film has also been criticised for its focus on the American soldiers. Absent the victims' voices or a qualifying narrative voice, Leimbacher argues, the positions expressed in the testimony of the grunts become confessions that function as excuses.[87] This legitimate concern threatens to collapse with a rejection of perpetrator narratives per se, save in a highly prescribed, condemning form. Yet the renegotiation of hegemonic images and narratives is as politically relevant as recovering space for the victims and should not be mutually exclusive. These subjectivities must be wrestled with in order to counter social denial and amnesia. Morris listens seriously to the soldiers' justifications and self-exonerations and asks his audience to do the same. During the testimonies, the Interrotron disrupts the possibility of a distancing, objectifying gaze. The perceived commonalities might feel uncomfortable, even offensive, but this 'enforced proximity'[88] also counterweights and dismantles the 'rotten apples' narrative. However, while the military personnel are given screen space and time to tell their part in the story, this does not automatically act in their favour. Some self-incriminate or attempt to dissociate themselves emotionally from their own responsibility, often revealing a distinct and rather shocking lack of perspective, self-awareness and empathy. Clearly not members of the intelligence community, they are struggling to comprehend what is happening to them. This limited display of moral and intellectual capacity indicts a chain of command that charged these soldiers with tasks they were neither trained nor qualified for. (The question of agency, including how much agency Morris grants his subjects, is key both within the film and within its making.[89])

A clear counter-weight to the idea that proximity to the soldiers results in forced identification is seen in the re-enactment of torture by waterboarding. As with the visualisation of metadata, the sequence is also an example of how the film strives to find a format to render visible,

> a point of view that by definition never existed. Waterboarding requires ... obscuring [the victim's] vision ... this is the same obscured perspective *SOP* adopts during its waterboarding scene. The scene literalises a purely empathic point of view to demonstrate what we imagine or what we think we can surmise about one particular torture the US. military inflicts on its detainees.[90]

Thus, Nichols's revulsion at Morris's decision to 'decontextualise' and 'fetishise' the images,[91] must be read as a feature not a bug, not a failure but the logical – and anticipated – reaction to the unavoidable complicity of watching. When we watch Morris's films, 'we become witnesses to the process of witnessing'.[92] Initially we study the soldiers, but increasingly the film's subject matter expands to include the performativity and temporality of speaking, questioning, writing, witnessing as well as the act of (watching the) watching, a self-reflexivity of the film that is in turn thrown back at the viewer. *Standard* interrogates and multiplies the voices and layered gazes that spread from the event. There is the gaze of the soldiers looking at the pictures in hindsight, describing and commenting directly; the investigators looking at the images as evidence; Morris's and the cameras' point of view; the implied gaze present in the Abu Ghraib pictures; the gaze of the soldiers looking at Morris and, via the Interrotron, *at us*, the audience, who are looking back.

Contemplating the images, again and again, attempting to wrestle meaning from them, is an activity shared between Morris, the audience and the soldiers. The spectator is watching characters who are themselves assiduously watching. They are also *performing* this watching, conscious that they will be or are being observed. This performance, too, is part of the story of Abu Ghraib, as in many of the images, the guards made their prisoners perform; but often they were also themselves performing. The film thus folds its audience into the concentric circles of rippling gazes from the event Abu Ghraib, who is acting and who is watching, who is performing and for whom, into what Williams referred to as the 'cluster fuck'[93] of accountability, responsibility and blame.

All interviews use complex lighting and make-up, and an unnaturally bland, unobtrusive background. Within this highly controlled environment, the focus is entirely on the interviewees: their words as well as their manner of speaking and mimetic behaviour. Both this interview setting and the dreamy re-enactments create a contemplative space, an effect enhanced by the fact that we generally do not hear the questions asked, while being involved in an intimate dialogue.

Jump cuts within the interviews – the digital repositioning of people within the frame so the talking heads appear to 'jump' from the right to the left side and reverse – disrupt any tendency to imagine the interviewees talking 'naturally' and serve as a reminder of authorial mediation. Such performative tactics in nonfiction cinema acknowledge the presence and inevitable intrusion of the filmmakers – as well as the anticipated future audience and their role in the construction of historical narratives – and present an 'alternative realness' and 'alternative honesty'.[94] They remind viewers of their own role in the construction of historical narratives, and of the fact that all attempts to recover past events (photography, narration or re-enactment) are mediated.

Often, the film lingers on a scene, long past the moments when it feels comfortable. One of Morris's trademarks is to *stay* with the interviewee after they have stopped speaking, focusing on their faces, and it is here that we often find moments of facial and gestural revelation.[95] These moments where 'nothing happens', usually cut in the editing process, point to those stories and images that are left out of the public discourse and perception.

Importantly, the acknowledgement of the limits inherent in any representation and the performative construction of truth does not suggest that all reframings are equally valid. Writing about Morris's seminal *Thin Blue Line* (1988), Williams suggests that 'the loss of faith in the objectivity of the image' is so hurtful because there was once so much of it.[96] The film, which cinematically reinvestigated a murder case, was interpreted as a prime example of the self-reflexive postmodern documentary. By staging competing narratives, it rejected the notion that truth can be fathomed as a totality. And yet, in the film, Morris succeeded in getting another character than the one who was convicted to confess to the murder on tape. As a result, the actual case was relitigated and the man who had been wrongly convicted of murder was exonerated. The film thus had a direct impact on reality, and it *had* a resolution. Two decades later, the point is rather to insist on the existence of a *piece* of truth – not in absolute terms, but truth nonetheless. Through 'strategies of fiction', Morris finds 'relative truths'.[97] Rather than using images as weaponised conveyors of absolute truth, as practices by the defence of King's attackers, the film's moral voice is found in the polyphonic truth of the layered interplay of gazes and voices and media formats.

Standard demonstrates that it *does* matter into which context the original Abu Ghraib images are inserted. The film guides the viewer away from reproducing a dominant and oppressive gaze, towards engaging with questions of accountability, complicity and the nature of the truth images can offer. Engaging with epistemological questions on the level of both content and form, the film does not overcome so much as problematise its representational difficulties, showcasing how today's media landscape filters what we know and believe, the struggle over the meaning of concrete, evidentiary images (and their absence). By reframing the images and by offering additional contextual information, the film does formally what it asks its viewers to do, namely to expand their view on the events in which the images originated.

Notes

1. Officials of the International Committee of the Red Cross visited Abu Ghraib twenty-nine times during the spring and autumn of 2003, reporting on prisoner abuse and practices amounting to torture. Cf. Danner, *Torture and Truth*. One of the first major pieces ran in *The Washington Post* in December 2002, and *The New Yorker* began its coverage in May 2004. 60

Minutes II showed images on prime-time US TV on 28 April 2004 (Grusin, p. 63).
2. For instance, amnesty was offered to soldiers voluntarily turning in their material. Cf. Mitchell, *Cloning Terror*, p. 169.
3. Coll, 'The Unblinking Stare'; McClintock, 'Paranoid Empire'. Sontag, 'Regarding the torture'.
4. Mayer, 'The Black Sites'.
5. Walsh, 'What stories we tell', pp. 154–5.
6. Mirzoeff, 'Invisible Empire', p. 23.
7. Walsh, 'What stories we tell', pp. 154–5.
8. Didi-Huberman, *Images in Spite of All*, pp. 32–3.
9. Mitchell, *Cloning Terror*, p. 113.
10. Rodowick, *Virtual Life of Film*, p. 146.
11. Hirsch, 'Surviving Images', p. 24.
12. Morris, 'The Most Curious Thing'.
13. Apel in Guerin and Hallas, *Image and Witness*, p. 207.
14. Williams, 'Cluster Fuck'.
15. Middleton, 'The Subject of Torture', pp. 5–6.
16. Butler, 'Photography, War, Outrage' and Butler, 'Ethics of Photography'.
17. Butler, *Frames of War*, p. 79. Hersh, 'Torture at Abu Ghraib'.
18. Cf. Carby, 'A Strange and Bitter Crop'; Hernandez, 'The Tortured Body'; Mitchell, *Cloning Terror*; Simpson in Bond, *Frames of Memory*.
19. Grajeda, 'Picturing Torture', p. 224.
20. Dauphinée, 'Politics of the Body in Pain', p. 147.
21. Hersh, 'Torture at Abu Ghraib'; cf. Mitchell, *Cloning Terror*; Grajeda, 'Picturing torture', p. 229.
22. McClintock, 'Paranoid Empire', p. 59.
23. Rejali, 'Convenient Truths', p. 221.
24. McNamara, 'Notes on an Ethnographic Scandal', pp. 4–5.
25. Cf. Hernandez' criticism of Hersh's inadvertent conflation of Muslims and Arabs. Hernandez, 'The Tortured Body'.
26. Butler, *Frames of War*, p. 129. Cf. Mirzoeff, 'Invisible Empire'.
27. Grajeda, 'Picturing Torture', p. 229.
28. Adelman, 'Tangled Complicities', p. 362. In deference to this argument and as my goal is to contribute to reflecting on the critical discourse *about* the images, as well as the affordances of their format, the images are not reproduced in this volume. See also Adelman, 'Atrocity and Aporiae'.
29. Jasbir Puar in Zimmer, 'Caught on Tape?', p. 92.
30. Carby, 'A Strange and Bitter Crop'. Cf. Faludi on the need to reassert a wounded 'US. national manhood'. Faludi, *The Terror Dream*, p. 3.
31. Philipose, 'The Politics of Pain', pp. 4–5.
32. McClintock, 'Paranoid Empire', p. 60.
33. Cf. Chuck Kleinhans's reading of the torture at Abu Ghraib in terms of recovering masculinity. Kleinhans, 'Imagining Torture'.

34. Rodowick, *Virtual Life of Film*, p. 149.
35. Cf. Peebles, 'Lenses into war', p. 139.
36. Sontag, 'Regarding the Torture of Others'.
37. Cf. Neroni, 'The Nonsensical Smile'.
38. Rodowick, *Virtual Life of Film*, p. 149.
39. McClintock, 'Paranoid Empire', pp. 62–3.
40. Grusin, *Premediation*, p. 89.
41. Regarding the necessity of proximity to develop empathy, see, for instance Boltanski, *Distant Suffering* and Butler, *Frames of War*.
42. Bronfen, *Specters of War*, p. 166.
43. Bégin, 'Ceci Est Mon Image, Livrée Pour Vous'. Cf. Didi-Huberman, *Images in Spite of All* and Reading, 'Globital Witnessing'.
44. Mitchell, *Cloning Terror*, pp. 148–9.
45. Bronfen, *Specters of War*, p. 2.
46. Cited in Bruzzi, *New Documentary*, p. 22.
47. Even the terms used in the Senate Report, such as 'rectal rehydration' were euphemisms.
48. Williams, *A Very British Killing*.
49. Semán, 'The Torture Consensus in US. Democracy'.
50. United States Department of Defense News Transcript. Rumsfeld liked the phrase enough to re-employ it as the title of his 2012 memoir, *Known and Unknown*.
51. CNN, 'Pentagon Press Briefing'.
52. Ibid.
53. Del Rosso, *Talking About Torture*, p. 17.
54. 'News Conference' *Obama White House*.
55. United States Office of the Press Secretary, 'Press Conference'.
56. Dreyfuss, 'Obama: "We Tortured Some Folks"'.
57. Danner and Eakin, 'Our New Politics of Torture'.
58. Smith, 'The Luckiest Man'.
59. The Megatron can use up to twenty cameras, allowing a wider range of angles and shots for the editing process. As Morris and critics continue to speak of the Interrotron after the introduction of the Megatron in 2001, I will follow their lead when referring to the structural effects of the device.
60. Ebert, 'Megatron'; Errol Morris, 'Eye Contact'. The underline and italic appear in the original.
61. Brown, *Breaking the Fourth Wall*, pp. 14–16.
62. Benson-Allott, 'Mediating Torture', p. 41.
63. Williams, 'Cluster Fuck'.
64. Morris, 'Will the *Real* Hooded Man Please Stand Up'.
65. Nichols, 'Feelings of Revulsion'; Nichols, *Representing Reality*, pp. 100–1; cf. Nichols, 'The Voice of Documentary'.
66. Turan and Hoberman in Benson-Allott, 'Mediating Torture'.
67. Arthur, 'The Horror', p. 112.

68. Arthur, 'The Horror', p. 112. Cf. Williams, Chaudhuri, 'Documenting The Dark Side'.
69. Fallon, 'Archives analog and digital'.
70. Bronfen, *Specters of War*, p. 165.
71. Tomasulo, 'I'll see it when I believe it'.
72. Benson-Allott, 'Mediating Torture', p. 44 and pp. 39–40.
73. Odorico, 'That Would Be Wrong', p. 170. Not all the soldiers who were punished are present in the images or interviewed for the film. Most notably, Morris did not gain permission to interview Charles Graner.
74. Ibid., p. 172.
75. McClintock, 'Paranoid Empire', p. 49. Cf. Caldwell, *Fallgirls* for an analysis particularly conscious of power and gender politics. In *Standard*, it is England who most directly indicts the US military as a misogynist institution.
76. Flood, 'Torture in Word and Image', p. 28.
77. Oyvind Vagnes cited in Andrews, 'Reframing *Standard Operating Procedure*'.
78. Nichols, 'Documentary Reenactment', p. 74.
79. Bronfen, *Specters of War*, p. 165.
80. Orgeron and Orgeron, 'Megatronic Memories', p. 247.
81. Mulvey, *Death 24x*, p. 187.
82. Orgeron and Orgeron, 'Megatronic Memories', p. 241.
83. For instance, Leimbacher, 'Facetime'; Arthur 'The Horror'.
84. Morris, 'Play It Again, Sam'; Morris, 'The Most Curious Thing'.
85. Bruzzi, 'Restaging History'.
86. Sontag, *Regarding the Pain*, p. 19.
87. Leimbacher, 'Facetime'. Cf. Kahana, 'Speech Images'; Westwell, 'The Hurt Locker'.
88. Bruzzi, 'Restaging History'.
89. Cf. Stjepan Mestrovic's reading of the film as demonstrating 'postemotional sadism': Mestrovic, 'Documenting the Documentaries on Abu Ghraib'.
90. Benson-Allott, 'Mediating Torture', p. 43.
91. Nichols, 'Feelings of Revulsion'.
92. Orgeron and Orgeron, 'Megatronic Memories', p. 238.
93. Williams, 'Cluster Fuck'.
94. Bruzzi, *New Documentary*, p. 155.
95. Cf. Morris's so-calledtwenty-minute rule in Ebert, 'Megatron'.
96. Williams, 'Mirrors without Memories', p. 10.
97. Linda Williams in Chaudhuri, 'Documenting The Dark Side'.

CHAPTER 6

The Presence of Absence in Contemporary Chilean Cinema

This chapter focuses on recent Chilean films that seek not only to show historical exclusions and absences but also to find expressions even for the *process of being erased* from history. Contextualised within the contemporary Chilean 'cinema of mood', selected close-readings demonstrate how the films invite an emotional access to history by evoking 'social moods': dispersed, opaque emotional fields, part of the collective aftermath of the dictatorship and its systematic torture. In this way, they help make emotionally available to the viewer what Raymond Williams calls a 'structure of feeling', which Aubrey Anable paraphrases as culture and art expressing 'emergent shared feelings that are not yet present in language, but in which we might sense the rhythms and emotional tones of new ways of being in the world'.[1]

This enables the films to expand the parameters of how we 'see' the past, and to tell perpetrator narratives that are not based on simplistic (dis)identification with the main character. By activating sensual modes of seeing, these films help to reconfigure what remains invisible and what is considered unspeakable, expanding the argument presented in the preceding chapters, that specific existential realities may need a new visual framework.

These strategies should be read not only as a self-reflexive meditation on the difficulties of 'doing' history on film, but also as political acts. They seek to counter *negacionismo*, revisionist narratives; to bring historical disappearances of various kinds into the present time of viewing; and to make structural invisibilities visible. The Chilean dictatorship used practices of *making disappear* that, to some extent, continue up to this day via the economic and structural violence of an extremely uneven distribution of resources. This inequality was further consolidated during the dictatorship and continued in the period of post-dictatorship: neoliberal Chilean society, argues Chilean scholar Tomas Moulian, is constructed on the corpses of Chileans.[2] A brief sketch of this historical development helps the understanding of this argument and the urgency for cultural production to counter a failure of visual epistemology, the suppression of imagination about the past and its connection to the present.

* * *

After the official return to democracy in 1990, the objective of post-dictatorship governments was to ease political tensions within a deeply divided society, and to dissipate the danger of a second coup. Pinochet's continued political presence as *Senador Vitalício*, Senator for Life, the legal securities he had put into place before relinquishing power, retaining the reins of military power, and the fact that the transition was negotiated, all contributed to a 'consensus' politics of the post-dictatorship governments. Negotiated on the basis of shared fear,[3] the Chilean transition left in place many of the dictatorship's institutions, most notably the constitution and the amnesty laws. The uneven playing field was unmistakably expressed in Pinochet's statement, on 14 October 1989, that 'the day they touch one of my men, democracy is over'.[4] Given this background, during the so-called transition,[5] official policy disciplined and excluded contentious issues. The pressure for reconciliation 'by means of an institutional pluralism that forced diversity to become non-contradictory'[6] led to 'consensus as the highest level of oblivion',[7] the repression, even negation of the past in official discourse.[8] In 1995, Pinochet claimed oblivion as the only solution to the 'problem' of human rights.[9] Chileans received justice 'within the limits of the possible'[10]: amnesty or impunity were named as the price for a free-market democracy. Forged by the political class and enforced by the judiciary and the media, a 'pact of silence' permeated all of society, and Chile was diagnosed as suffering from collective amnesia.[11] Thus, the films respond to the experience of social amnesia and paralysis. Certainly, alternative memories cannot be and have never been truly 'erased'. But the suppression of these memories, alongside the impunity of perpetrators, the neglect of survivors and the denial of collective costs, are all part of the legacy of torture.

Both torture and disappearances involved a state apparatus that had perfected a concoction of demonstrative threat, silence and a web of deception and disinformation. Because the power of state terror resonates most strongly when it is both visible and invisible, leakages about officially disavowed torture sites were useful to the regime,

> the mere threat of entering a place like [the Chilean torture centre] Villa Grimaldi gave the state's dirty work an omnipresence in the nation. Although archival documents declare Villa Grimaldi's absence ... its existence was the dictatorship's most broadcast national secret.[12]

This public secret, alongside the unpredictability of targeting – 46 per cent of torture victims exhibited no known political militancy[13] – created a pervasive sense of fear and terror. The practice of 'disappearing' people was part of the same strategy to create visible invisibility: for everyone who knew a disappeared, 'there is nothing more visible, and more eloquent, than their disappearance'.[14] The specific horror of erasing even the evidence of murder, what Rancière calls the crime of 'double elimination: of the Jews and of their elimination',[15] has been expertly investigated in relation to the Holocaust. 'Because the dead were never sufficiently "obliterated" ... the Nazis concentrated ... on "leaving no single trace", and on *obliterating every remnant* ... [including] the *obliteration of the tools of the obliteration*'.[16]

In Chile, too, the victims of state terrorism were stripped of their death as a legal narrative, and their families of the right of *habeas corpus* and the closure that mourning might have provided. The victims of torture were facing a different form of obliteration. Their experience was negated by post-dictatorial pressure for reconciliation, and a state-sponsored official amnesia.

> During the transition to democracy in the 1990s, tens of thousands of torture survivors were all but forgotten by the Chilean state ... torture fashioned and sealed a culture of silence ... torture survivors [became] the nation's living ghosts.[17]

The films analysed here address these multiple processes of double erasure, of past and ongoing *being-made-invisible*. Showing these processes counters the process of 'forgetting extermination [as] part of extermination'.[18] The idea is not only to combat forgetting but to show that the forgetting has already happened and has become part of the event.[19] These films invite the viewer to return to a familiar terrain of the past, to explore it from different angles,[20] which leads back to Rosenstone's call to 'make familiar events of the past strange ... to make one see them anew', or Steven Connor's demand for 'systematic unseeing'. They aim not only to make visible what is covered up but also to expand the parameters of seeing.

Social Hauntings

Torture survivor Jean Améry finds the feelings that result from torture are 'as incomparable as they are indescribable. They mark the limit of the capacity of language to communicate'.[21] The films discussed in this section do not seek to represent the pain-event in total, aware of the folly and hubris of such attempts. Yet they do succeed at making *something* about torture emotionally available.

This analysis is informed by recent approaches in cinema theory, which emphasise the medium's sensual capacities. The move towards a more expansive model of affective spectatorship, rather than empathic identification with characters, is built on the phenomenological notion of an embodied spectator and the cognitivist suggestion that actual emotions, including empathy, need not be necessarily character- and narrative-driven, goal-, action- or object-orientated.[22] Such an approach examines the overall atmosphere or 'feel' of a film. Some cinema and media scholars have used this approach to 'push the boundaries of commonly accepted notions of cinematic empathy', and to argue that sensual modes of vision can make what Raymond Williams calls 'structures of feeling' experiential by recreating these social moods with a film's toolbox.[23]

For contemporary Chilean fiction cinema in particular, this approach is useful. The idea of 'representing indirectly' is a recurrent theme in Chilean cinema, which employs various strategies to evoke in the spectator 'a state of mind that escapes direct representation but which can be recognised in the formal construction'.[24] Characterised by melancholia, uncertainty and alienation, a 'poetics of malaise', contemporary Chilean cinema is frequently discussed as 'a cinema of mood'.[25] What Nelly Richard calls 'unprocessed mourning'[26] is reflected in the post-traumatic melancholy of Chilean cinema in the 1990s and linked to the pervasive mood of depression, fear and paralysis of post-dictatorial Chile that sociologist Eugenio Tironi diagnosed as 'learned hopelessness'.[27]

Thus, the scarcity of Chilean fiction films dealing explicitly with political topics has mostly been read in reference to this socio-historical context and in terms of traumatic latency; less attention has been given to structural impediments which originate in the censorship and suppression during the dictatorship period.[28] The absence of more overt political stances is then either considered as a capitulation or as an expression of politics through form.

In the first interpretation, the avoidance of political subjects is considered evidence of 'internalised' neoliberalism, a privatisation of pain, where cinema, too, was seen as suffering from the neoliberal policies, from a 'repression of mourning',[29] a 'truncated past'.[30] Lack of faith in political solutions resulted in an 'apolitical' cinema,[31] where ethics is replaced by aesthetics, style takes priority over substance, and narcissist expression evidences a successfully depoliticised daily life.[32]

> The exorcism of the political and the 'social' ... celebrated as artistic and critical advance of the individual may well be considered the ultimate triumph of military and market forces.[33]

The second, oppositional reading suggests that the shattering of grand narratives resulted in a 'cinema of intimacy',[34] which focuses on small, subjective stories. From this intimate arena, 'local truth' emerges, previously subordinated points of view of vertiginous subjects, individuals in crisis.[35]

> Chilean films today express the human tragedy of individualism that was installed [sic] in us in such a violent way. That's the reason why the films are also a little bit dark and harsh, from the most absurd TV to the most experimental cinema, and even comedies ... – they all speak a lot about loneliness. It is like a ghost that haunts our society, and I think that ghost, that absence, is what unites Chilean cinema; a loneliness that somehow drags us along as a collective.[36]

Besides the structural impediments outlined above, I would like to add a further reading dimension to this issue, namely the focus on *dispersive and opaque* emotional fields. In the films analysed here, emotions such as depression and dread, released from their attachment to particular characters, address a collective dimension. Read in terms of the social aftermath of systematic, institutionalised torture, they help to reconfigure the parameters of the non-visible.

On the other hand, such 'structures of feeling' also relate to a malaise of the present: none of these films are *only* about the past, but rather about the continuation of the past in the present. By creating an emotional opening, the communal and political effects of social hauntings are better understood.

In Larraín's dictatorship trilogy – *Tony Manero* (2008), *Post Mortem* (2010) and *NO* (2012), discussed in depth in the following chapters – for instance, we are 'invited to feel'[37] 'historical' emotional structures: *Manero* recreates the feelings of fear, paralysis and gloom that permeated Chilean society under the dictatorship; *Post Mortem* evokes what director Larraín called, in the DVD commentary, 'the smell of the coup'; and *NO* tells the story of the return to democracy from the point of view of those campaigning to incite people to vote NO to continued dictatorship, translating the giddy tension between hope and fear around the plebiscite. Thus, the trilogy, which offered the first comparatively mainstream films to depict the Chilean dictatorship in fiction film, invites the viewer to enter such collective states, socially pervasive moods and to recollect or empathise with a historical era.

The Absent Signifier

Two scenes from *NO* help illustrate how the presence of absence can be evoked. Although characters refer to the regime's abuses several times, torture appears in the image only once: in a diegetic TV spot for the NO-campaign, hence doubly mediated and distanced from the spectator. This very first spot of the campaign (that we see) is a montage of the facts of Pinochet's human rights abuses, with graphic images, including torture. The spot is shown to the protagonist René Saavedra, an ad man, played by Gael García Bernal. His reaction seems emotionally cold – 'Is that all? Don't we have something more, I don't know … happy?'[38] Subsequently, the question whether or not to include such footage ignites a heated discussion among the members of the campaign regarding the goals and focus for the campaign. The side arguing for a 'strategically happy' approach prevails. In an obvious parallel to post-dictatorship Chile, the crimes of the dictatorship are sidelined in the *NO*-campaign. The spot is pulled and not shown to the Chilean population. However, as the diegetic members of the campaign watch the spot, so does the spectator. In this way, the topic *is* raised within the diegesis, while pointing to its historical exclusion and marginalisation. As the statistics referenced in the spots – the numbers of the disappeared and of the tortured – would be unlikely to have existed before the Truth Commissions of 1990 and 2004, the intended audiences of the spot seem to be not those of 1988, but contemporary spectators.

A second spot of the NO campaign shows historical footage in the form of a testimonial video of relatives of the disappeared. In the sense of the open terror for the relatives and pervasive social fear, I include disappearances here under the heading of psychological torture. Mainly mothers and sisters, the women wear similar dresses, they are framed in the same way in the image, and they present information in identical structure: their own name, their relation to and the name of a disappeared. This (historically accurate) intentionally repetitive formula emphasises quantity and solidarity. The women then dance the *cueca*, a traditional Chilean couples' dance, without their partners.

For a certain generation of Chileans, this scene would raise memories of President Patricio Aylwin's inauguration ceremony in the National Stadium on 11 March 1990, where women from the Association of Family Members of the Disappeared-Detainees danced this national dance 'to symbolize the human losses that had been caused by the authoritarian regime'.[39] A later generation might recall the original moment of being confronted with these images of public memory. Private histories of viewing and the (public) history of the image intertwine. Calls for (self-)

Figure 6.1 *NO*.

censorship to avoid fatigue through repetition imply that only the 'original' emotional response is 'truthful', an approach that does not allow room for the ways in which additional reviewings, and new viewers, may also expand perception and understanding.[40]

The recent Chilean documentary *Pena de Muerte* (*Pena*) provides another example of a successful translation of an invisible constellation, in ways that recall Nichols' idea of an 'absent signifier': 'Absent signifiers ... occupy our minds but not the screen ... [our] understanding ... depends on an awareness of what is absent but nonetheless alluded to'.[41] *Pena* investigates a series of unsolved murders in the Chilean city Viña del Mar (Viña) in the early 1980s. Despite the deployment of all the methodology of objectivity – maps, clips, diagrams – the film is unable to entirely solve its central 'whodunnit' crime mystery, a comment on impunity for past crimes, and also about the difficulty of establishing historical truth.

The film combines original documentary footage – Super 8 mm, 16 mm, Betamax, U-matic – in different stages of decay, mixing re-enactments, newspaper articles, animation, interviews and the testimony of various historical witnesses. The interviews take place in identical, highly stylised environments. By contrast, the re-enactments switch between the grainy

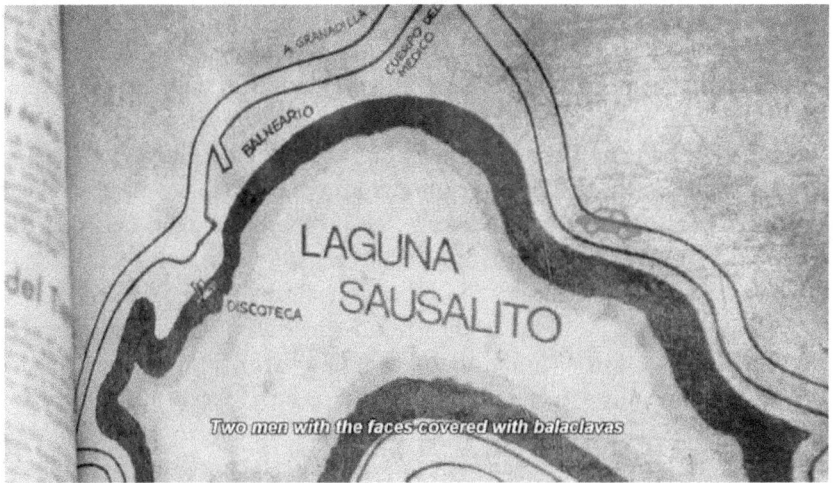

Figure 6.2 *Pena de Muerte*.

feel and low resolution of a purposely aged look, and hyperbolically artificial scenes, expressively lit and coded in terms of cinematic genres such as *film noir* or the gangster movie. Through this self-reflexive, performative construction, *Pena* emphasises how much each kind of historical narrative is shaped by its transporter medium.

Pena begins with a Pinochet speech, set to grainy black and white images of what appears to be original footage of people sleeping in a Valparaíso metro (a transit light train system used in the coastal cities of Valparaíso and Viña). As the speech ends on the menacing admonition to 'stay at home in order to avoid innocent victims' – the camera zooms in on the face of one passenger. Suddenly, this man opens his eyes, distorts his mouth into an ominous grin, and the image switches to colour. The juxtaposition insinuates that the character, who seemed to be sleeping, has in fact heard the speech. The montage confuses the viewer as to the rules of the film – which part is *faux* footage and which is real? – which is part of the 'particular appeal to films that begin with the awakening of a character ... it appears as though it's the real world that is a dream'.[42]

Twenty minutes into the film, another formal switch demonstrates the limits of vision to offer a complete picture and understanding of the film's narrative, and by extension, the historical events being told. Until now, the interviewees had appeared alone in the image, each seated before the same background, facing the camera, thus creating the impression that the interviews have taken place separately and consecutively. Now two interviewees, a police investigator and a neuropsychiatrist, suddenly begin interacting. This switch is only conveyed through sound; there is no visual change in the static composition. Each interviewee continues to be framed separately in the image, the camera remains stationary, and the two interviews are linked via montage. But there is change *within* the image as their faces reveal the expressions and reactions of listeners. The audience sees an image of *one* person, listening, and from the off-screen space, we hear the words of the *other* interviewee. The evolving dialogue between the interviewees is edited as an *aural* shot-reverse shot structure while visually, each character still seems to look at and speak to the audience.

Usually, camera movements convert off-screen space into screen space, but here it is the flow of sound that makes us aware of the existence of the off-screen. This off-screen space turns out to be different from what we imagined it to be; it becomes the space where we confront the limits of our perception and knowledge. The viewers must reconfigure their mental idea of how these interviews took place, must acknowledge the existence of several cameras, each filming one interviewee as they respond to the other. This revelation remains partial: we are never actually given visual confirmation of the characters' joint presence, only the sound maintains spatiotemporal continuity. And at the same time that we know more, we feel as if we know less, and remain encouraged to wonder what else we might be wrongly assuming.

The tendency of Chilean cinema to emphasise what is off-screen as much as or more than what is inside the frame, has led Carolina Urrutia to define contemporary Chilean cinema as 'centrifugal',[43] that is, as a cinema which tends to move away from the central conflict. As we will see, in the films analysed here, history – the authoritarian repression in *Manero*, the coup in *Mortem*, a history of torture in *Carne* – is not excluded but overbearingly present, distinctly felt, as if encroaching from the off-screen. In her analysis of Michael Haneke's *Caché*, Libby Saxton proposes that the film attends

> to our blind spots – not only to personal and collective traumas that have been silenced, forgotten or excluded by commercial cinema and the mass media, but also to the *sites of non-seeing which structure cinema and spectatorship*. In according priority to the hidden, the invisible, the unknown, [such] secretive fiction exposes the margins of blindness which frame and limit our look, but are also, it suggests, a condition of our seeing.[44]

Such centrifugal forces do not restore the off-screen spaces of official history and memory to visibility but their *erasure* is made present. Formal emphasis on what is visibly, palpably, absent, reflects our fragmented, contingent knowledge of history, and connects this particular historical event to the larger issue of impunity and amnesty in the present.

Early in *Pena*, a neuropsychologist explains that the psychopathic behaviour demonstrated by the murderers did in fact mirror the conduct of the authorities. Taunting the police, these serial killers did not even bother to cover their traces. Such a sense of inviolability appears also with the perpetrators in *Los Archivos* and *Manero*, and in each case it is expressed through a consciously *cinematic* self-presentation of the killers, who stylise themselves in ways that mimic cinematic conventions.[45] In each example, the films are careful to show but also aesthetically undermine this performance, deconstructing the fear and awe that it might have inspired historically. In *Manero*, Raúl is at bottom a pathetic figure who cannot actually dance and does not look much like John Travolta; in *Los Archivos*, the perpetrators are shown also in moments of fright and confusion; in *Pena*, the aesthetic hyperbole of the re-enactments disrupts the smugness of impunity. Overlit and amateurishly acted, the re-enactments add a sense of ridicule, and highlight that the killers' narrative is just that – a narrative. As a central dimension of torture's power dynamic is its emotional grip on the collective imagination, its power to shame, to ostracise and taint, these aesthetic choices can be read as a deliberate political act.

Sensual Visualities: Sound, Breath and Touch

In *Pena*, the dynamics of shame and terror are denaturalised via aesthetic hyperbole and hypermediation.[46] In *Carne de Perro*, the emotional tone is made palpable by a sensual mode of vision. This film shows a week in the life of former torturer and present-day taxi driver Alejandro. The marketing focus for *Carne* relied heavily on public knowledge centred on the *body* of its protagonist. Actor Alejandro Goic, well known in Chile, who portrays the former torturer, is in fact a torture survivor. Reinforced by extradiegetic promotion and continually insinuated on a narrative level, though never explicitly mentioned, Alejandro's past is present as absent signifier. The film begins with a phone call Alejandro receives, after which he explodes in rage. In the next scene, he attends a funeral – as it turns out, a former colleague has killed himself. The following days are haphazardly punctured by random encounters and sudden fits of anger, but mostly spent in crushing isolation. Similarly to Argentina's seminal *La historia oficial* (Luis Puenzo, 1985), torture appears in symbolic and displaced forms, 'ever present, even though it is not directly presented. It is there by allusion, by suggestion rather than by direct representation [as the film] make[s] us feel the physical effects'.[47]

In *Carne*, Alejandro's buried past creates a claustrophobic present. Glaring absences and silences palpably weigh down on Alejandro, encroaching on him. The film 'makes us feel' these physical effects by restricting our range of perception: objects are tightly framed; and the camera focuses almost constantly on Alejandro's face and torso; there is always a sense of tightness, a lack of (breathing) space. The soundscape, too, weighs down with silences, the absence of extradiegetic sounds, the pronounced silence of its protagonist, and the sounds that trigger Alejandro's attacks.

Carne begins *in medias res*, and never resorts to explaining the events via flashbacks. Viewer and protagonist are imprisoned in an artificially orphaned present, left without context, without narrative explanation, without familiar sense-making schemes. The film translates Alejandro's subjectivity in this spatial, temporal, sonic and intellectual confinement. Bits of a larger story can be inferred through Alejandro's proclivity towards violence and through insinuations of a violent past. Unable to deal with frustration, tension or fear in socially acceptable ways, Alejandro reacts even to minor incursions with violent and destructive behaviour. During his first panic attack, Alejandro smashes a mirror, hurting his own hand. When he speaks to his ex-wife, he insists that he wants to change but, repudiated, he blows up at her. He smashes and burns a tape that he intended to give to his daughter, whom he is not allowed to see (a history of domestic violence is heavily implied). Shortly after he notices his trashed washing line, we watch Alejandro calmly boil water (a dog barking off-screen) and are then shocked to see him throw the boiling water into that off-screen, followed by yelps of pain.

Alejandro is completely isolated in a world of silence and unpleasant noises. A scene at a clinic begins with a heaving Alejandro, framed alone in the image, as a bodiless voice gives him instructions to breathe. In this case of de-acousmatisation – splitting body and voice – *Carne* uses (the absence of) sound and language to create a sense of Alejandro's subjectivity. A young doctor explains Alejandro's panic attacks and feelings of 'electricity' in the spine as post-traumatic stress. These metaphors – of electricity of the spine, Alejandro's smashed hand, the dog's burnt flesh, even the noise-drowning water of the swimming pool he frequents – evoke torture techniques.

Carne is almost exclusively filmed in close-up or medium shots of Alejandro in shallow depth of field, recalling what Tiago de Luca called the 'hyperbolic' dimension of the close-up.[48] Excluding all extraneous information and blurring the background, the flat focus restricts the audience to a myopic point of view, confined to a perceptual space shared with Alejandro. Yet this spatial proximity hinders rather than helps intimacy, access, or empathetic attachment. The physical closeness to a largely unlikeable subject is sometimes rather uncomfortable. Where mere exposure may create attachment, as 'we tend to react more positively to people we see repeatedly',[49] the joint perceptual space in *Carne* does not lead to emotional contagion or identification. Neither do we experience the same emotion as Alejandro: his actions suggest that he feels pain and rage, neither of which we share and the precise reasons for which we can only surmise.

The film's soundscape provides another layer of perceptual alignment that does not lead to ideological bonding. Alejandro seems to suffer from a symbolic aphasia, recalling Richard's 'cultural aphasia', the loss or impairment of the power to use or comprehend speech, as a result of brain damage. This aphasia also informs the film's formal language. Filmed with no extra-diegetic sound, the film emphasises silences, 'inner' or in-between sounds such as his breathing and acousmatic forces.

Carne fictionalises the result of a culture of silence, both for the perpetrators and for the society as a whole. In Chile, only a few perpetrators or collaborators spoke out. Their perspective, Bilbija and Payne suggest, 'remains novel, even if the information they provide is not ... overexposure may prove less dangerous than its opposite, underexposure'.[50] The silence of the torturer means that something of the nature of torture is 'lost to our understanding ... something of what ties the torturer to the ordinary citizen who shuts his or her eyes to the presence and persistence of systematic torture is then not understood'.[51]

Carne's protagonist is a perpetrator who hardly speaks. Language fails Alejandro as a means of social interaction, bonding or self-expression. Every verbal communication is shown to be problematic, characterised by misunderstandings, conflict and fights, and often prematurely aborted. In Western society's model of communication, 'speech is the norm'[52] and silence implies distance. But silence – such as pauses in speech – can also make the speaker sensuously, physically present. Everyone has experienced how, when punctuated by long silences, words weigh more; they become almost palpable. Or how, when one talks less, one begins feeling more fully one's physical presence in a given space.[53] In *Carne*, Alejandro's silences as well as his inept speech foreground the presence of his unwieldy, resisting, failing body. Even when he uses language, his body seems to overwhelm his voice, with sudden outbursts of anger, stammering or shaking. The breakdown of language is thus symbolic of Alejandro's incapacity to redefine his existence and to find meaningful connection to his community.

Usually, cinema's visual impact is heightened by sound, giving a body to the two-dimensional image. In *Carne*, the absence of sound seems to flatten the image. The lack of extradiegetic sound is combined with a camera that seems glued to this character. Excluding more varied or stimulating visual information, the film intersects visual and aural paucity. Alejandro's sparse sonic surroundings reach us in snippets: a television report, military music on the radio, white noise in public places, waiting rooms, the nightly traffic of Santiago. Along with a sombre colour palette, the absence of recreational or pleasant sounds aurally render Alejandro's depressed state.

Withholding a musical score further aligns us perceptually with Alejandro's diminished sensual radius. In this sound-poor world, discursive forms outside language gain prominence and express Alejandro's emotional state. These sounds, which disturb Alejandro, are exclusively transmitted in *acousmêtre*, Michel Chion's term to describe a voice we cannot connect to a body.[54] As Chion describes it, we imagine the *acousmatic being* as all-seeing and all-knowing. Such voices or sounds retain their 'aura of invulnerability and magical power'[55] until the voice is connected to a body, to mouth and face. In *Carne*, acousmatic sounds trigger Alejandro's attacks: shouts from his neighbours through the walls; his dog's barking from off-screen; the voice on the phone telling him about a colleague's suicide.

At the funeral, a stone-faced Alejandro does not pray along to a priest's verbose and saccharine words. Oyarzún proposes that the silence in mourning seems closer to truth than the 'impotent' lament, the most 'undifferentiated' aspect of language.[56] Initially, Alejandro's silence indeed acknowledges the inadequacy of language for certain experiences; increasingly, however, the silence suffocates him. Later in the narrative, Alejandro visits a former colleague in a mental hospital, who prattles on compulsively, seemingly oblivious to Alejandro's presence. Alejandro's silence is the counterpart to his friend's babbling, equally helpless and inadequate.

It is not only Alejandro's own inability to communicate and his failure to read his surroundings adequately, but also his social set-up that inhibits speaking. He lives alone in an isolated area; his taxi has broken down; during his regular swimming exercise he cuts himself off sonically from his environment. He is also literally silenced: at a meeting with former colleagues, Alejandro is threatened not to break their pact of silence. Here, the meaning of Alejandro's silence changes from a form of agency or resistance, and most likely also an obstruction to justice, to a passive *being silenced*. Thus, both the absence and the conflictive presence of language reflect on voluntary and enforced silences, a comment on the society that emerged from the dictatorship.

For the audience, it is often impossible to distinguish voices and non-verbal sounds or to isolate concrete words within the acousmatic soundscape. As the sources of these sounds remain off-screen, while perfectly believable within the diegesis, they could also be an aural flashback; a figment of Alejandro's imagination. Privileging sound also privileges time; as Chion points out, 'the eye is more spatially adept, and the ear more temporally adept'.[57] The temporal mode of *Carne* is a permanent present: while the origin of the sound might be in Alejandro's past, the sound itself, unstoppable, always keeps us in the present. This of course is suggestive of trauma, where the victim is locked into a temporal loop.

Conveying Alejandro's posttraumatic state to the audience via sound, or its absence, captures the state of being frozen, locked in: silence where there *should* be sound is terrifying, as Edvard Munch's famous *Scream* series of paintings demonstrate. The audience, like the PTSD victim, cannot escape the perception and experience: we cannot shut our ears to sound. This is the sensation to the image which ends the film: the dog is buried, Alejandro is 'born again'; he turns off the lights and leaves camera and spectator imprisoned inside his newfound church. There are the sounds of being locked in, and the camera remains completely static, immobile, as if staring at the doorknob. This last image can be read as a metaphor on the locked door to the past – and an escape on the part of Alejandro, who at last liberates himself from the camera's scrutinising gaze.

Only after Alejandro has wounded the dog do we see images of the animal: bloody insides, visible in a large wound. It is as if, for Alejandro, the dog only now appears as a physical, embodied being. He now bandages the animal, and as nurses it, he aligns his own breath to that of the animal. It seems that through pain, and then through synchronous breathing, he gains a form of interconnectedness which he fails to obtain with people. As interface between inside and outside, the dog's wounded skin crosses the inside–outside boundary. Alejandro rips the skin to cross the intersection between self and other, individual and social. (The film's central metaphor is of course the dog and his eponymous flesh; the expression *carne de perro* – dog flesh – signifies thick skin, resilience.)

Dog and man are linked in a montage, when they move in similar ways in their sleep. (In his ineptitude at verbal communication and instinctive defensive behaviours, Alejandro acts a bit like an animal.) A form of communication independent of language seems to evolve between them, a moving and breathing together in time, similar to the connection in certain group activities where an expansive synchrony links bodies, an encounter of 'kinesthetic empathy', rather than emotional identification.[58] The spectator is invited to become part of this affective, 'breathing encounter between filmic bodies and the bodies of the viewer'.[59]

Quinlivan extends Marks's concept of 'haptic visuality' to other sensual modes of perception in her analysis of *Breaking the Waves* where she frames the 'act of *hearing* breath … [as] an aural form of haptics'.[60] As the viewer responds to the protagonist's diegetic breathing, breath offers a potentially inter-subjective nature of viewing and hearing.[61] In *Carne*, the tactile dimension of haptic perception relates closely to textures of breath and of noise.

Breathing tends to incite mimicry: conscious, strong breathing has the potential to cross and connect inner and outer spaces. Like sound and skin, breath is an interface, both internal and external, produced, felt and heard both inside and outside the body. Breathing is intrinsically something more heard than seen, and more *felt* than heard. Breath indicates life – a thing that breathes is a living thing – as well as some form of authenticity, as breath can never be 'fully articulate artifice'.[62] We cannot *not* breathe; neither sound nor breath can be stopped without being destroyed. Breath becomes visible through its supporting medium: the body that produces and lives the breath.

Even before the pivotal dog scene, the act of breathing connects the audience with Alejandro's experience: *Carne* opens with a panic attack that is mainly aurally transmitted – watching a dark screen, we hear someone gasping for air. Brief images of an open water tap, Alejandro staring motionless into a bathroom mirror are followed by a longer shot, which begins as a close frame of Alejandro's back. He is on the phone, breathing heavily. He hangs up, smashes the phone, then his body against the wall, the door. The camera remains still. As Alejandro moves away, he merges with the unfocused background. The whole image becomes blurry at this point, as if no longer able to 'see clearly'. In combination with his ragged breath, these initial moments of the film seem to approximate Alejandro's inner state, they make his pain perceptible.

Following Quinlivan's suggestion that 'film's formal attributes can become suggestive of breathing, especially the rhythms of editing techniques, composition, colour and camera movement',[63] the scene can also be conceived of as visualised breathing, as the blurring and attempted refocusing of the lenses translate the rhythmic heaving visually. The image's unfocused surface highlights its haptic and sonic-epidermic dimensions. It comes to resemble a kind of skin, or even a heaving lung, whose alveoli membranes are polluted. Additionally, the heavy breathing of the soundtrack overwhelms the sonic space; there is no ambient sound

Figure 6.3 *Carne de Perro*.

in the sequence. The blurred surface and the sound of compressed breathing produce an affective congruence between aural, haptic and visual dimensions.

Contrary to this reading direction, which suggests that the image *performs*, even embodies Alejandro's loss of control and perceptual acuity, such images can also be read as programmatic of the camera's relentless but futile pursuit of Alejandro throughout the film. As with the excessively and uselessly close initial image of Alejandro's back, the camera in *Carne* does not look, it *touches* – but not with Marks's soft touch, Quinlivan and Irigaray's notion of the caress, which links the touched and the touching (the one being touched also touches). Here, this touching is connected to an element of intrusion, of scientific probing, even of violence. It is as if this camera wished to invade, to dissect this character. The resulting close-ups do not promote clarity but destabilise our sense of space and proportion, as discussed by Mary Ann Doane: such excessive proximity flattens the image and, by dissolving shapes, threatens with 'a certain monstrosity', to disfigure the legibility of the image, 'annihilating all sense of scale'.[64] Human bodies and faces are isolated in the frame, as their surroundings dissolve into blurred backgrounds. Such a compression of space suggests the characters' isolation, pointing to the destruction of community. There is a brutality to such a fragmentation of the living. When the dog is hurt in *Carne*, this inquisitive camera shows us its wounds in close-up, linking spatial proximity and pain, yet neither the snout of the panting dog nor his

Figure 6.4 *Carne de Perro*.

entire body are ever completely visible in the frame. The image remains always myopic, too close to its object to be properly seen.

Usually, the body and especially the face of an actor invite a particular kind of encounter with the audience.[65] Close-ups in particular exploit that we are hard-wired to respond strongly to the language of facial expressions. Yet the protagonists of the Chilean films analysed here – *Carne, Manero, Post Mortem*, even *NO* – give barely a mimetic clue. They all remain rather inexpressive, or rather, their expressiveness resides in a strained facial blankness, the very present *absence* of stronger expressions. We are so distanced from Alejandro's inner world that we cannot anticipate what he will do with the boiling water or what his motives are for entering the ocean – is it a rebirth, a suicide attempt? Alejandro clearly desires human contact and to have his existence recognised, specifically through touch (on visiting a prostitute, all Alejandro wishes to do is to cuddle in her lap). What he seeks is to take possession of himself through being addressed through 'embodied self-perception ... made possible through the perception of another'.[66] The need for 'good touch' also appears at prominent places in the other films discussed here: the protagonists of *Post Mortem* and *Manero* seek (but fail to create) satisfying sexual encounters and *Nostalgia* features a woman who helps survivors heal through physical touch. Skin knowledge is part of an intelligent body memory, which can evolve and help the mind heal and 'to move into contact with' sense memory.[67]

The camera in *Carne* cannot extract and present the historical and subjective knowledge hidden in Alejandro; in spite of its almost violent attempts, the image offers only an incomplete view. The relentlessness of this persecuting camera destabilises the perpetrator – victim boundary, for what right do we have to demand explanations and to force our entry into Alejandro's world? The machine gaze does not offer a compassionate and empathic perspective. That possibility is reserved for the spectator: *we* may decide how to see Alejandro, whether to acknowledge his existence and those like him, and whether our gaze amounts to judgement, pity, condemnation or indifference.

Often described in personal terms, or in the case of affect, as simply a 'hardware' part of human nature, emotions are in fact often harnessed to psychological, social, cultural and ideological concerns and constructs. Feelings such as disgust, shame and compassion 'derive from social training, emerge at historical moments [and] are shaped by aesthetic conventions'.[68] Such 'social feelings' circulate, they are relational and attach to certain bodies; 'certain people are made to carry the affects of another'.[69] Following Ahmed's suggestion to focus not on what emotions *are* to but what they *do*, the attention shifts towards the processes that taint some bodies and leaves others free of the emotional mark of torture.[70]

Contrary to the fear of 'emotional contagion', which resonates with the paradigmatic rejection of perpetrator narratives in representation- and identification-based criticism, many of the films discussed here offer an emotional space within perpetrator stories, without inviting emotional identification with the perpetrators. These films render 'socially circulating' emotions perceptible and invite access to an emotional dimension that is not in opposition to rational thought.

* * *

Supported by affective scholarship, this chapter has explored various approaches taken both to find visual metaphors to fill historical erasures, to show the limitations of such metaphors and to make a historical structure of feeling and a more contemporary paralysis perceivable to the viewer. The analysis of *Carne*'s use of sound, breath and haptic images illustrates one such strategy in detail. The exploration of how we receive, speak of and show history also entails an engagement with the medium that allows and shapes access to these stories. The next chapters discuss questions ranging from the body of the medium itself to the discourse on the presumed *objectivity* of the machine and the question whether a framework based on visual dominance and indexicality is still able to represent today's new existential realities.

Notes

1. Anable, *Playing With Feelings*, p. 11.
2. Moulian, *Chile Actual*.
3. Jocelyn-Holt, *Espejo retrovisor*; de Zárate, 'Terrorism and Political Violence During the Pinochet Years'.
4. 'El día que me toquen a alguno de mis hombres se acabó el estado de derecho'. Cf. 'Las 40 frases macabras del tirano'.
5. The beginning and end of the transition, and even the term itself, are highly contested.
6. Richard, *Cultural Residues*, p. 16.
7. Moulian, *Chile Actual*, p. 2.
8. See for instance Jelin et al., *State Repression*; Mitnick, 'La Persistencia'.
9. 'La única solución para el problema de los derechos humanos es el olvido'. Cf. 'Las 40 frases macabras del tirano'.
10. This phrase was coined by the first post-dictatorship president, Patricio Aylwin ('justicia en la medida de lo posible').
11. Jocelyn-Holt, *Espejo retrovisor*; Gómez-Barris, *Where Memory Dwells*. For the aggressive media campaign to self-impose forgetting, see Villarroel, *La voz*.
12. Gordon, *Ghostly Matters*, p. 46.
13. Cortínez and Engelbert, 'El cine chileno de los sesenta'.
14. Jocelyn-Holt, *Espejo retrovisor*, p. 89.
15. Rancière, *Future of the Image*, p. 127.
16. Didi-Huberman, *Images in Spite of All*, p. 21, emphasis in the original
17. Gómez-Barris, *Where Memory Dwells*, p. 77.
18. Godard quoted in ten Brink and Oppenheimer, *Killer Images*, p. 3.
19. Rojas, 'Profunda superficie'.
20. Rosenstone, *History on Film/Film on History*, p. 86; Connor, 'Sounding out Film'.
21. Améry, *At the Mind's Limits*, p. 33.
22. Cf. Smith, *Film Structure and the Emotion System*.
23. Stadler, 'Affectless Empathy'. For the various applications of Williams' concept, see for instance: Gordon, *Ghostly Matters*; Pribram, *Emotions, Genre, and Justice*; Sprengler, *Screening Nostalgia*.
24. I adapt Estévez' observations on a different set of Chilean films ('narra aquello que no se puede nombrar ... un estado de ánimo que escapa a la representación directa, pero que es posible reconocer en la construcción formal'.) Estévez, 'Dolores Politicos', p. 16.
25. Urrutia, 'Hacia una política en tránsito'; Urrutia, 'Turistas'.
26. Richard, 'Reconfigurations', p. 274.
27. Cf. Moulian, *Chile Actual*.
28. Barril and Cruz, *El cine que fue*; Pino-Ojeda, 'Latent Image'; Henríquez, 'El cine chileno de ficción'; Trejo Ojeda, *Cine, Neoliberalismo y Cultura*; Broderick and Traverso, *Interrogating Trauma*.

29. Tal, 'Memoria y Muerte'.
30. Draper, 'The Question of Awakening in Postdictatorship Times'.
31. Shaw, *Contemporary Cinema of Latin America*.
32. Trejo, 'El cine chileno'; Klubock, 'History and Memory in Neoliberal Chile'.
33. Cortínez and Engelbert, 'El cine chileno de los sesenta', pp. 16–17.
34. Saavedra Cerda and Horta, *Intimidades Desencantadas*, p. 22.
35. Masiello, *The Art of Transition*, p. 5. Cf. Urrutia, 'Hacia una política en tránsito'; Podalsky and Soto take this approach for documentary. Podalsky, *The Politics of Affect*; Soto *(Un)Veiling Bodies*.
36. Director Andrés Waissbluth in Diestro-Dópido, 'Children of the coup', para 9.
37. Smith, *Film Structure and the Emotion System*, p. 38.
38. '¿No tenemos algo más … no sé… alegre?'
39. Bilbija and Payne, *Accounting for Violence*, p. 20.
40. Cf. Sontag's description of seeing the photographs of Bergen-Belsen and Dachau for the first time in *On Photography*, pp. 19–20.
41. Nichols, 'Irony, Cruelty, Evil', p. 28
42. Chion, *Film, A Sound Art*, p. 283.
43. Urrutia, *Un Cine Centrífugo*.
44. Saxton, 'Secrets and Revelations', p. 15, emphasis added.
45. Compare the recent discussions on the aesthetics and ethics of the documentary *The Act of Killing* (Joshua Oppenheimer, 2012), in which the murderers of thousands of Indonesians in the 1960s, who remain in power to this day, restage and partly re-enact their killings, stylising their clearly self-serving white-washed version of history according to various movie genres.
46. Cf. Bolter and Grusin, *Remediation*.
47. Hart, *Latin American Film*, p. 123.
48. de Luca, *Realism of the Senses*, p. 9.
49. Eder, 'Ways of Being Close', p. 72.
50. Bilbija and Payne, *Accounting for Violence*, p. 31. Among the most famous and widely discussed cases of victims-turned-perpetrators were Luz Arce and Marcia Merino. Cf. *La Flaca Alejandra* (Carmen Castillo/Guy Girard, 1994); Arce, *The Inferno*.
51. Gordon, *Ghostly Matters*, p. 74.
52. Kurzon, *Discourse of Silence*, p. 114.
53. Sontag in de Luca, *Realism of the Senses*, p. 97.
54. Chion, *Voice in Cinema*, p. 21.
55. Ibid., p. 28.
56. Oyarzún, *La Letra Volada*, p. 227.
57. Chion, *Audio-Vision*, p. 11.
58. Reynolds and Reason, *Kinesthetic Empathy*; cf. Blackman, *Immaterial Bodies*.
59. Quinlivan, 'Breath Control', p. 159.
60. Ibid. Cf. Marks, *Touch, Skin of the Film*.

61. Cf. Sarah Wright's interpretation of this scene as staging a 'crisis of (mimetic) identification' between spectator and perpetrator, in which the hurt dog symbolises both the 'spectral manifestation of past torture victims', and an 'intersubjective manifestation of Alejandro himself'; victim and perpetrator are intersubjectively bound in pain. Wright, 'Tough Love'.
62. Quinlivan, 'Breath Control', p. 159.
63. Quinlivan, *Place of Breath in Cinema*, p. 19.
64. Doane, 'Scale and the Negotiation of Cinematic Space', p. 73.
65. Balázs, *Early Film Theory*.
66. Elsaesser, 'World Cinema', p. 10.
67. Bennett, *Empathic Vision*, p. 44.
68. Berlant in Walsh, 'What stories we tell', p. 7.
69. Brennan in Blackman, *The Body*, p. 48.
70. Ahmed, *Cultural Politics of Emotion*.

CHAPTER 7

The Politics of Realism in Chilean Cinema

Many contemporary Chilean fiction films form part of what has been discussed either as a renewal of realist trends in non-Hollywood productions – a tendency to feature a realist aesthetics – or in reference to preceding cinematic movements, from Italian neorealism to revolutionary Third Cinema of the 1960s and 1970s.[1] Following scholars from Bazin onwards, film critic A.O. Scott suggests discussing 'the realist impulse [as] less as a style or genre than as an ethic that finds expression in various places at critical times'.[2] Following this characterisation of realism as an *ethic emerging at critical times*, the question follows: why realism here and why now? Which factors encourage the emergence of this style at this specific historical and cultural moment?

After a brief spike in the early 1990s, after the return to democracy,[3] Chilean fiction cinema had all but avoided the topic of the recent national past. Possible reasons range from institutionalised and internalised censorship, the historical experience of mediatic betrayal and collaboration,[4] the discrepancy in economic risk in comparison to documentary, where such topics continue to dominate, lack of infrastructure and state support to a perceived lack of audience: since 1999, the Chilean audience for Chilean films has settled at 6 per cent of total spectatorship, or about 1 million, even though production has considerably increased. As Antonio Martínez pointedly remarks, 'Chilean cinema does not appear when it wants to but whenever it can':[5] only around 10 per cent of films shown in Chile are not from the US; if more than a dozen Chilean films come out in a given year, these will compete amongst themselves.[6]

Here the contemporary global film industry and festival landscape acts in both enabling and constraining fashion, wielding influence and creating streamlined aesthetic expectations in their own right, geared towards a particular kind of global cinephile audience. International festivals increasingly function as producers and distributors, helping films to be produced, to gain exposure and (potentially international) distribution. The spread of the festival circuit has coincided with the resurgence, or in some cases the emergence, of several 'small national cinemas'. Changes in the festival landscape, often concomitant with changes in national funding policies, particularly affect these cinemas.[7]

> What the Chilean film industry really lacks is producers ... Aside from rare cases such as Fábula [Larraín's production company] Chilean cinema depends largely on state subsidies as well as co-production treaties signed with Brazil, Argentina, Venezuela, France and Canada [as well as] the money that comes from European institutions ... which ... for a while ... seemed to encourage 'an anthropological stance'.[8]

For lack of alternative forms of funding, filmmakers often employ strategies to render their films globally accessible, and in particular, to appeal to cinephile audiences at global film festivals, who in turn seem to have adapted and been trained to expect certain standards and to favour a particular aesthetic. As a result, the festival circuit can have the effect of creating films 'made to order',[9] and international co-production or funding can erase cultural specificity. Thus, the international film festival scene offers a space, but also sustains universalised ideas of 'the national' and promotes a particular aesthetics.[10] In the case of Chile, Maria Peirano suggests that the influence of international festivals results in a 'Chilean-cosmopolitan aesthetic', which uses national identity strategically to appeal to a specific set of transnational film communities who share a 'global cinephilia'.[11]

The precise ways in which procedures and requirements – whether foreign or national – impact the type of film proposed and selected for (national or international) funding, are difficult to measure.[12] What *can* be empirically demonstrated though, is that an internationalised circuit of dissemination has become the established routine in Chile too: films are first screened abroad at international festivals and only then (if at all) exhibited and potentially distributed in Chile.[13]

Perhaps to counter international festivals' pull towards what Montañez and Martin-Jones call 'auto-erasure',[14] these films are layered in ways that appeal to a transnational audience and their shared type of cinephilia, but also to the national home audience, and here the realist aesthetics are key. Italian neorealism had a strong influence on Latin American revolutionary filmmakers, including the celebrated 'Nuevo Cine Chileno' or 'New Chilean Cinema' of the 1960s and 1970s,[15] which in turn remains an important reference point for contemporary film and national (media) history.[16] The aesthetics perceivable in contemporary production which seem to echo these cinematic trends have led some Chilean academics to propose that we are presented with a 'Novísimo Cine Chileno', a 'Newest Chilean cinema'; other scholars, such as Cortínez and Engelbert, dismiss this notion as a marketing ploy.[17] Accordingly, contemporary Chilean cinema's realism is operating within a paradigm that is familiar to global cinephile festival audiences, but its realist style could also specifically appeal to its home audience, once the hurdles of the festival circuits are successfully jumped.[18] The realist aesthetic offers a sense of ambiguity and a transnational appeal for filmmakers who attempt 'to produce a "crossover" that will successfully address a national audience as well as one beyond geographical boundaries and maximise profits'.[19]

Confirming the need to appeal to both national and international audiences, Larraín has argued that while the current, younger generation of filmmakers must use festivals,

> [they also] have to make films about our reality, our behavior, our customs – you must always shoot for a Chilean audience, first, otherwise you will not have a connection with them – but, at the same time, they have to be somehow universal.[20]

This quote also corroborates the characterisation of Contemporary Latin American cinema generally as marked by stylistic hybridity as well as by what Juan Poblete terms 'supplementarity': narratives that extend beyond the surface, adding further, subordinated information and double-entendres and thereby inscribing political critique. Similarly, Haddu and Page consider Latin American 'hybrid aesthetics' as an alliance of aesthetics and politics.[21] Aesthetic multiplicity makes this cinema accessible and productive for García Canclíni's 'glocal' publics – citizens global in consumption but local in 'languages, memory, and national sensibility'.[22] While not homogeneous, such interpretative communities share common frames of reference, 'everyday games of hide-and-seek that only "natives" play, unwritten rules of behavior, jokes understood from half a word, a sense of complicity'.[23]

The realist style also resonates with Art Cinema and its international festival audiences: 'Realist conventions [have been part of] the tradition of international art cinema ... [and] central to the creation of the "global literacy" of an incipient "cosmopolitan citizenship"'.[24] Art Cinema has been defined as an 'impure'[25] or 'ambiguous' form, even as an aesthetic *practice*.[26] This leads back to Bazin's praise of neorealism as an *ethics* and for 'giv[ing] back to the cinema a sense of the ambiguity of reality'.[27] Bazin championed neorealism as the realisation of cinema's ultimate potential: to capture reality itself. The favoured long take and deep focus shot capture elements of chance and ambiguity inherent in reality, instead of constructing meaning through framing and montage, thus producing the image without (or with minimal) intervention. But Bazin also found neorealism's aesthetics inextricably interwoven with its political agenda. As Richard

Allen points out, 'neorealism has a canonical status in Bazin's thought *because* it is more than a style; it directly engages social history'.[28]

Taking place at the end of World War II, neorealism sought to enable a different kind of emotional engagement, and also to contribute to a distinctively national cinema. In his 1952 proclamations on what distinguishes neorealism from 'the American cinema', Cesare Zavattini advocates a cinematic style that looks directly and *for extended duration* 'on the real things, exactly as they are', that the responsibility of cinema is to help audiences arrive at 'a moral discovery' and that this practice of cinema would create emotions that are 'more effective, morally stronger, more useful'.[29]

Likewise, the renewals of realist commitments in 'world cinema'[30] have been discussed in terms of political and ethical intent. Lúcia Nagib defines this realism by its reliance on exclusive, not simulated profilmic events, real physical activity and 'real time' shots. Her 'ethics of realism' hinges on indexicality – 'what Rancière termed "the inherent honesty of the film medium" ... that is to say, the film's indexical property' – and the element of chance which generates 'the truth of the unpredictable event'. For her, world cinema's new realism is informed by a political ethics: 'To choose reality instead of simulation is a moral question'.[31]

Perhaps something about the aesthetic thrust of an 'impure' art cinema realism even seems to lend itself particularly to the topic of what is hidden or invisible about the national past? Realism's claim to make visible what otherwise goes unseen meshes with art cinema's attempt to represent the forbidden or unspeakable. And yet, as Schoonover reminds us, precisely because aesthetic devices do not have a fixed meaning, it is possible to 'appropriate a logic of the image' of neorealism while rejecting its political, humanist project. In his work on the reception of neorealist cinema in the US, Schoonover is critical of monolithic understandings of neorealist aesthetics which bind a type of audiovisual strategy to a particular political meaning. Stylistic commonalities may suggest shared concerns or might well hide very different agendas.

The Chilean films discussed here adhere to some of the formal characteristics of neorealism – such as

> a predominant use of location shooting, deep-focus and long-take photography, non-professional actors, a loose form of narration, and a documentary look ... the intermingling of fiction and nonfiction, the privileging of marginal and subaltern groups, and a focus on contemporary situations[32]

– but they also diverge from this aesthetic in crucial ways.

Bearing in mind Schoonover's intervention, economic limitations and the explicit or implicit requirements of the festival circuit, the following analysis explores the ways in which these films purposefully both invoke *and* depart from aesthetic modalities originally associated with neorealism, which were received, reverberated and explored in Latin American filmmaking of the 1960s and onwards to contemporary realist movements. The analysis focuses on the prominent use of long takes and of a corporeal metaphor – what Schoonover has elaborated as the 'indulgence of corporeality' in neorealism. Like their predecessors, these Chilean films engage with the national history through 'small stories', banal 'dailiness', the normal qualities of the past, with protagonists who are not so much heroes as everymen, which results in 'conflicting temporalities ... the complex dialectic between big history and small everyday lives'.[33]

In contrast to the realist style sketched above, in these films directorial interference is highlighted, temporal unity disrupted through editing, professional actors – even stars – complement the amateurs; technical imperfections foreground the material, 'living' and ageing nature of the medium, and there is little reliance on contingency. As such self-referentiality locates the position of the narrative agency firmly in the present, their argument is not only about the past but also about the present in which they are telling their histories.

This engagement with these aesthetic and epistemological approaches opens a conceptual space in which to consider the realism's ethical and political agenda from the vantage point of the present. Considering that contemporary Chilean cinema is still frequently accused of 'failing to take up a critical position with regard to [contemporary] neoliberal policies'[34] (see Chapter 6), often in explicit comparison with famous predecessors, the argument proposed here is that the evocation of a particular type of realist aesthetic *does* make a political argument.

Post Mortem

Pablo Larraín's *Post Mortem* opens with an 'impossible' view of history. Introducing the film, a long-take shot from beneath the undercarriage of a military tank passing over a street littered with debris announces a self-aware camera through a point of view physically inaccessible to human perception, as the position and perspective of the shot create an image that is beyond the reach of the human eye. It is a slow-exposure shot almost completely devoid of human movement. Space seems reduced on the screen and in the frame, as if pressed under a tank, suggestive of 'something blind, mechanic, advancing, unstoppable, ready to crush everything

Figure 7.1 *Post Mortem*.

in its way'.³⁵ As a result, while this long take actively renders visible an otherwise inaccessible view, it also, despite its length, shows very little. What is not shown, what is crushed under the tank, emerges into the foreground as visible absence, a metaphor of history. Often associated with 'natural' human perception – in avoiding the cut, the viewer remains in the present, free to roam the image, subjected neither to Hollywood's illusionism nor to intellectual montage – the long take also always flaunts its artifice in its intentionality. In *Post Mortem*, its perspective is unequivocally associated with the machine. What is not shown, what is crushed under the tank, emerges into the foreground as visible absence, a metaphor of history.

Post Mortem tells the story of Chile as experienced by one of those whom history has forgotten: the third person present at the autopsy of the just deposited president Salvador Allende, a coroner's assistant named Mario Cornejo.³⁶ Set in the weeks from shortly before until shortly after the coup, Mario pursues his plans to win the heart of his neighbour Nancy, when the coup d'état interrupts his cocooned world. An obsessive, occasionally voyeuristic observer of his love object, Mario seems largely uninterested in the political events unfolding around him. The military takeover and Allende's death are psychologically central to the audience, yet visually and dramatically deprioritised. The decision to tell a momentous moment in Chilean history through the eyes of 'very ordinary people, people who are invisible in society'³⁷ evokes the 'mundane' quest to recover a stolen bike in the classic *Bicycle Thieves* (Vittorio de Sica, 1948).³⁸ As history is unfolding in the background, the film tells the 'small' story of Mario's struggle with the unfamiliar typewriter during Allende's autopsy. His humiliation at being replaced by a more capable (younger and handsome) cadet appears to have more impact on him than the historical event he is witnessing. By showing such 'banal "dailiness"',³⁹ one might argue that the film seeks 'to replace official narratives and popularise culture through a renewed responsiveness to contemporary experience ... [and to render] even the most mundane and everyday events uniquely compelling'.[40]

Yet a significant departure from realist style is how the film's first long take fractures diegetic time. The opening shot seems situated in the days of, or right after, the military takeover. When the narrative trajectory begins, diegetic time is pushed back to before the coup: Mario seeks to conquer his neighbour Nancy, a dancer at the *Bim Bam Bum* (a variety theatre famous at the time), and only few corpses arrive at the morgue. Politics take place literally in the background, as when Mario's employer is heard – not seen – pontificating over lunch; when Mario cannot continue driving because a Unidad Popular[41] demonstration is blocking the road. The camera remains focused on Mario, we barely see the demonstrators, whose chants sound menacing and aggressive.

The chronological trajectory is punctured again fifteen minutes later when the autopsy of a woman is carried out in the morgue, identified by an examiner (whose head remains outside the frame) as Nancy Puelma. A seemingly unfazed Mario types up the cause of death, determined as starvation and dehydration, and helps to carry away the naked corpse. This premonitory scene is preceded and followed by scenes of Nancy alive. As she is introduced as an anorexic, the implications of this shot are not immediately clear. Only at the end of the film, where we see Mario effectively incarcerating Nancy, can the audience understand this scene of Nancy's autopsy and charge it with political significance. Nancy, a fictional figure, will not be written into official history, yet she is linked to the historical figure of Allende by the repeated motif of the autopsy.

By breaking the temporal unity of the film, these jumps distort chronology and modify narrative unity. Instead of following an unpredictable, contingent reality as it unfolds, there is clearly a structuring agency that finds it necessary to order the narrative differently, to begin with an image that stands for the presence of the coup as already happened, and to present the audience with a scene mid-film that presages Nancy's death. In these instances, the film exits most clearly the selective perception of the protagonist. The coup itself takes place halfway through the film, off-screen, invisible but sonically present and temporally encoded for a knowledgeable audience: the bombardment of the presidential palace took place in the early morning and the image shows the protagonist showering. While the camera remains with Mario in the shower, it also records what he does not hear, alerting us to the presence of an extra-diegetic consciousness. The protagonist is ignorant of what is happening, but the machine knows – and yet the narrative agency chooses to document Mario *missing* the coup. We hear the sound of low-flying jets, barking dogs, glass smashing, shouting, objects being destroyed.[42] And then, only eerie silence, as Mario steps out into a deserted street full of debris and into his neighbour's demolished house. Here, there is finally the *visual* evidence of the coup in the form of its aftermath. Next, the morgue is inundated with corpses, followed by the pivotal scene of Allende's autopsy – crucial for the audience but deprioritised within the film in terms of its position.

The final scene of *Post Mortem* is another extremely long take during which we see Mario piling up furniture destroyed in the raid in front of a shed in his neighbour's garden. Taken with a static camera, unrelated to human movement, this shot lasts over three minutes. Strategies such as long takes and close-ups typically increase viewers' awareness of *their own* bodies, their own physical presence, as well as the corporeal dimension of the representation, the physical, material presence of the screen and of cinema.[43] But here, the odd, even 'brutal' frame and motionless position make us aware that it is a *machine*'s choice: the fixed stare of the machine cuts off Mario's upper body mid-chest, as he exits and re-enters the frame. His movements connect on-screen with off-screen space, or at least draw attention to the existence of the off-screen – metaphorically, the invisible, that which falls through the cracks. Nancy is hiding in this shed, together with her lover, an active member of the Unidad Popular. The camera's gaze remains fixed on these invisible humans inside the shed. This metaphorically beheaded (and de-hearted) Mario is imprisoning the bodies of the moribund, those who *will be dying*, seemingly without love or compassion. In a sense, the entire film is an enacted *futur antérieur*, an exercise to show '*This will have been*', beginning with its title and its anticipation of the hauntings of already past events. As the image is being filled with trash, it transforms into a flat, somewhat abstractedly patterned surface, in visual analogy to the scenes of the dead piling up at the morgue, connecting the disappeared and this future past that is being covered up, a visual link to the narrative mirrored by the nonlinear temporality.

Pondering the reason for the lack of major tonal change in the film after the coup, the cinematography consistently in the palette of pale discolorations, Jonathan Romney argues, 'It is not clear precisely what Larraín is saying about 1973 Chile. The suggestion perhaps is that the nation was already in a state of somnambulistic denial ... even before the coup'.[44] This persistent aesthetic of death is one of the reasons why the film was attacked as coming from the ideological right – perhaps adding to the pervasive suspicion of a filmmaker whose parents are associated with Chile's political right.

But I suggest that at the end of *Post Mortem*, we understand that for Mario, life after the coup returned largely to how it was before. We

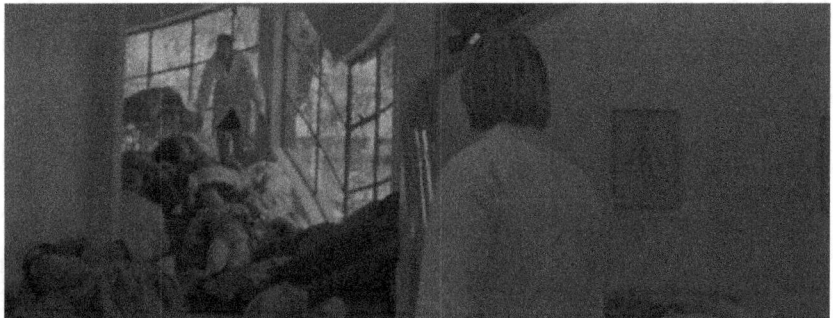

Figure 7.2 *Post Mortem.*

may therefore interpret this figure as representative of an amnesiac and blind(ed) Chile, a character in denial, a *Mitläufer*. Although at the end of the film it becomes clear that Mario has acquiesced to the right, we have also witnessed moments of courage and danger: at one point, Mario tried to smuggle a survivor in the piles of corpses into the adjacent clinic – only to find him among the pile of dead of the next day, together with the nurse who took him in.

In all of Larraín's films, the visual is deprioritised as a means of verification or understanding. We never see clearly in these films; our vision is blocked by objects, cut into odd frames, thrown back as reflections. The final take's brutal framing is only the last in a long line of images that show the characters of *Post Mortem* trapped, compressed in frames, positioned in stage-like spaces, or with parts of their bodies ruthlessly cut off. For instance, during Nancy's autopsy, the head of her examiner is outside the frame; when Mario searches his neighbour's house, his torso is cut off; and during Mario's and Nancy's brief sexual encounter, the image of Nancy comes from a point of view that cannot be Mario's, a strangely angled close-up on her face and parts of her torso, as if extrapolated from the rest of her body.

As some audiences will clearly recognise, the first long take in *Post Mortem* is built on the same symbolism as the opening (and closing) shots of the seminal Argentine film *Garage Olimpo* (Marco Bechis, 1999). *Olimpo* begins with an aerial view, shot from a plane, of the Río de la Plata in Argentina, symbolically linking the river as mass grave with the 'disappearance, the economy, the political climate', as the shot is accompanied by the sound of a weather forecast on the radio. Both films strive to work against its 'naturalizing frame of unpunished crimes' (the death flights in *Olimpo*), and to 'problematize the afterlife of the dictatorship by showing how it involves a kind of framing that works to imprison the gaze'.[45] This 'militarized gaze' translates as an aerial view connected to the death flights in *Olimpo*, and a mechanical view in *Post Mortem*, which fractures and leaves most of the human (cost) outside its image of history. The central issue concerns again the framing gazes through which we learn about history, the mediation of the machine and how historical reality is conveyed through mechanical means. The audience is made aware of the different actors involved in creating the gaze(s): the camera, the narrative agency, the perspectives adopted by the protagonists, the machine itself.

When discussing which points different audiences may pick up on, we may recall that President Allende's death was also a global event, devastating to a transnational socialist dream that had many people around the world captivated at the time, who would remember where they were when they heard of his death or when they heard the iconic radio speech. The director is clearly aware of the diverging reactions of his transnational audiences: 'International audiences laugh at different moments ... In Chile, nobody laughed at any point in the entire film ... nobody considered it a black comedy, either'.[46]

As in *Carne*, the characters in *Post Mortem* seem to be visually 'touched', as if acknowledged, by the camera. Yet this gaze is unmistakably marked as complicit, inhumane and brutal in *Post Mortem*, and as obsessive and relentless in *Carne*. Here, one may return to Schoonover's analysis of how in neorealism 'an imperiled body is offered to a bystander's gaze as an opportunity to exercise ethical judgement'.[47] Both the corpse of Allende and the bodies of those killed in the first months after the coup appear in *Post Mortem*, manifesting the ghostly figures that possess and haunt the country with their traumatic absence.[48] When the morgue team is taken by military men to examine Allende's dead body and determine the cause of death, a row of soldiers is standing behind them. The setting of the autopsy resembles a stage, with the military men lined up as witnesses, guards and audience. We watch them watching the morgue team looking at Allende.

The presence of the military in the background of the image suggests a less than free decision in determining the cause of death and visually implies the unreliability of the emerging account. When the principal doctor concludes that it was suicide, an ominous smile flits over Mario's face. After the autopsy, Mario encounters his colleague Sandra: she insists that the president has been killed, a stony-faced Mario repeats, almost pleadingly, that it was suicide. Mario and Sandra embody the two (medical) positions that have historically transpired, as the cause and circumstances of the former president's death have been subject to much debate and contestation in Chile. The characters not only *see* the dead body, surrogates

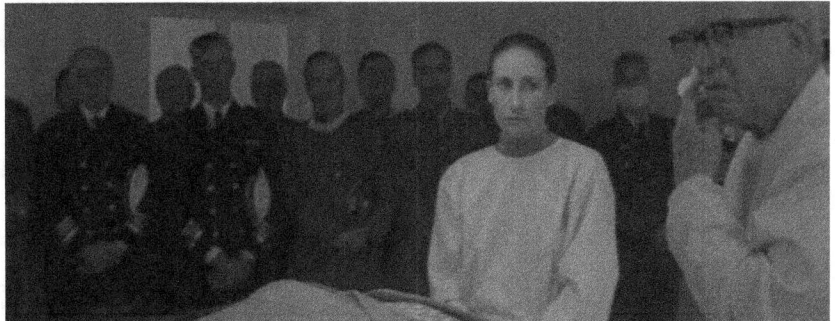

Figure 7.3 *Post Mortem*.

for the Chilean public, but they even *touch* it. Yet, despite the literal dissection of Allende, the ultimate cause remains unconfirmed.

As with Nancy's autopsy, the juxtaposition of one particular death of a mythical figure and the many deaths of the unnamed point to a parallel in the uncanniness of the sudden, traumatic disappearances – be it of a close loved one, a publicly visible historical figure or even the sudden disappearance of one's world in the form of the current democratic nation-state, and the dream of a socialist Chile. Along with political opponents and those caught in the crossfire, this political dream was violently shattered. Giving the dead president a body can also be read as an attempt to humanise this idealised, petrified and haunting figure. Instead of reanimating Allende, *Post Mortem* resurrects his corpse, re-embodying the traumatic loss of this singular publicly visible body, as well as the bodies of the many disappeared.

The brutal violence of the coup is expressed indirectly, by showing its fallout. In the first part of the film, there was the occasional autopsy every other day, in the second part, after the coup, the morgue is inundated with corpses. The bodies of those killed in the first months, unknown and unnamed, are piling up in corridors and on stairwells, filling the morgue and the screen.

These bodies are infused with a symbolic meaning that surpasses their physical reality. Similar to the re-enactments in *Los Archivos* or in *Standard* (and the 'fictional archive' I will discuss in the next chapter), such a referential, haunting presence of on-screen bodies may counter invisibilities, without erasing the history of their disappearance. For even as we are watching, we lose them yet again, as they are 'processed' without anyone finding out their names, sufferings or precise cause of death. (As the number of victims far exceeds their capacity, the small morgue team is told by the military to resort to a fast-track version of their trade.) This fictional reappearance of the first victims of the coup creates a metaphorical, alternative truth, a kind of *restorative corporeality* for those bodies that went missing, or that were perfunctorily quantified and discarded into mass graves. In the Chilean context of a violated social body, imaginarily *having*, visually possessing the missing bodies becomes a powerful gesture.

Tony Manero

As with *Carne*'s fragmentation of the human body, or the compression of space in *Post Mortem*'s mechanical images, *Tony Manero* obliterates the sensation of sky and horizon through its cruel framing. The destruction of community is carried to extremes in this film. In *Manero*, the figure of a psychopath functions to 'represent the unrepresentable'[49] of the military dictatorship, the extreme *embodiment* of a system of institutionalised psychosis.

Protagonist Raúl Perralta wants to win a Chilean television look-alike contest, specifically the round calling for the star of *Saturday Night Fever* (John Badham, 1977), John Travolta's Tony Manero. The titular quest can be read as an allegory of the Chilean nation at that point in its history. Just as the protagonist mimics his Hollywood idol, the country wanted to emulate the glittery appearance of the USA. What Carlos Flores defined as Chile's 'mania of the copy', a sociocultural tic,[50] is certainly not an exclusively Chilean obsession, but it lends itself easily to the interpretation of Raúl rejecting his national identity. In one scene, Raúl's lover reminds him he is Chilean and he responds: 'No, not me ... not any more'. Raúl's delusion is that he does not want to be 'the Chilean Tony Manero', he wants to *be* Tony Manero – not only change his appearance or nationality, but become an entirely different, and fictional, person. This delusional ambition of the protagonist is comically frustrated by his lack of visual resemblance to Travolta's Manero. He resembles the crazed protagonist of *Breathless*, who also bases his identity on an American actor, Humphrey Bogart.[51]

Raúl is walking the fine 'line between the criminal (the extreme embodiment of the system itself, which takes the system at its word) and the resister/contester of the system'.[52] He is a psychopathic criminal, who has internalised the promises of neoliberal capitalism to the point of delusion. Raúl murders an old woman to steal her television set, and he murders a projectionist to steal the film reels of *Saturday Night Fever*. His desire to be free to choose his identity is completely self-centred, and this very absence of any larger social or political inclination or vision makes his character political. As Urrutia suggests, Raúl's psychopathology reflects the 'psychopathic' historical moment in which the character lives, both result of and a metaphor for the

Figure 7.4 *Tony Manero*.

military dictatorship. In an insane world, Raúl's delusion appears a rational response, a survival instinct, to escape into the dream world of cinema from a society in which public space and social bonds have been dissolved. Ostensibly apolitical, Raúl is a true creature of totalitarianism; oppressive circumstances enable him to brutalise and exploit others *with apparent impunity*, his own crimes fading into the background in a society that is itself institutionally homicidal.[53]

This dictatorial state obfuscates what Butler identified as the precariousness of all human life and that we are all bound to and dependent on each other, precisely through our vulnerable, irrevocably material bodies. Raúl's obsession also resonates with Butler's notion of the unacknowledged and ungrievable life. In *Frames of War*, Butler argues that a life must first be perceived as living in order to be grievable. Raúl certainly does not grieve for the old lady he has killed and not even the members of his dancing troupe, who will be imprisoned or killed, taken by the DINA (the secret police during the dictatorship, later CNI, see Chapter 4) as he is hiding. And if Raúl died, no one would grieve for him, and he would be one more erased existence. From this vantage point, his desire to be someone whose existence is acknowledged, a public figure and a star, and consequently to be grievable, emerges as logical.

La Danza de la Realidad

Alejandro Jodorowsky's *La Danza de la Realidad* (*Danza*) offers another example for Chilean cinema's epistemological quest to go 'beyond the visible'. Promotional material on the film's official website describes *Danza* as an 'imaginary autobiography' but 'not in the sense of fiction, because all the *characters, places and events are real*'.[54] The film meshes memoirs about Jodorowsky's childhood, magical realism and public history and makes references both to the dictatorship under Carlos Ibañez del Campo (1927–31, 1952–8, thus long before Jodorowsky's lifetime), and the Pinochet dictatorship (during which Jodorowsky was in exile), occasionally in overlapping form. Jodorowsky himself appears as guardian-angel for his on-screen self, which is portrayed by his son, and the film generally pairs close attention to historical faithfulness – to objects, actors and *mise-en-scène* – with techniques echoing magical realism and modernist *Verfremdung*.

What further stands out about *Danza* is the aesthetic and narrative logic of its torture scenes. In contrast to other moments of violence, the lengthy torture scenes in *Danza* are not subjected to modernist strategies. They materialise with little narrative framing: as suddenly and inexplicably as they begin, they then resolve, without closure or explanation. The particular torture techniques used are specific to Chile, modelled on techniques as documented in Chile's national Museum of Memory:[55] the protagonist is bound spread-eagled onto a metal 'bed' and electroshocked, a technique called *La Parrilla*. In stark contrast to the rest of the film, the scenes are aesthetically blunt and unembellished but for a red filter. Then, near the end of the last torture sequence, black blood suddenly spouts from the protagonist's mouth and spreads over the image. Read metaphorically, rather than reifying that 'truth' which the fiction of torture claims resides here, the inside of the body remains unfathomable. In other scenes of the film, too, the body becomes a metaphorical space to express abstract concepts – for instance, amnesia cripples the protagonist's hands, until he regains both memory and movement, and a long scene features the mother urinating on the father, thereby healing him from the plague.

While the cold aesthetic of the images underscores the realness of the torture, its unforgivable nature and its pain, the narrative disrupts the link between torture and intelligence gathering or truth. Neither the protagonist nor the viewer understands what the torturers might be after because we never leave the perceptual alignment with the tortured. The protagonist does not possess any information, and he is constantly asked senseless questions about a minor character. The question is irrelevant; the prisoner tries all kinds of variations in his attempt to find an answer that will satisfy his tormentors: '[he] is your father/your son/you/me'.[56]

In *Danza*, the logics of the interrogation are revealed to be meaningless, and the physical body is unable to reify conceptual truth. Jodorowsky thereby disrupts the 'standard narrative' of torture – as a tool to extract information – which is not even deconstructed in films as central to the topic as *Rome, Open City* (Roberto Rossellini, 1945) or *Battle of Algiers* (Gillo Pontecorvo, 1966). Although these two films clearly denounce the horror of torture ethically, the link between truth and torture is not broken. Deeply embedded within the neorealist tradition, though not part of the canon, *Algiers* is not only a seminal film for the representation of torture but also for its strange career in terms of transnational viewership and reception.[57] In *Algiers*, the French army's use of torture successfully produces intelligence, allowing them to win the battle but lose the war. *Rome* explores the dynamics of seeing/nonseeing through spectatorial alignment with a witness who hears but cannot see the torture. In this film, torture fails in the sense that the tortured Manfredi dies rather than divulge information. However, this narrative not only marks him as a heroic, 'nontorturable' body, but also maintains the torturer's narrative regarding its purpose (see Chapter 1), so that 'the idea of torture itself remains intact because it is still believed to [seek to] *extract the truth*'.[58]

In his analysis of the centrality of corporeality in neorealism, Schoonover had shown how these films used 'scenarios of physical suffering to dramatise the political stakes of vision [to an] outside extranational eyewitness'.[59] Neorealist films' political-ethical appeal had been made to a broadened international audience, encouraging an ethically problematic 'benevolent receptivity'. But the parallel between a transnational address then and now ends here, as the Chilean films emphasise the *limitations* of vision to convey historical reality, to access historical truth. In the films discussed here, access to the 'real' is not pure or direct. Perhaps 'reality can be analysed by ways of fiction' but it is clearly impossible to look directly 'on the real things, exactly as they are'.[60] Instead of a transparent phenomenal world revealed by cinema, these films point precisely to what is hidden, disappearing or inaccessible about the past. They highlight the intrusive organisation of a narrative agency, the mediation of history, the scepticism towards visual evidence.

In conclusion, the films offer a conceptual reworking with its predecessors' political agenda through their aesthetics. Invoking and reshaping key features associated with neorealism and the Latin American filmmaking movements it inspired such as the New Chilean Cinema, as well as contemporary realist movements, enables a political critique of and through the form and can be read specifically and in supplementary fashion in reference to Chile's lost socialist dream and the more utopian cinema of its time. Such cross-connections with preceding, often more politicised cinematic movements, link past and present of media and political history through aesthetic engagement.

Challenging realist modes is key to the enterprise of problematising epistemological access to the past through visual means. Where Bazin presupposed the existence of a reality to be depicted – that in front of the camera – and the capacity of cinema to document it, scholars like Elsaesser frame world cinema's 'new realism' as questioning preceding aesthetic forms and the capacity of its techniques to convey this or any 'reality'. Such a 'post-epistemological concept of realism' may begin as 'perceptual insecurity', suggests Elsaesser, and move on to 'a more directly ontological doubt'.[61] And yet, such questions are already dormant in neorealism, as Schoonover explains with regard to the effect created by (neorealism's) long shots.

> The image invites us to watch while telling us that we are just watching. In other words, the image is a visual field that is becoming, something that just is, but it also asks to be witnessed ... this cinepresence confronts the viewer with the profound ambiguity of the real.[62]

This is the tendency that the films pick up on: not the Bazinian relation between cinematic realism and reality, the cinematic image as change mummified, nor an aesthetics of the accidental and contingent,[63] but an orientation towards what is ambiguous, self-referential, doubled: there is trouble, in this kind of realism. By both evoking and modifying the aesthetic of preceding cinematic, more politicised movements, the films enable a political critique of present grievances which are no longer aptly addressed through the categories of this politicised cinematic past.

The next chapters follow this thread of ontological and epistemological doubt. Larraín argued that the era of the plebiscite was 'just printed in my body, and in everybody else in Chile too'.[64] The last of his 'dictatorship trilogy' in fact features not just Chileans but specific historical 'persons of interest', whose known bodies and faces not only evidence the dictatorship period but also the passing of time since then. Bazin suggested that the presence of non-professionals results in an 'osmotic' effect and creates a 'general atmosphere of authenticity';[65] the next chapter will explore what kind of (doubled) authenticity is created through this strategy, in order to discuss the ways in which authenticity can be anchored in the corporeal, including the physical, material presence of the film itself.

Notes

1. Nagib and Mello, *Realism*. For discussions on neorealism's strong influence on Chilean cinema, see: Barril and Santa Cruz, *El cine que fue*; Corro,

Retóricas del cine chileno; Elsaesser, 'Third Cinema between Hollywood and Art Cinema'; Estévez, 'Cine contemporáneo chileno'; Gaines, 'Political Mimesis'.
2. Scott, 'Neo-Neo Realism', cf. Nagib, who points to a close connection between the realist mode and new cinema movements in the 'cyclical re-emergence of realist approaches to cinema around the world'. Nagib, *World Cinema*, p. 3.
3. The spike includes the belated exhibition of *Imagen Latente* (Pablo Perelman, 1987) in 1990, *La Luna en el Espejo* (Silvio Caiozzi, 1990), *La Frontera* (Ricardo Larraín, 1991), *Amnesia* (Gonzalo Justiniano, 1994), as well as foreign productions such as *Missing* (Costa-Gavras, 1982) and *Death and the Maiden* (Roman Polanski, 1994).
4. Recognising media power, the junta either prohibited images completely, in classic anti-pictorial fashion, or used them for spectacular social deceit. Media were involved in public deception and hoaxes, peaking perhaps with the so-called *Operación Colombo*, a campaign orchestrated by Chile's secret police to make political opponents disappear, and which involved the publication of the so-called 'list of 119' in one-edition magazines to conceal their disappearance. *El Diario de Agustín* (Ignacio Agüero, 2008) shows the level of involvement by the official media in these processes of strategic disinformation, and more importantly, the state of impunity and power, which centrally involved authority figures continue to enjoy.
5. 'El cine chileno no aparece cuando quiere, sino cuando puede', quoted in Mouesca and Orellana, *Breve Historia*, p. 213.
6. Estévez, 'Cine contemporáneo chileno'.
7. Montañez and Martin-Jones, 'The Aesthetics and Politics of Auto-Erasure'.
8. Carolina Urrutia in Diestro-Dópido, 'Children of the coup'.
9. Elsaesser in Montañez and Martin-Jones, 'Uruguay Disappears', p. 29.
10. Cf. Villarroel, *La voz*, pp. 167–8.
11. Peirano, 'Towards a "cosmopolitan" national film industry'.
12. Cf. Shaw, 'Transnational Latin American Film'.
13. Stock, *Framing Latin American Cinema*.
14. Montañez and Martin-Jones, 'The Aesthetics and Politics of Auto-Erasure'.
15. Groundbreaking Latin American films on taboo subjects of respective national pasts – Puenzo's *historia* and Bechi's *Olimpo* come to mind – have been formative for Chilean films seeking a form to speak about their past. Among the Nuevo Cine Chileno were seminal works such as *Largo viaje* (Patricio Kaulen, 1967), *El chacal de Nahueltoro* (Miguel Littin, 1969), *Valparaíso mi amor* (Aldo Francia, 1969), *Tres tristes tigres* (Raúl Ruiz, 1969).
16. Cf. Estévez, 'Cine Contemporáneo Chileno' discusses neorealism's strong influence on contemporary Chilean cinema, cf. Gaines, 'Political Mimesis', p.102.
17. Coined by Ascanio Cavallo, the 'Novísimo Cine Chileno' has attracted considerable scholarly national and even international attention. Cavallo and Maza, *El Novísimo Cine Chileno*; cf. López Barraza, *Nuevo Cine Chileno 2005–2010*.

Cortínez and Engelbert, 'El cine chileno de los sesenta'; Cavallo and Díaz, *Explotados y Benditos*; Flores, *Excéntricos y Astutos*. Cf. Cavallo, Douzet, and Rodríguez, *Huérfanos y perdidos*.
18. Cf. King, *Magical Reels*; Barril and Santa Cruz, *El cine que fue*.
19. de la Garza, 'Realism and National Identity', p. 109.
20. Matheou, 'The Body Politic'.
21. Poblete, 'New National Cinemas in a Transnational Age', p. 223. Haddu and Page, *Visual Synergies*; Alberto Moreiras's 'savage hybridity' is cited in Kantaris and O'Bryen, *Latin American Popular Culture*.
22. Quoted in Poblete, 'New National Cinemas', p. 221.
23. Boym, *The Future of Nostalgia*, p. 42.
24. McGrath in de la Garza, 'Realism and National Identity', p. 109.
25. Galt and Schoonover, *Global Art Cinema*, p. 17.
26. Bordwell, 'Art Cinema'.
27. Bazin, *What is Cinema?* Vol. I, pp. 23–40, p. 37.
28. Allen, 'There Is Not One Realism, but Several Realisms', p. 77–8.
29. Zavattini, 'Some Ideas', p. 58.
30. Despite the evidently problematic implications of 'world cinema' or 'cinema of small nations', as they necessarily lump together a vast array of different films and styles as non-Hollywood cinema, itself an imaginary monolith, I will nevertheless use these terms here, following the cited authors.
31. Nagib, *World Cinema*, p. 235 and p.10.
32. Landy, 'Rome Open City', p. 404.
33. Brewer, 'Neo-realism and re-enactment', p. 88.
34. Page, 'Neoliberalism and the Politics of Affect and Self-Authorship in Contemporary Chilean Cinema', p. 269.
35. 'el sentido que reviste para nosotros; algo así como una cosa ciega, mecánica y compacta que avanza ... imparable ... irrefrenable, dispuesta a arrasar con todo o destinada a estrellarse'. Corro, *Retóricas del cine chileno*, pp. 239–40.
36. As the military destroyed almost all existing records, the only concrete historical file available to the filmmakers was a record of Allende's autopsy, featuring the unknown coroner assistant's name and inspiring the film. Matheou, 'The Body Politic'.
37. Matheou, 'The Body Politic'.
38. Although Zavattini was a principal scriptwriter for *Bicycle Thieves*, the film is (often) mistakenly 'thought to be an enactment of a distinct neorealist poetics', according to Nowell-Smith. Nowell-Smith, 'Bicycle', p. 424.
39. Zavattini, 'Some Ideas', p. 54.
40. Bertellini and Ritter, 'Zavattini', p. 3. Bertellini and Ritter's argument refers to Zavattini's engagement with painting, television or newsreels. Compare Corro, *Retóricas del cine chileno* on the political implications of Chilean film's focus on the mundane, the everyday and the intimate.

41. The Unidad Popular was a left-wing political alliance in Chile that stood behind the successful candidacy of Salvador Allende for the 1970 Chilean presidential election.
42. With regard to this image-sound combination, cf. also Landy's notion of 'conceptual realism' in *Rome, Open City*. She argues that the openness of the film's images 'subvert[s] cinematic clichés by making self-conscious its application of image and sound in relation to their past uses'. Landy 'Rome Open City', p. 419.
43. Margulies, *Nothing Happens*, p. 47. Cf. de Luca, *Realism of the Senses*.
44. Romney, 'Staying alive', pp. 46–7.
45. Draper, *Afterlives*, pp. 189–90.
46. Smith, 'Larraín, *Post Mortem*'.
47. Schoonover, *Brutal Vision*, pp. xiv–xvi.
48. Burucúa and Kwiatkowski, 'The Absent Double'.
49. Urrutia, 'Hacia una política en tránsito'.
50. Cited in Mouesca, *Plano secuencia*, p. 167.
51. This precursor is further evoked by the use of jump cuts, when Raoul escapes and abandons his troupe as they are taken by the secret police.
52. Elsaesser and Buckland, *Studying Contemporary American Film*, p. 276.
53. Romney, 'Staying alive'.
54. 'La danza de la realidad', emphasis added.
55. Author interview with producer Xavier Guerrero in October 2013.
56. A reference to *The Count of Monte Cristo* and perhaps referring to the lasting post-traumatic changes derived from wrongful imprisonment.
57. Screened at the Pentagon in 2003, the film played a role in the development of the torture programme; it is an example of how a single film 'can turn into a transnational memory, part of a collective open archive'. Pisters in Martin-Jones, 'Archival Landscapes', p. 716. Cf. Harrison, 'Yesterday's Mujahiddin'.
58. Zivin, 'Seeing and Saying', p. 111. For a closer reading of the relation between *Rome* and Larraín's trilogy, see Jung, 'Realist Aesthetics'.
59. Schoonover, *Brutal Vision*, pp. xiv–xvi.
60. Zavattini, 'Some Ideas', p. 51.
61. Elsaesser, 'World Cinema', p. 10.
62. Schoonover, *Brutal Vision*, p. 27.
63. Contingency, improvised acting and 'real time' are not characteristics employed in the films discussed here; there are, however, examples within contemporary Chilean fiction films which use improvised acting and 'real time'; for instance, *Sábado, una película en tiempo real* (Matías Bize, 2003) or *La sagrada familia* (Sebastián Lelio, 2005).
64. Rohter, 'Pablo Larraín and His Unintentional Trilogy'.
65. Bazin, *What is Cinema?*.

CHAPTER 8

Cinema as Poetic Archive

Just as the 'cinematic bodies' discussed in the first part of this volume have become battlefields in a war of images – where multiplied screens, remediated and distorted images reflect the prevalent aesthetics of modern warfare – the Chilean films discussed in this chapter also use their own material bodies to address recent technological developments in relation to competing truth claims. The question for cinema theory is whether we are confronted with a new type of image or a new dispositif; the question for the films, already facing absent or contested documentation, is how to offer interventions on historical truth. In other words, how does the epistemological challenge posed by the digital turn intertwine with these films' attempts to create conditions of belief in the truth of their images?

By reframing the question of indexicality as just *one* way to theorise cinema and cinema's potential to establish links to the real, it is possible to better understand how the analysed films establish a referential connection. They turn to affective registers, for instance, and to their own material dimension, or they locate the indexical in other aspects of the film, such as sound or specific places. They also offer figurations which substitute for those images that are visibly missing, all the while flaunting these compositions' constructed nature. The result is a kind of relative authenticity, one that is aware of its own limitations but does not forego claims to historical truth and that expands what we can see or perceive as existing.

Rethinking Indexicality

In cinema studies, indexicality defines the paradox of the cinematic image as the presence of the photographed body, which, though pointing to the absence of the actual body, bestows upon the image an evidentiary status. CGI and simulation technology challenge and historicise this notion and definition of cinema as perforce an 'indexical' medium. As a result, the revelatory automatism of a filmic trace is often contrasted with the unprecedented ease of producing identical copies of digital images, the alleged lack of distinction between an original from a computer-based image destabilises the idea of an *original* body.

These technological changes impacted on and challenged *all* images' relation to the real.[1] Yet this binary between the loss of truth value in digital images and the direct link to truth in photochemical film has never been fair to either side. Metadata reveals that digital copies only *seem* flawless. There are no identical copies; data is always lost in copying; and the material base of the digital also deteriorates – though more slowly and invisible to the unaided human eye.[2] Digital media have expanded the possibilities of manipulation only in magnitude and degree, and their capacity for tricking the eye comes with an impressive pedigree. In some ways, the digital even promises *more* truth, by allowing data visualisation to move from the conceptual to perceptual realm.[3]

Moreover, examples such as the Charlie Hebdo shooting in January 2015 or the Mohammed caricatures in the Danish newspaper *Jyllands-Posten* illustrate that what is considered indexical – in the sense of *derived from, tied to the real* – is at least partly a socio-culturally derived agreement of perception. Generally, 'trust in the moving image as an index of truth is of fairly recent standing'.[4] In other words, the current 'theoretical fix' has preceded the digital: what is considered authentic has always been an agreed upon form of trust, shaped by social convention.[5]

Hence, and in defiance of scholarly debates, the reception of the image, of that which 'counts intuitively as an image has changed very little for Western cultures'.[6] Against the implied capitulation before the manipulability of digital images, Doane argues that especially 'images [of pain, death and suffering] ... point to the persistence and strength of an indexical imaginary even in the realm of digital photography'.[7]

What this means is that establishing an image as indexical in the sense of *authorised to make evidentiary claims*, may reside in different aspects of the film. Doane's formulation of an 'indexical imaginary' explicitly anchors this relation within the spectator.[8] As this argument rests on the *perception* of indexicality, the following analysis will pay attention to both aesthetic cues and cultural context to make inferences on how these films *ask to be read*.

* * *

The first phenomenon to discuss is how audio footage can be used as an indexical anchor. *Pena* opens with the historical radio transmission of Pinochet's declaration of military takeover, a document which points to its doppelgänger and counterpart, President Allende's last speech. With this opening, the film announces its exploration of the discourse of the perpetrators, and large portions of the film feature historical footage from a media which had been largely under the regime's control.

Heard now, the speech is not only interesting for its content but even more so for its sonic texture. The speaker's stilted way of talking, typical for the time, encodes pastness. Crackling sounds and interferences of the radio transmission evidence decay and evoke a sense of obsolescence regarding this previously dominant medium. Its warmer sound and granular texture lend a particular *body*, an almost haptic character to both voice and transporting device, heightening its authenticity. This recalls what Barthes called the 'grained voice', 'the materiality of the body [of the recording medium is] speaking its mother tongue'.[9]

Unlike the image, audio material seems to have rarely been viewed as losing its indexical qualities, and recorded sound remains closely identified with its own original. Although we are trained to focus on image-centred modes of hearing, sound in fact always possesses spatial, haptic and temporal qualities. Digital or analogue, sound is always three-dimensional, penetrating and describing space. It creates a tactile contact, making objects 'closer to touch and even to smell than to sight'.[10] As there is no total silence, sound is omnipresent; we cannot refuse it. These qualities of sound function to anchor authenticity. Sound material seems to connote the truth of contingency, even though sounds that were present in reality may be lost on or filtered out of the recording, and in this case, the performance of the original Pinochet speech and its purposeful insertion in the film indicate that the sound is clearly mediated, and functions possibly as 'a *representation of sound*, not an "innocent" reproduction'.[11] The recorded tape here offers the 'surrogate proximity' usually applied to cinematic presence,[12] compensating for the audience's absence when the (audiovisual) reality was documented.

Where an image can appear to freeze a moment in time, sound stretches on, it only exists in duration. The 'projective' temporal movement of the recordings is fascinating to consider in light of Tom Gunning's and Mulvey's remarks on movement, time and cinema. Gunning proposes the *animation* of images as the defining essence of cinema, and Mulvey suggests that through movement, cinema is able to preserve a sense of 'now-ness' into the future, namely into the time of our viewing – or hearing – the material. Both refer primarily to moving images, but their ideas can be extended to sound. Gunning even suggests in passing that the debates on the ontology and phenomenology of modern media of reproduction 'can be extended to *both moving image and sound recording*'.[13] 'Motion always has … a progressive movement in a direction, and therefore invokes possibility and a future'.[14]

The recordings in *Pena* combine pastness, presentness and future: their duration takes the audience into a prolonged past moment that is happening in the present and projects towards the future. Our perception of these indexical and temporal qualities intertwines with sound's primary function in the film, that is, to provide emotional access and to evidence the 'realness' of its narrative. Along with smell and taste, sound is a primary instigator of memory recall, often even inducing a reflex or *mémoire involontaire*. The sound in *Pena* presents a way to bypass the visual index, which the film's texture and collage-like montage shows to be clearly problematic. By contrast, the sound anchors authenticity, establishes complicated temporal pointers and may evoke subjective emotional states and memories in the audience. The ghostly qualities of photographs have been observed by many scholars,[15] but recordings of the *voices* of people known to be dead might be even more haunting, even more evocative of involuntary body memories.

Moving on to the second phenomenon, from sound to space, *Pena* in fact offers a soundscape that intertwines these sonic qualities with particularly and culturally relevant *locales*. The film begins with the sound of a bullhorn, and then, accompanied by maritime sounds, the recorded speech sets in. Threading in and out of its various sections, this non-diegetic marine soundscape identifies the film as a whole. Rendered sounds evoke the washing of waves at sea, the creaking of sails, describing its topic: past atrocity and impunity that happened in a seaport location. A visual support is provided by the repeated shot of the backside of a deck of cards depicting the (in)famous training and torture ship *La Esmeralda*, whose home harbour lies in the municipality of Viña and Valparaíso.[16]

The strategy of using the real place reverberates more deeply, perhaps, in the context of Latin America where consumerist, postmodern and posttotalitarian urban spaces often pre-empt the possibility of engaging in 'a continuing history of a real place'.[17] For instance, *Post Mortem* was shot in the actual mortuary where Allende's autopsy took place. As Larraín explains,

> For some reason, that hospital, which belonged to the military, was returned to the state. The building is in midtown and was going to be destroyed for another hospital. They decided not to touch it and the rooms were still there – the lights, the beds, the instruments – everything used in those days at the hospital. But that's a place, not a record. The military destroyed almost all existing records.[18]

And yet, many of the films exhibit a faithfulness to locale that goes beyond the familiar attention to historical detail or implicit links to location shooting in realist tradition (see Chapter 7). *Danza* is shot in and peopled with extras from Tocopilla, the town where Jodorowsky grew up. But Jodorowsky also decided to rebuild his childhood home, as if creating a re-enactment of factual history in spatial terms. This same strategy was also used in *Zero*, where Bigelow reconstructed the bin-Laden compound. How are we to recognise such efforts at authentication, if they are not marked as such? As prop, Jodorowsky used the real saddle of real dictator Carlos Ibañez del Campo, lent to him by the Ibañez' granddaughter; information which is only conveyed in extradiegetic material.[19] How, one might ask, can this saddle or a rebuilt place anchor authenticity, if one needs to be told about it? Is this perhaps simply proof of the awareness that in today's media landscape, a film is expected to be dissected online, that the means of meaning-making collaboration between viewer and text have expanded beyond aesthetic codes and historically situated viewing habits?

The next section will discuss the indexical links proposed in *Nostalgia de la luz*. Facing the absence of the missing bodies of those who were disappeared, this film establishes its referent through the material connection between the stars and humankind. The painful gap between past and present is softened by making the relativity of time in relation to space and movement experiential in the film's timelapse technology, linking stars, cinema and humankind in an 'existential bond' that can appropriately be called indexical.

Nostalgia de la luz

That certain spaces seem to store memory is a notion familiar from site-specific memorials and museums, the affectively charged 'guilty landscape' of concentration camps.[20] Patricio Guzmán's *Nostalgia de la luz* (2010) and his follow-up film, *El botón de nácar* (2015), are set in complementary examples of such 'woundscapes': Chile's desert north and the Patagonian south, both spaces that have been used as graveyards for disappearing people.

Nostalgia remains in this same space but navigates across various times. Guzmán follows three groups performing historical excavations in the Atacama Desert in the north of Chile: women combing the sand for corporeal remains of their disappeared family members, archaeologists studying pre-Columbian mummies conserved by the aridity of the desert, and astronomers examining distant galaxies in search of the origin of the universe. The film thus speaks about the entanglements, traces and disappearances of Chile's distant and more recent history, focusing in particular on the losses caused by the dictatorship. To approach these topics,

Guzmán uses traditional documentary methods such as voiceover narration and interviews with survivors and members of a post-memory generation, but he also sets up filmic space, various objects and the technology of time-lapse photography in such a way that they come to function as non-human witnesses and metaphors for conceptual themes. In this way, the film reflects the recent turn in memory studies 'toward a focus on entanglements of embodied and emplaced memory'.[21]

Such people, objects and places, who have 'been there', can acquire a testifying presence even when they do not speak. In *Nostalgia*, we encounter a couple who were faced with the choice between having their granddaughter taken away or revealing their daughter and son-in-law's hiding place. A living archive, they are present in the image, sitting silently side by side, but their story is being told by their granddaughter. There are interviews with survivors of the Chacabuco concentration camp, such as architect Miguel Lawner, who memorised the dimensions of the camp in his own body's physical dimensions. He can perform *embodied* memory by walking the physical measurements of the prison camp. Created in 1970, Chacabuco, the largest concentration camp under the Pinochet dictatorship, held 60,000 political prisoners, many of whom were later disappeared. This is but one example of the 'evocation of landscape as archive ("page after page")'[22] in this film. Today the most arid desert on Earth (which used to be an ocean), Atacama conserves the past well, often in palimpsestic layers: a new road is built on the old one; the barracks of nineteenth-century mining towns, premised on indigenous slave labour, are repurposed as concentration camps, and now function as a graveyard.

Atacama is depicted as *auratic*, in the sense of being imaginatively endowed with the capacity to return our gaze.[23] There are literally faces in the desert, which seem to be looking back at us: sketched figures carved in stone by pre-Colombian shepherds; the photograph of a disappeared is laid on the desert floor; and the audience watches the faces of Vicky Saavedra and Violeta Berríos, two women who comb the desert for remnants of their loved ones. Through their dusky clothes and tanned faces, Guzmán links the women tonally to the hues of the desert and lets them speak *for* it. 'There is a strong sense here that the landscape speaks through Berríos … the affective landscape appearing as a face talking of the occluded past whose secret it keeps'.[24]

Nostalgia proposes mimetic-magical correspondences between object, place and person, channelled through cinema. Both desert and cinema work like 'a time machine',[25] and we see a mummy and petrified amber, some of Bazin's famous metaphors for the cinematic capacity to embalm time.

Figure 8.1 *Nostalgia de la luz.*

Like analogue cinema, the light of the stars is a spectre, hovering in a space between there (the materiality of the stardust) and not there (we are seeing the light of stars long dead, their indexical trace). As with the disappeared loved ones, the origin has been extinguished, yet their effect on those touched by them continues to this day. Where Benjamin's concept of the aura reminds us of the human element in things and objects, *Nostalgia* also reminds us of the forgotten celestial element in living beings. Desert and cosmos point to 'the material origin – and finality – that human beings share with non-human nature, the physical aspect of creation'.[26] Thus, *Nostalgia* establishes a link

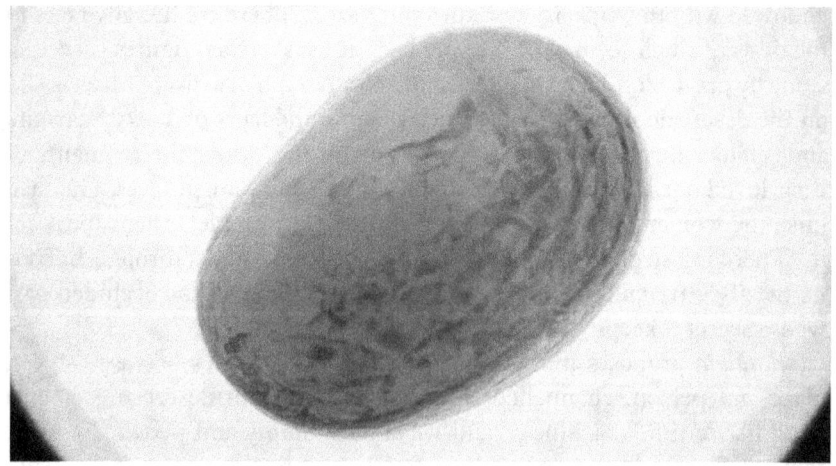

Figure 8.2 *Nostalgia de la luz.*

CINEMA AS POETIC ARCHIVE

and correspondence between the disappeared, audiovisual imprints and the light of the stars. All are indexical traces of the past; both metaphorically and literally, the dead are within us.

Before the film arrives at this poetic solution, it must address the absence of that which is so central to our experience of documentary film and its 'relentless demand of habeas corpus':[27] the presence of the body. Faced with the absence of both bodies and documented evidence of the disappearances, Guzmán turns to the ostensibly 'empty' space of the desert as their tomb or shrine and to various kinds of objects as witnesses. Already in his previous films, such as *El caso Pinochet* (2001) or *Salvador Allende* (2004), Guzmán had used real objects and places in such an authenticating function, expanding the mnemonic function of photography to other 'physical objects and places as memory anchors'.[28] In *Nostalgia*, the investigated objects range from deeply emotional and mnemonic 'ghosts' – long-lasting memory traces, 'buried books, faded photographs, fragmented testimonies, exhumed bodies, harvests of bones'[29] – to technical objects, including obsolete tools of astrology and cinema.

Central among these archival objects explored in *Nostalgia* are the photos of the disappeared, whose iconic status derives from context, quantity and repetition. These images appear both in their private and collective memorial dimension. A single photograph of José Saavedra is laid down on the desert floor which his sister combs daily in her search for Jose's remains. Near the end of the film, the camera lingers on the images of the disappeared at the *Museo de la Memoria* in Santiago, zooming and retracting, panning along the faces united on the wall. And the images also appear in 'embodied' form, carried by those protesting their disappearance.

In the context of these protests, the images substantiated the 'realness' of these lives and of the crime committed against them; today, they point to the event of their disappearances *and* to the resistance against this practice. For the protesting Mothers in Argentina and Chile disrupted the 'perverse tactic of invisibility' of state terror by making it visible: photographs pinned to their chests, they lent their own bodies to the floating face or head, 'embodying' a number or statistic. (For practical reasons, and frequent lack of other visual documentation, most images were taken from identity cards. Originally supposed to make a person comparable and countable, pushed further towards being a *thing*, this purpose was here productively harnessed to find strength in numbers.[30]) In doubling their own bodies' proprietary function, the women both made visible and fortified the original pointer to the disappeared because,

> To put it bluntly, there was no corpus. No body. Dead or alive. The photo became a substitute for the body that the government officials contended had never been arrested, a way of bringing into visibility someone who was at that very moment being hidden from view.[31]

The public display of these images was therefore 'itself already an instance of an oppositional political imaginary at work, an act of sedition'.[32] For this act, the protesting women were able to use *any* photograph of their disappeared relative. 'The photographs had hardly to be melodramatic, but they did need to conjure the ghosts and the haunting quality of disappearance'.[33]

The intrinsic ghostliness, the spectral qualities and temporal ambiguities of the photographic image lent themselves easily to this particular cause. As photographs, the images of the disappeared insist both on their objects' having-been-here (lived) as well as the attempted erasure of their existence, their having-been-disappeared.[34] This effect derives from the (perceived) indexicality of the photograph in combination with the particular history or biography of these images. The indexicality of the photograph is here harnessed not as Barthes' *futur antérieur* but to evidence an as-yet-undetermined temporality of an existence (are they still living, are they already dead?).

Ahmed's notion of an 'affective economy' illuminates the intuitively evident affective attachment to certain objects. The cultural, social and personal meaning and value of things does not reside in themselves, Ahmed points out, but is produced as an effect of their circulation in social contexts, outside or in surplus of their worth in terms of labour and commodity. This is especially pertinent when objects are connected to loss.[35] Vicky Saavedra carefully enumerates the few parts that have been found of her brother: several teeth, some bits of his head, a foot with the shoe and sock still on it. What is this object: a foot, a thing, a body part, something that once lived? Heartbreakingly, Saavedra recounts how she caressed this foot, how she sat in mourning with it, observing every detail, only then being able to realise the fact that her brother was dead.

Violeta Berríos, sister of a disappeared man, lucidly describes herself and her fellow searchers as 'the lepers of Chile'. The comparison is powerful in its evocation of how the horror of the past seems to *stick* to the bodies of these women who describe being shunned by society as if they carried a contagious disease. As long as their relatives remain disappeared, these women refuse to let go, thereby disrupting the narrative of reconciliation. They are thus *abject*, in the sense described by Kristeva, as that which 'disturbs identity, system and order'. Here, this abject disrespect for 'borders, positions, rules'[36] relates to the parameters of the official post-dictatorship discourse of a smooth flow of transition. Their pain remains so *raw* that others feel as if threatened to empathise against their will, but *Nostalgia* encourages its viewers to move into this pain.

Nostalgia both features and creates such affective encounters, not only with people but things and spaces, from dusty spoons and self-made telescopes to the ruins of Chacabuco. The film is saturated with attention to archival objects and places, which are approached from unusual perspectives and scales and, with the time-lapse, in unusual duration. An image that resembles a close-up of the surface of the moon, preceded by images of galaxies, is revealed to be a close-up of a human skull; Chacabuco is explored through archive aerial footage, present-day recordings of its ruins but also through a close-up shot of a wall, on which are scratched the names of the prisoners held here, partly disappeared. Through its own attending and attentive gaze, the film encourages us, too, to *unsee*, to *see anew*.

Certain objects, Elsaesser writes, attain a 'particular kind of presence or agency',[37] a signifying dimension beyond their presence as a thing 'to be looked at'. Such objects may evidence their biography, exhibiting indexical traces of time; which is why they can serve as mnemonic device or as historical document. They carry an embodied heft or 'auratic' presence. But even when there are no visible traces, by their sheer existence in time, such objects are witnesses to historical reality. The obsolete media featured in *Nostalgia* are objects in this sense, estranged, yet affectively saturated and evidence of a historical reality. The film shows the technical tools we use to access time, history and memory: the high-tech telescopes in Atacama, the 'old German telescope [that] is still working', and the self-made (but functional) telescopes constructed by the prisoners in Chacabuco. By offering various histories within their various temporalities – cosmological, archaeological, subjective-personal and national notions of time – *Nostalgia* liquefies time and creates space for unofficial narratives on and experiences of the past.

The film also *performs* different ways of representing time. The first move to create a temporal-spatial change in perception consists of the 'moment[s] of stillness'[38] introduced by the presence of photographs in the film. With the changing speed we also change the gaze: we are looking *again*, looking more *closely*. The second move is created by the inclusion of time-lapse sequences, which compresses long periods of time by changing the frames-per-second rate.

The time-lapse highlights that human temporality, perceived as natural and normative, is only one among many. Aided and confirmed by the camera as 'technologically enhanced visions of [different] temporal realities',[39] the time-lapse delimits our senses and opens the possibility to investigate our place within larger scales of time and space. Thus, time-lapse photography offers a means to translate entities and concepts that are beyond the range of human vision into a visible analogue. As with computer simulation, this method allows 'the conceptual world to enter the perceptual one'.[40] Through their poetic shape and slowed-down temporality, time-lapse allows room for contemplation, opening a gateway for the audience to engage in an affective and experiential conversation with history. In the last time-lapse sequences, the camera also slowly tilts, further enhancing audience engagement by adding the 'dramatic quality of the movement itself'.[41] In this way, *Nostalgia* uses the technical capacities of the cinematic apparatus to offer its critique of history(-writing) by opening potentialities of perception that lie beyond unaided human capacity. Like telescopes as elongations of the human vision, the time-lapse offers a non-anthropocentric perception of time. We construct time spatially, contrasting the recent with the *distant* past. The time-lapse sequences reveal the arbitrariness of the human-centred counting of time. In the film, the astronomer Gaspar Galaz explains how our subjective present, our 'objective reality' is the illusion, and a fictional construct, for the speed of light, which determines and circumvents human perception, always causes a minuscule delay between an event taking place and our perception of the event. In fact, what we perceive as or believe to be the present is always already the past: as Galaz points out, the past is all there is. Because our image of time is spatial, when something happened a long time ago, we imagine traumatic events to move away, to become smaller, and less emotionally urgent. *Nostalgia* nudges us to question these inherited notions of the fading of memory and the progress of time. The visual demonstration that events do not actually recede into temporal distance is an argument against the narratives of amnesia, the gradual disappearance of historical pain, and enforced looking forward.

The way in which *Nostalgia* links literal archaeology with various technical ways of listening to and looking at time, thereby creating 'alternative temporalities', resonates with the battle cry of media archaeology: to understand the new via the old, to explore alternative history/-ies of obsolete, failed and even imaginary media technologies as equally relevant. Especially with its emphasis on obsolete media, the film visualises Siegfried Zielinski's 'archaeology of hearing and seeing by technical means'.[42] The realisation that *it could have been otherwise* interrupts the hegemony of the present and the winners of history, countering the 'dictates of progress' which see 'time and history as straight lines'.[43] This disruptive momentum links *Nostalgia* with *NO*, a film which has been accused of vain superficiality. But in both cases, the films use the capacities of cinema to make a political argument. As the next section will show, in *NO,* the surface is indeed the message, as the materiality of the medium is linked to its narrative core.

NO

Drawing attention to how the unprocessed national pasts of both Chile and the US rear their heads in contemporary cinema, a *New York Times* article suggested that '*NO* has provoked a *Zero Dark Thirty*-scale controversy in Chile'.[44]

Chilean critics suggested that Larraín's films carry a conscious or unconscious right-wing point of view due to the fact that he is the son of prominent politicians of the right-wing UDI party; *NO* was considered an oversimplifying misrepresentation at best, and historical revisionism at worst.[45] While interpretations of *NO* as conservative and ideologically distorted dominated in Chile, Western reviewers tended to focus on the film's superficial and sentimentally infused aspects, sometimes missing its ironic and bleak tones and contextualising the film's style symptomatically in terms of postmodern self-absorption, and alleging it used historical footage 'to lend historical context' (presumably to a North American audience): 'If you can shake off the inherent grossness of mining the Pinochet years for yet another *Mad Men*-style deification of zeitgeist-grasping salesmen, this is moderately interesting stuff'.[46]

Both criticisms misread the level of self-reflexivity inscribed in the film's aesthetic and formal strategies. While there are omissions and condensations (for instance, the film does not depict the anti-Pinochet forces' grass-roots efforts to bring out the vote, which were pivotal to the referendum's success), the film does depict competing discourses and points of view; precisely this polyvocality is its strength. The celebrated ousting of Pinochet by a national referendum was achieved by little more than 50 per cent of the popular vote, and the film juxtaposes various ways of experiencing the result of the plebiscite at the end of the film: joyful celebrations, genuine tears and hugs among the *NO* camp; a stupefied René Saavedra, a wary expression on his face; the loneliness of the *Sí*-campaign's chief ad man, whose superiors had excluded him, a lower-class member, from their planned victory party.

Rather than a success story, *NO* shows how the victory of the NO vote was also a little bit of a yes vote, won through the very means installed by the system it was rejecting: Pinochet was ousted by the very commercialism he brought to Chile.[47] Narratively, the world of sales speaks to the particular way in which the transition to democracy was *negotiated* in Chile. The melting of market, publicity and politics creates a clever and apt metaphor for contemporary Chile, where 'the official discourse is one of advertising'.[48] Ad man René is able to use the same tagline – 'What you will now see is deeply embedded in the contemporary social context of Chile ... Today Chile thinks of her future'[49] – at three different occasions: to sell a soft drink, to present the *NO* campaign, and at the end of the film, to sell a new TV show. Each time the pitch works, and its vague grandeur also serves as a caption, introduction or advertisement for the film itself, for the 'contemporary social context of Chile' can refer both to the diegetic time, or to the time of viewing for the film's audience.

Formally, the montage of historical and *faux* footage suggests continuity between or the continuation of the past into the present; repetition and leitmotifs seem to suggest a cyclical time. René is watching his food rotating in the microwave or playing with his son's toy train: but the train – symbolically evoking modernity, linear progress of time, and the arrival of cinema, change, travel, transit – is going in circles.[50] Combined with the aesthetic tension between surface and depth in video, suggests Urrutia, these loops introduce a reflective quality and express one of the central questions of the film: what has really changed? Has there been (lasting) progress? The old medium allows us to look anew at the past: what else is left out of hegemonic discourses, public and private memory; what else was maybe not told?

Conversations spill over from one scene to the next: the scenery – the image – changes, but the discourse continues. Ellipses call attention to absences in the plot, and by extension, to comparable absences in narratives on history. What transpires between the scenes can only loosely be based on the available visual and narrative information and must be filled by paratextual knowledge or memory. As these gaps do not match expectations according to genre rules or continuity editing, they demand an active reading position where 'what is being seen is in excess of what is being shown',[51] allowing for a different, subjective experience of mediated historical time.

NO tells the story of a historical transformation and event, but also of a media transition and the disappearance of a previous medium: *NO* is a *film* shot in *video* largely about the impact of a *television* campaign. Media and cinema history speak about a larger history, a method evidenced in other moments of Larraín's trilogy as well. Each film raises the spectre of spectacle inside the spectacle: *Post Mortem* conjures aspects of melodrama and reminisces about the *Bim Bam Bum* in Santiago; in *Manero*, the protagonist kills to steal a television and film reels; in *NO*, the ad men want their latest commercial to be shot in 'James Bond Style'. The manic desire for imitation[52] in *Manero* (whose protagonist strives to emulate an American icon and movie star) ends with *NO*, where one character chastises the campaign as postmodernist simulacra, 'the copy of the copy of the copy'.[53] *NO* recognises that historical memory can be turned into a product: the medium that sells soft drinks, that helped the historical advertising campaign to 'sell' democracy, is now selling this film. Larraín creates what Benson-Allott, building on an eloquent expression from Paula Massood, calls 'an aesthetic appropriate to the conditions'[54] by critiquing the removal of Pinochet through the same capitalist principles he helped introduce to Chile: a story about media manipulation is told in mediated, manipulated images.

If we consider the cinematic apparatus as the cinematic narrator, then enmeshing old and new footage is a way of foregrounding this authorial voice, and of drawing attention to the film's, and by extension the historical, construction. Foregrounding the medium disrupts the illusion that content is all there is and refocuses our attention on the transporter medium.

The replication is never meant to be exact, never attempts to suffuse with the original form. As in a palimpsest, in the remediation of analogue aesthetics, the past shimmers through into the present. In *NO* we can, as proposed by media archaeology, *watch the medium showing something*, listen to the noise of the transmitting system itself. As if performing the 'epistemological reverse engineering' that Wolfgang Ernst and Jussi Parikka advocate, *NO* uses its medium as 'both a method and an aesthetics of practicing media criticism'.[55] By making its machinery visible, the film reflects on how our epistemological systems are bound up with the technology used to mediate representations.

In *NO*, twenty-one of the historical figures who literally embody the historical experience were cast to reperform their roles, to re-enact *themselves*. Patricio Aylwin, the first post-dictatorship president, portrays himself, as does Patricio Bañados, presenter of the NO-campaign, or the sociologist Eugenio Tironi. This play with not-quite-the-same repetition bluntly interrupts any suspension of disbelief: an elderly Patricio Aylwin waddles in, shakes Saavedra's hand and sits in front of the diegetic camera. Then the camera tilts downward to a diegetic television screen that shows Aylwin's younger self announcing the importance of the vote.

These filmic bodies establish the link to the real, precisely *because* they have aged. It is through their aged bodies that these historical figures affirm change, or at least, given the historical amnesia, the passing of time. The point of engaging these bodies is to draw attention to the *perception* of the real, again, the frames through which we receive history, our view on

Figure 8.3 *NO*.

the past *from* the present. These human bodies of historical players complement what the film does technically, meshing the original and the re-enactment on the 'authentically old' cinematic body. The lenses and the real bodies anchor the real, while the narrative agency clearly signals the telling of these stories from a later vantage point. Rather than having old vintage stock and cameras working as unquestioning tools for the authentication of the narrative, archive footage is juxtaposed with the re-enacted genesis of this material. The combination of *genuinely* old film stock with *real* archive material effectively sutures two kinds of documentary. The result is an authenticity that acknowledges its artificiality, both evoking and deconstructing the concept of what is 'the real', a 'double realness' that alerts the viewer to the culturally inherited nature of claims regarding the (transparent) truth of footage material generally.

While the use of vintage video cameras, lenses and film stock in the fictionalised parts in *NO* allows for a softened, often imperceptible suture between archive material and fictional re-enactment, the idea is never to trick the audience: the star presence of Gael García Bernal in almost every one of the new scenes ensures that even those unfamiliar with Chilean history never lose sight of which part is re-enacted. The central presence of Bernal's well-known star body enhances this play with metalepsis. Bernal's popular star persona, his record in acting and producing politically liberal and Latin-American-focused productions is interesting to consider, given that the film was accused of being reactionary, selling out to Hollywood aesthetic and narrative structure.

In addition to the casting, in *NO* the medium itself becomes an indexical anchor. Footage of the actual ads from the 1988 plebiscite and other archive material, such as Pinochet being embraced by Jimmy Carter, Ronald Reagan, Margaret Thatcher and Pope John Paul II, amount to 30 per cent of the film.[56] These are meshed with new scenes, shot using the same material, tools and style. Even though the archive look is extended to the whole film, the boundedness of the NO campaign clips clearly delineate which parts are archival and which form part of the diegesis.

Shot with a 1983 U-matic video camera, the new scenes flaunt the idiosyncrasies of this particular medium – overexposure, discolouring or bright but bleeding colours, narrow depth of field, flickers and flares, low resolution – and the clips faithfully reproduce aesthetic mannerisms and the style of the era, such as a tendency to frame single figures and small groups recorded in close-ups and medium shots. In interviews, Larraín described how he did not want the historical footage to 'interrupt' and break the illusion of the film, and Benson-Allott suggests that Larraín creates a 'cohesive experience of a media moment rather than an historical truth... By making his fiction look archival, he underscores the fictive quality of the archive and of politics in general'.[57]

Expanding on this argument, I suggest the film makes possible an experience of a *historical moment* that seems real precisely because it is so consciously fictional: both the film and the original NO campaign are clearly media creations. Having aged, video footage is coded as a material that has 'lived'. This appeal of and nostalgia for an old form which, paradoxically, seems more stable due to a materiality that guarantees decay, can then also be considered a reaction to digital technology, and the ephemeral character of the digital, as a yearning for a 'sensuous connection to physical reality in a universe dominated by simulation and information saturation'.[58]

The 'truthiness' of video constitutes a specific aesthetics which evokes particular sensibilities and invites a certain reading, as 'grainy moving images have become a marker of the real'.[59] Yet the way in which such material support is culturally embedded also inflects on the mode of attention these media invoke. How to read a certain aesthetics and materiality is a negotiation, evoking not intrinsic qualities but rather culturally or nationally specific potentialities, which depend on historically particular reception contexts.[60]

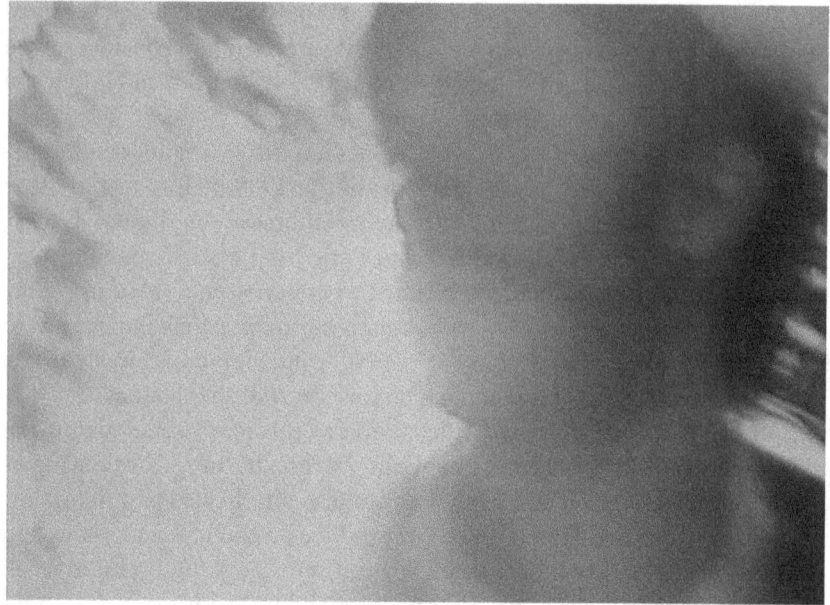

Figure 8.4 *NO*.

Video in *NO* is included not only as an obsolete object *inside* the film but as an *active*, performing partner, testifying not only to a general pastness but also a *culturally specific* history or identity. Video images were used by the regime to spread disinformation, but also as a weapon of resistance. Alongside documentary and photography, U-matic, VHS-C, Hi-8, Super VHS and Betacam video helped shape an alternative 'imaginary' of Chilean society by developing a language for the *NO* campaign and defined the way in which Chilean documentaries were made during the 1980s and 1990s.[61] This collective social imaginary and cultural history resonates strongly in a Chilean viewing context, harnessed by the object qua object, by emphasising the style and specific look of the medium.

The now apparent limitations of video – failures, glitches, overexposure – help to experience the 'thingness' of the transporting medium. The interruption causes us to look not through but *at* the object in its opacity; its qualities come into sharp relief.[62] Thus, in opposition to the logic of immediacy which 'dictates that the medium itself should disappear', the medium in *NO* is determinedly present. Precisely by drawing attention to itself, this hypermediation makes us 'aware of the artificiality of the original'.[63] In other words, the pronounced mistakes remind us that this is a mediated representation of history.

This aesthetic strategy offers a political critique by commenting on historical progress or lack thereof, on the historical experience of deception, hoax and absence of images. Reading Chile's history in dialogue with its media history, the form(at)s of *NO* make us aware of the constructed nature of the image and the inherited claims to a transparent truth attached to it, denaturalising the presumed normality of the present and drawing attention to the gaps in the official construction of history.

The link between a specific medium identity and specific audiences can be further refined by recent reassessments of nostalgia, which emphasise how its affective powers contain critical and even transformative potential to challenge hegemonic historical narratives or notions of progress.[64] Such nostalgia provides a 'space of *shameless* emotion and longing', not 'a freedom from memory but a freedom to remember, to choose the narratives of the past and *remake them*'.[65] Remaking, of course, implies an element of fiction, while it is the excess of emotion, its *shamelessness*, which can provide a valuable critical tool. Nostalgia never pretends to be objective. Allowing nostalgia a place in critical analysis provides a corrective to the historical devaluation of emotion as separate from and inferior to the faculties of reason where 'to be emotional is to have one's judgment affected'.[66] Etymologically a pain for a *place*, the critical potential of nostalgic longing resides in its capacity, or even insistence, to imagine a temporally or spatially alternative world.

In the context examined here, nostalgia also provides yet another layer of Poblete's 'supplementarity'. Rather than looking at the image in terms of representation, *NO* uses the surface of its own medium, the skin of its metaphorical 'body', to strategically evoke a nostalgic mode across generations and uneven memory landscapes. The materiality of video, and its evocation of a foregone temporality, may trigger subjective memories for different audiences, including non-Chilean ones, as such footage is associated with home movies, family memories and the emotional and sensual experience triggered by feelings of intimacy, as Martine Beugnet points out: 'It is the material and aesthetic characteristics of the medium [of video] itself that endow its images with a specific corporeal and synesthetic appeal'.[67]

The format seems able to create affective and nostalgic effects even for those who did not experience the medium when it was new. Roger Odin describes how home movies are able to evoke such an emotional appeal, even when we are not in the image – 'these images are a little like me and they speak to me of people like me'[68] – but he criticises this affective trend, 'When I see a document that I know to be excerpted from a home movie, I have a tendency not to ask the truth question.'[69] By contrast, what

I argue is that the medium itself can be asked perhaps not *the*, but *a* 'truth question'. As an historical emotion, both in the sense of an emotion with its proper history and one that is acquired and learned, nostalgia reads differently across different audiences. *NO*'s aesthetic quotes imitate and cite the audiovisual products of the era as a style to make it possible for the audience 'to feel what it was possible to feel [then]', not unlike Dyer's suggestions with regard to pastiche, an aesthetic strategy that 'suggests that we can enter into the feelings of our forebears through immersion in their art'.[70]

In *NO*, the nostalgic mode is activated not towards identification with the characters, but to invite the viewer to something resembling an affective identification, to 'feel close' to the iconic 1988 documentary footage and to the medium itself. *NO*'s protagonist is not an entirely sympathetic character – a mediocre father, indifferent to politics, a careerist who embraces capitalism and consumer culture: 'phlegmatic, apolitical, and depressed', an anti-hero on his way to a divorce.[71] Where we remain emotionally disengaged from the characters in the film, the affective relationship to the material is both personal and potentially communal, 'liberated' from the vicissitudes of narrative immersion and anthropocentric discourse. Kinaesthetic empathy towards objects may well include a strong affective relation between audience and the metaphorical 'body' of a film – as when Marks speaks of 'loving a disappearing image', and Nagib of an '*identification* through cinephilia, rather than through manipulation and illusionistic catharsis'.[72]

The nostalgic register helps account for cultural variation in affective response and attitude towards a medium. Bypassing identification with historical personnel, this strategy invites us to relate sensually and affectively to the images, and through them, to the past. Both *Nostalgia* and *NO* use media history to look askance at general history and historiography. In *Nostalgia*, the cinematic medium helps render tangible invisible processes of memory or the passing of time, evoking recent challenges to the anthropocentric framing of history, letting objects speak as enchanted witnesses, whereas *NO*, by letting the medium speak, helps the viewer become aware of naturalised assumptions regarding historical progress.

* * *

Many Southern Cone documentaries, prominently including Guzmán's films, are self-consciously planned as and have become part of their country's archive. Centrally built around the surviving images and their use by the resistance, such films construct 'a testimonial space … an entire visual and auditory arsenal for mourning work'.[73] (Guzmán's position in these memory debates and his sense of his own films' importance have been subject to numerous critical interventions in Chile.[74]) Guzmán's documentation is partly a rescue of memories and their bearers from suppression and displacement, partly the *creation* of a type of 'poetic' archive, through the filmic spaces and objects, and eventually, by the existence of the film itself as a document and mediator of public memory.

While the idea of such a cinematic, poetic archive recalls Rosenstone's questions on film as method of historical inquiry and the legitimacy of film as *document* – 'Can a metaphoric or symbolic truth, a poetic truth, similar to that of oral history ... take precedence over specific items of data and documentation?'[75] – the suggestion that some images may expand but not surpass the archive is indebted to Jaimie Baron's notion of the 'archival effect'. Building on Vivian Sobchack's notion of a 'documentary consciousness' – defined neither by object nor style but by a viewer's attitude towards the screen – Jaimie Baron has reframed archival documents as an 'archival consciousness ... not as objects with inherent qualities but as a spectatorial experience or a relationship between viewer and text'.[76]

In a context where the authority of the archive is being challenged, not only on ontological grounds but also as material praxis, in the tension or rupture between the archive and its subsequent use, the creation of such an alternative archive makes sense. In Chile, the state of the archive remains politically charged. For reasons ranging from the 'absence of a conversationist conscience [and state policies]', to intentional or accidental destruction of culture and documentation, falsifying, neutralising, excluding, marginalising and killing by neglect, Chile's cinematographic archive faces a perilous existence.[77]

In reference to the idea of poetic justice, this kind of 'cinematic poetic archive' (which from now on will be referred to as 'cine-poetic archive') offers a way to address a lack of, or lack of access to material. Proliferating outside of official archives, these texts gain authority through a certain kind of encounter with the spectator which produces an affective experience of 'historical presence'.[78] This pool of images renders transparent both its fictional dimension *as well* as its rootedness in the historical real. Shifting between original and restaged registers, archival and *faux* footage both question and affirm the original. Such images are reflexive, and openly performative in the sense identified by Bruzzi, *pace* Butler and J. L. Austin 'namely, that they function as utterances that simultaneously both describe and perform an action'.[79] These images stand in for the parts that are known to be missing, performing both by offering some level of solace and by pointing to the absence of an original through their artifice. This establishes a kind of authenticity that is aware of its own limitations and that does not seek to replace what has been lost or erased. Not to be seen in opposition to traditional forms of documentary, this cine-poetic archive exceeds the (filming of) actual artefacts to encompass fictional additions, re-enactments and re-imaginings of resonant events, such as the Viña killings in *Pena* and the autopsy of Allende's body in *Post Mortem*.

Notes

1. Hediger, 'Lost in Space and Found in a Fold'; cf. Doane, *The Emergence of Cinematic Time*.
2. Cubitt, 'Archive Ethics'.
3. Wolf, 'Subjunctive Documentary', p. 290; Parikka, *What Is Media Archaeology?*, p. 120.
4. Kay Hoffmann in Manovich, 'To Lie and to Act', p. 166.
5. Elsaesser, 'Digital Hollywood', p. 317. Of course, one reason for audience trust is digital images' frequent 'mimicry' of photography which creates indexicality as an '*effect* of the digitally produced image ... a consequence of its resemblance to an imagined referent'. Rosen in Page, 'Digital mimicry'; Philip Rosen coined the term 'digital mimicry' to describe how the digital imitates photography and other 'preexisting compositional forms of imagery'. Belton, 'If Film is Dead'.
6. Rodowick, *Virtual Life of Film*, p. 11.
7. Doane, 'The Indexical and the Concept of Medium Specificity', p. 129. Cf. Gauthier, 'What Will Film Studies Be?'.
8. Doane, 'Indexicality: Trace and Sign', p. 5.
9. Cited in Quinlivan, 'Breath Control', p. 160.
10. Connor, 'Sounding out Film'.
11. Rick Altman in Lury, *Interpreting Television*, p. 57.
12. Schoonover, *Brutal Vision*, pp. 32–42.
13. Mulvey, *Death 24x*, p. 188. Gunning, 'Moving Away from the Index', p. 100, emphasis added.
14. Gunning, 'Moving Away from the Index', p. 42.
15. Richard, *Políticas y Estéticas*, p. 166; Sontag, *On Photography*, p. 15; Hirsch, 'Surviving Images', p. 21. Gunning includes audio material in his discussion of the ghostly. Gunning, 'To Scan a Ghost', p. 117.
16. For a film discussing how *La Esmeralda* has become a stark symbol of ongoing impunity, and especially the case of tortured and killed British-Chilean priest Michael Woodward, see *The Dark Side of the White Lady* (Patricio Henríquez, 2006).
17. Sarlo, *Tiempo pasado*, p. 287.
18. Smith, 'Larraín, *Post Mortem*'.
19. Author interview with producer Xavier Guerrero in October 2013.
20. Stijn Reijnders in Pribram, *Emotions, Genre, and Justice*, p. 113.
21. Ribeiro de Menezes, 'Memory Beyond the Anthropocene', p. 102.
22. Martin-Jones, 'Archival Landscapes', p. 711.

23. Cf. Buck-Morss, *The Dialectics of Seeing*.
24. Martin-Jones, 'Archival Landscapes', p. 718.
25. Darke, 'Desert of the Disappeared'.
26. Marleen Stoessel in Hansen, 'Benjamin, Cinema and Experience', p. 212.
27. Nichols, *Representing Reality*, p. 232.
28. Martin-Jones, 'Archival Landscapes', p. 716; cf. Rodríguez, 'Framing ruins' and Guynn, *Unspeakable Histories* and his criticism of Guzmán's 'disjunctive' style.
29. Franco, *Cruel Modernity*, p. 9.
30. Kopytoff, *The Cultural Biography of Things*; Richard, *Políticas y Estéticas*, pp. 165–72. Many of the victims came from poor communities where photography was not widely available, and it was difficult to amass images for all the disappeared. Apart from the infamous burning of films, books, and film stock, as documented in *La Ciudad de los Fotógrafos* (Sebastián Moreno, 2006), the photographers as well as the photographs themselves taken were attacked, culminating in a brief spell where photographs in magazines were forbidden altogether. For the role of photography in the resistance see also *Imagen Latente* (Pablo Perelman, 1987), which was screened at the Festival de La Habana and then immediately censored in Chile until 1990, according to its page on the website *cinechile*, 'Imagen Latente'.
31. Dorfman, 'Globalizing Compassion', pp. 276–7. Cf. Bossay, 'Cineastas al rescate'.
32. Gordon, *Ghostly Matters*, p. 110.
33. Ibid.
34. Déotte, 'El arte en la época de la desaparición', p. 156.
35. Ahmed, *Cultural Politics of Emotion*, p. 45. Similarly, D'Aloia argues that we can even feel 'empathy' towards objects: 'empathy can also concern relationship to objects rather than exclusively intersubjective relationships with other people'. D'Aloia, 'Cinematic Empathy', p. 19.
36. Kristeva, *Powers of Horror*, p.2.
37. Elsaesser, 'World Cinema', p. 9.
38. Mulvey, *Death 24x*, p. 186.
39. Lavery, 'Time-Lapse Photography', p. 6.
40. Wolf, 'Subjunctive Documentary', p. 274.
41. D'Aloia, 'Cinematic Empathy', p. 19.
42. Zielinksi, *Deep Time of the Media*.
43. Parikka, *What is Media Archaelogy?*, pp. 11–13.
44. O'Hehir, 'How you overthrow a dictator'.
45. Eminent critics include Manuel Antonio Garretón, who called *NO* 'ideological trash' and Raquel Olea, who detected a 'perversion of the truth'. Garretón in *Emol*, 'basura ideológica'; Olea, '*NO* ... La perversión de la verdad en la pelicula' (13 August 2012; this article used to be available from the Radio Tierra website, but this has closed down, along with the radio station); cf. Rohter 'One Prism'. Part of the virulence in *NO*'s reception might be owing

to the historical moment of its release, which coincided with the election of the right-wing government of Sebastián Piñera, after decades of rule by the Concertación, <http://www.radiotierra.cl/node/4741> (accessed 13 August 2012)
46. Jones, 'No'.
47. Director Larraín observes that 'we said no to Pinochet but yes to his system. There's a piece of the Yes that won'. Palacios, 'The Problems of Fiction'.
48. 'el discurso oficial es el de la publicidad', Lübbert in Villarroel, *La voz*, p. 136.
49. 'Lo que van a ver a continuación está enmarcado en el contexto social del Chile actual ... Hoy Chile piensa en su futuro.'
50. Urrutia, '*NO*'.
51. Willemen in Jeffries, 'Comics at 300 Frames Per Second', p. 237.
52. Mouesca calls this 'mania de la copia'. Mouesca, *Plano secuencia*, p. 167. Cf. Schmöller, *Kino in Chile*.
53. 'Es la copia de la copia de la copia.'
54. Benson-Allott, 'Appropriate to the Conditions', pp. 61–2.
55. Ernst and Parikka, *Digital Memory and the Archive*, p. 55.
56. Rohter, 'One Prism'.
57. Benson-Allott, 'Appropriate to the Conditions', p. 62.
58. Rodowick, *Virtual Life of Film*, p. 158.
59. Scott, 'Neo-Neo Realism'; Chun, *Programmed Visions*, p. 68.
60. Cf. Belton, 'Psychology of the Photographic, Cinematic, Televisual, and Digital Image'; Brunsdon, 'It's a Film'.
61. Liñero, A*puntes para una historia del video en Chile*.
62. Brown, 'Thing Theory'.
63. Bolter and Grusin, *Remediation*, p. 4 and p. 47.
64. Boym, *Future of Nostalgia;* Cook, *Screening the Past*; Niemeyer, *Media and Nostalgia*; Sprengler, *Screening Nostalgia*.
65. Boym, *Future of Nostalgia*, p. 54, emphasis added.
66. Ahmed, *Cultural Politics of Emotion*, p. 3.
67. Beugnet, Cinema *and Sensation*, p. 133.
68. Odin, 'Reflections on the Family Home Movie', p. 264.
69. Ibid.
70. Dyer, *Pastiche*, p. 178.
71. O'Hehir, 'How You Overthrow a Dictator'. Based loosely on Antonio Skármeta's play 'The Plebiscite', *NO* deliberately changed the qualities of the play's protagonist, who is fiftyish, politically engaged, idealistic and happily married.
72. Nagib et al., T*heorizing World Cinema*, p. 156. Cf. Barker, *The Tactile Eye*.
73. Aguilar, *New Argentine Film*, p. 156.
74. Klubock, 'History and Memory in Neoliberal Chile', p. 276. Guzmán's acute sense of his own films as archive can be seen in *Chile, Obstinate Memory* (1997), in which he remediates his own trilogy *La Batalla de Chile* (*1975– 1979*) by staging, and documenting, an encounter between his film as archive

and a contemporary audience. To the dismay of other members of his team, Guzmán did not consent to give his *Batalla de Chile* to Chile's national Museum of Memory for free. The museum has established a bottom line of not paying for any film, on the grounds that they cannot pay everyone and that it would be impossible to establish a price for other memory objects, often of inestimable personal value, such as last remnants or clothes of a disappeared. This information is based on interviews with former and current audiovisual directors at the museum, José Manuel Rodríguez Leal and Maria Teresa Viera-Gallo in Santiago, Chile, June/July 2013. Guzmán on the other hand, takes a stance against the notion that documentary should be given for free, which he perceives as the devaluation of the documentary. By withholding the film from the public sphere, however, he also participates in the commodification of memory and contributes to the privatisation and limitation of memory to those who are able to pay for it (*Nostalgia* was shown only on Sky in Chile, hence available only to those who could pay for satellite dishes).

75. Rosenstone, *History on Film/Film on History*, p. 4.
76. Baron, 'Archive Effect', p. 102.
77. Jacobsen and Lorenzo, *La imagen quebrada*; Traverso and Crowder-Taraborrelli, 'Political Documentary Cinema in the Southern Cone'. Villarroel and Mardones, *Señales contra el olvido*. Troncoso, *El espejo quebrado*.
78. 'Baron, 'Archive Effect', p. 102.
79. Bruzzi, New Documentary, p. 186.

Conclusion

The doppelgänger of visible, spectacular horror – the mediated terrorist attacks and execution videos, designed for widespread dissemination – is the terror of the invisible. In the common imagination, terrorists threaten by 'passing', like Baudrillard's shadowy figures,[1] sleepers of uncertain quantity or power, contagious, deceiving and multiplying like a virus. Torture, on the other hand, makes visible: it materialises or reifies a truth through the tortured body, and so serves as the symbolic antidote to terrorism.

And yet, the power of factual contemporary torture relies fundamentally on being half-known and half-invisible, an open secret. In such situations, where information is censored and facts are disputed or obscured by visual excess, there is immense political potential in striving for visibility and transparency. In both sets of cinematic texts explored here, the films seek to express the invisible of history, that which is forgotten, erased, obscured, but also to push categories of what counts as perceivable beyond the visible, from film as collective experience of emotional repercussions, creating a sense of shared social pain, to enlarging the frames of our perception, the relation between visual mediation and reality.

The Invisibilities of Torture in US and Chilean Cinema

The first part of this book investigated what kinds of images cinema has created within the situation of visual excess – if not in variety, then in quantity – that resulted from the circulation of the Abu Ghraib and Guantánamo images. The films discussed here focus centrally on the *visibilities* of torture, showing typical scenes, narratives and images of torture, and often operating with the terrorist attacks of 9/11 as reference point. Increased surveillance and the unequal access to and distribution of visual information express differentials in knowledge and power, and anxieties about the failures and potential manipulations of machines. Yet these films, too, explore invisibilities in the shape of epistemological vulnerabilities, emerging from the superimposition of clichéd representations which impede understanding, known but denied facts, verbal pirouettes which by now have become alternative facts and false statements.

In the second part of the book, the analytical focus shifted from the visible towards the invisible, towards other ways of accessing the past and of anchoring our cinematic experience. Beyond the framework of aspirational political visibility and accurate representation, the close readings of the films showed that invisibilities can be made known in many different shapes, and not all of these rely on the visual. For instance, in *Post Mortem*'s and *Manero*'s off-screen space, the unseen and invisible become an overbearing presence. These films explore the traumatic national past and its repercussions of emotional pain in the present, the borders of visibility, socially circulating emotions, sticking to some bodies and not to others. Where the US films position themselves in relation to the overbearing *presence* of (some) images, the Chilean films explored here lack confirmation through *images* of the body in pain, the absence of visual evidence. By conveying this *presence of absence*, these films extend the traumatic feeling of 'not knowing', 'not having' the body.

At the same time, in both cases, the films use the capacities of cinema to emphasise the *limitations* of the visual to authenticate historical reality. Translating invisibilities means giving a shape, body, form, a metaphor. Yet precisely this body, in cinema, is experiencing a transnational trend of 'visual stress', as Garrett Stewart suggests, one of the discernible consequences of the historical shift in the cinematic medium's own material constitution.[2] These films' plots are often 'obsessed [with] human temporality and human memory'[3] and, I would add, human perception, converging medium and theme. Through images that are self-aware and performative, through aesthetic hybridity or alliances of documentary and fictional modes, the films mimic, even perform, such 'regime changes' in current media. These formal explorations were here both contextualised within their respective national contexts and considered in relation or as responses to a more general challenge to the domination of the visual epistemological. Locating these films' disparate aesthetic responses in a similar moment of epistemological quest should not collapse all differences between them. Instead, the hope had been that the transnational link may help us understand something fundamental about how we currently relate to our past and present reality through our images.

This also means that the ethical question about torture on-screen has been reframed in this volume, from the focus on how to avoid appropriation and to create empathetic identification in the viewer towards the question of how to legitimise belief in the truth of a representation – whether documentary or fiction – in light of often unreliable, biased or contested documentation. In reference to 'post-continuity' cinema, Shaviro suggests that the understanding of spatiotemporal relations through continuity editing has become less central to articulate the narrative, elevating other structures: 'What unites [post-continuity films] is not just a bunch of techniques and formal tics, but a kind of shared episteme (Michel Foucault) or structure of feeling (Raymond Williams)'.[4]

Both an epistemological quest and a socially expressive affectivity are also shared characteristics in the films analysed here, though they have not been explored under the rubric of post-continuity. Their subject matter feeds into an epistemological quest going beyond the question of indexicality, beyond the question of material basis of analogue and digital imaginations,[5] towards discourses on and the generation of knowledge per se. In summarising how these poles of emotional politics and epistemological quests take form in the examples analysed in this volume, I hope to have highlighted how they impact on our understanding of torture through the films.

The Politics of Affect

A major impetus for my research journey was to develop a political critique of and through films that would go beyond representation- and identification-centred approaches. Representation matters, and countering historical invisibilities continues to be a political act against marginalisation and erasure, an argument forcefully made for the historical protest against the dictatorship: 'Making [the regime's] violence globally visible was a particularly apt response to disappearance because that extreme form of repression originates, in fact, in a strategy of a dictatorship that had a global component from the start'.[6]

Yet films can also reconfigure what is considered invisible, unspeakable or imaginable, thus disrupting the rules or limits of the playing field, helping to 'sketch new configurations of what can be seen, what can be said and what can be thought and, consequently, a new landscape of the possible'.[7]

Butler's critique of media frames aims precisely at the affective dimension, arguing that these differentiate 'the cries we can hear from those we cannot, the sights we can see from those we cannot, and likewise at the level of touch and even smell'.[8] Turning to affective and material registers can expand what we can 'perceive as existing'.

And indeed, rather than comprehending by seeing the world at a distance, some of these films hold us close and encourage us to feel our way in. Instead of fostering empathic identification only with *characters*, these films create an affective space: sound in *Pena*, the time-lapse in *Nostalgia* and breath in *Carne* as sensual forms of looking. Evoking body and sensory memory, they involve the viewer physically and object to the 'distanciation from the body and to the objectification and control of self and others'.[9]

Here, the analysis of the Chilean films and the concept of 'presence of absence' excavates absences in the US films as well, beyond the readily apparent failure of many of them to give more space to the gazes and voices of the immediate victims of torture under US responsibility. For instance, attention to the affective registers of visuality present new aspects for reading the US films' torture scenes. In *Zero*, the embodied perception through the anonymous first-person camera and in *Syriana*, the sensual, haptic visual language belongs to the victim, in contrast to the more spectacular and distanced torture scenes in *Rendition* or the self-reflexive focus on the *mediation* of torture in *Body*. Offering such a visceral somatic experience projects an epistemological entry point to affective structures.

The analysis of the television shows emphasises the social dimension of affective registers, encouraging audience involvement through growing and changing relations between viewer and characters. Fostered by melodramatic traditions, increasingly complicated storylines and longer screen time available throughout several seasons, the format of serial television allows the exploration of ambiguities through changing perspectives and uncertain knowledge, the examination of collective structures and systemic problems. As far as these films make a 'historical structure of feeling' emotionally perceivable to the viewer, they enable not only an individual encounter with history between public and private memory(-ies), but also hold the potential for an emotional public space, a sense of shared social pain, sometimes perhaps merely a space of ambivalence.

Epistemological Quests

Shaviro's claim of a shared episteme reflects on the transformation of vision and what counts as visual evidence. Elsaesser, for instance, links the 'crisis in representation' to how contemporary mainstream cinema

> meets the challenge of visibility and visualisation when more and more phenomena that govern our lives are not visible to the human eye because they are either too big or too small, too fast or too slow, or deal in magnitudes and quantities we cannot comprehend other than in visual metaphors.[10]

Similarly pondering the effects of a changed visual paradigm, Grusin suggests 'mediality' has supplanted 'representationality' in mass media: where the regime of representationality was concerned with truth or 'referential fidelity to its object', mediality is concerned 'with mobilising people or populations, or as Massumi and others would put it, with modulating affect'.[11] And yet, visual knowledge remains central. Programmatically, software scholar Wendy Chun urges to interrogate its precise changes:

> By interrogating ... the visual knowledge [software] perpetuates, we can move beyond the so-called crisis in indexicality toward understanding the new ways in which visual knowledge – seeing/visible reading as knowing – is being transformed and perpetuated, not simply rendered obsolete or displaced.[12]

Combining the analysis of these transformations of 'seeing/visible ... as knowing' and the category of the witness, human or material, a figure so central to theorisations of both torture and cinema, I suggest that the films and TV shows analysed here suggest at least two witnesses, whose material groundedness anchors their visual capacities: the body of the film text and the body of the spectators.

The investigation of one's own mediating 'body' characterises all these audiovisual texts – from the failing lie detectors and surveillance blank spots to the film *Zero* itself as a Rorschach test. Frequent references to the medium's own material base mediate anxieties about the reliability and selectivity of mechanically generated visual evidence, the disappearing index in today's audiovisual landscape, the effects of the decreasing dominance of the visual on the visual image's capacity to establish a sense of authenticity and authority. The films always ask the viewer: what kind of truth do you see here, and how certain can you be of what you see?

Far from assuming a straightforward procession from visual evidence to knowledge, these films foreground their own representational difficulties as well as the ambivalences of watching. *Standard* for instance not only highlights the mediation, selection and framing of the Abu Ghraib images, but also explores the problems digital media pose for photographic epistemology, deconstructing the known forms of producing knowledge through photography by adding metadata.

* * *

In her discussion of 'empathic vision', which she defines as 'a process of embodied perception through to a kind of critical awareness', Jill Bennett ends on a political outlook:

> The registration of affect is ... a manner of doing politics ... And it is certainly timely for art theory to review its approach to the political at a point where the old 'communication' models that rest on the assumption that content is transmitted via text and image begin to haunt discussions around imagery relating to war, violence, terror and trauma ... the preponderance of work conducting its politics through an

imagery of affectively charged space signals, in itself, what amounts to a theoretical strategy in practice: a counter to the return to the real.[13]

Bennett contrasts art that works with affectively charged space with art that returns to the referential. But the 'imagery of affectively charged space' does not have to be read in opposition to a 'return to the real'. Concurrent with highlighting gaps of knowledge and epistemological uncertainty, the films also often insist on a strange fidelity to truth: offered through the cinematic body, anchored through the affective response of the spectator.

Some texts, like *Standard Operating Procedure* or *Los Archivos* supplement or differentiate existing official texts with additional images. Culturally specific knowledge may even be encoded in the specific properties of the media formats being used, as in *NO*, where the unmasked imitation of the historical material acknowledges both the historicity of the past mediation and the present moment of production. Such staged confrontations between ways of producing the real point to the distance between then and now, presenting an argument not only about the cinematic past, but also about that past's political projects. (Compare how the recent film *Vice* (Adam McKay, 2018), similarly to *Zero*, marries fidelity to verisimilitude – most notably Christian Bale's embodied performance of Dick Cheney, including considerable weight gain – with permanent meta-critical reflections on and parodies of typical cinematic framings, an increasing emphasis on gaps in information, and the inability of film to offer a 'complete' account.)

In this way, the films also assert their own importance: their fictional approximations provide a cine-poetic archive for absent images, artistic responses to blank spots and erasures in public history and official memory, reimaginations of past events that can offer a relevant intervention, and as materially embodied objects, films themselves provide the anchoring presence. Used as a cine-poetic archive or in a palimpsestic fashion, such images draw attention to the gaps in the official construction of history, inviting the viewer to look again at the familiar, and recreates images and stories which have been invisible or 'missing' from the canon, offering a partial, symbolic recovery of such 'small' stories. These films openly acknowledge their own mediated and fictional dimension, but *also* insist on being rooted in the historical real. While the emerging truths are not absolute, their plurality does not capitulate to deconstruction or relativisation.

Not only are we often watching characters who are watching and being watched, but both the cine-poetic archive and hyper-mediated images of war or operational images throw back the gaze at the viewer. Images may tell us that something happened, but not what it means; and the 'blind' output of the camera as 'scientific witness' needs human decoding, first within the diegesis and, eventually, through an extradiegetic spectator. This need for visual literacy connects the embodied spectator with diegetic moments of expertise and reflection – the image-decoding CIA agents in *Zero*, the failing lie detector in *Homeland* and the meta-data analyses in *Standard* – or with the cine-poetic archive, paratextual information on profilmic objects such as the emperor's saddle in *Danza* or cultural knowledge about actors' bodies and biographies in Larraín's trilogy.

The Spectator and the Torture of Others

All the audiovisual texts explored here have to address the ethical dimension expressed in Sontag's question, namely, how to respond to the pain of others. As both torture and cinema need an audience, viewers have often been framed as inherently complicit, repeating visual power relations and subjugations. But this problem of complicity might also be the solution.

Each film emphasises the role of the media in the process of historical narrativisation, the nature of cinema as spectacle and visual dispositif, and the performance of watching and witnessing. They also align the viewer with these activities, as the audience is watching people watching media: television in *Los 80*; surveillance cameras in *Rendition*; experts in *Zero*; the Abu Ghraib images in *Standard*; archival footage in *Nostalgia* and *No*.

While the facts of historical truth must be confirmed and defended, we also need spaces where the plurality of different subjective experiences and its resulting tensions can play out. Such spaces can at times feel uncomfortable, sometimes even painfully complacent, and yet precisely in this space of indeterminacy, cinema can be potentially emancipatory, empowering and 'genuinely political – that is, as cinema'.[14] As far as these films enable such a space to explore ambivalence, the spectator – *any* spectator – is positioned alongside with those who are working to make sense of their history. Layering their content for different audiences, the films are able to speak to different transnational constituencies. Instead of searching for a 'transnational, a global historical literacy or global historical understanding'[15] in visual media, by giving 'an opportunity to exercise ethical judgement' to an extra-national Western, self-proclaimed 'humanist audience'[16] of privilege, it might be more useful to hold space for the *glocal* historical imagination, the vernacular character of knowledge.

Rather than remaining with the 'pedagogical model' of art,[17] and its analysis of representation in terms of historical veracity or distortion, the films empower spectatorial agency by demonstrating that there is no such thing as an impartial gaze. These films do not strive towards determining the truth of a transparent reality; their trace is an imprint on us. The invitation to an emotional experience of the past described above is filtered through and fractured by the perceptually diminished world of the protagonists or the mediating machine. The films highlight the discrepancy between these two kinds of eyes, the mechanical and the human. While people filter material selectively, recording devices are indiscriminate, perceptually superior, but they fragment and distort, too, and sometimes even need expert decoding. The machine also ensures that there is always already more in the image than intended by the filmmakers (or the photographers in Abu Ghraib), a surplus of information, the excess of Benjamin's optical unconscious. But only a human and embodied reader is endowed with the possibility of an understanding and compassionate gaze, able to acknowledge what Butler calls our common vulnerability, to give a compassionate gaze on obscure characters and on history itself. Such gestures ultimately affirm the power of the spectator – at the same time, these images ask *all* its viewers to take a stance. We have all seen by proxy, and we cannot claim ignorance.[18]

Notes

1. At a lecture series in Vienna, Baudrillard, modifying Marx, claimed that 'a spectre is haunting the global world order – the specter of terrorism'. ('Ein Gespenst geht um in der globalen Weltordnung – das Gespenst des Terrorismus.') 'Jean Baudrillard'.
2. Stewart, *Framed Time*, p. 8.
3. Ibid., p. 3.
4. Shaviro, 'Post-Continuity', p. 60.
5. Cf. Kara, 'Beasts of the Digital Wild' and Page, 'Digital mimicry'.
6. Dorfman, 'Globalizing Compassion', p. 277.
7. Rancière, *The Emancipated Spectator*, p. 103.
8. Butler, *Frames of War*, p. 51.
9. Sobchack, *Carnal Thoughts*, p. 133.
10. Elsaesser, *Film History as Media Archaeology*, p. 303.
11. Grusin, *Premediation*, p. 79.
12. Chun, *Programmed Visions*, p. 92.
13. Bennett, *Empathic Vision*, pp. 152–3. Cf. Grusin, 'Post-Cinematic Atavism'.
14. Aguilar, *New Argentine Film*, p. 123.
15. de Groot, 'Illusions of History', p. 271. Cf. Rosenstone, *History on film/film on history*.
16. Schoonover, *Brutal Vision*, pp. xiv–xvi.
17. Rancière, *Dissensus*, p. 136.
18. Shapin quoted in Leach, 'Scientific Witness', p. 194.

Bibliography

Aaron, Michele (2007), *Spectatorship: The Power of Looking On*, London: Wallflower.
'About those black sites' (2013), *The New York Times*, 17 February, <https://www.nytimes.com/2013/02/18/opinion/about-those-black-sites.html> (accessed 3 July 2018).
Adelman, Rebecca A. (2012), 'Tangled Complicities: Extracting Knowledge from Images of Abu Ghraib', in Esther Cohen, Leona Toker, Manuela Consonni and Otniel E. Dror (eds), *Knowledge and Pain*, Amsterdam/New York: Rodopi/Brill Press, pp. 353–79.
Adelman, Rebecca A. (2014), 'Atrocity and Aporiae: Teaching the Abu Ghraib Images, Teaching Against Transparency', *Cultural Studies ↔ Critical Methodologies*, 14.1, pp. 29–39.
Agamben, Giorgio (1998), *Homo Sacer: Sovereign Power and Bare Life*, Stanford: Stanford University Press.
Aguilar, Gonzalo Moisés (2011), *New Argentine Film: Other Worlds*, New York: Palgrave Macmillan.
Ahmed, Sara (2004), *The Cultural Politics of Emotion*, Edinburgh: Edinburgh University Press.
Allen, Richard (2014), '"There Is Not One Realism, but Several Realisms": A Review of Opening Bazin', *October*, pp. 63–78.
Améry, Jean (1999), *At the Mind's Limits: Contemplations by a Survivor on Auschwitz and its Realities*, London: Granta Books.
Anable, Aubrey (2018), *Playing with Feelings. Video Games and Affects*, Minneapolis, London: University of Minnesota Press.
Andrews, David (2010), 'Conference Report: Reframing *Standard Operating Procedure*: Errol Morris and the Creative Treatment of Abu Ghraib', *Jump Cut*, 52.
Arthur, Paul (2008), 'The Horror: Paul Arthur on Errol Morris's *Standard Operating Procedure*', *Artforum International*, 46, pp. 111–12.
Avelar, Idelber (1999), *The Untimely Present: Postdictatorial Latin American Fiction and the Task of Mourning*, Durham, NC: Duke University Press.
Arce, Luz (2004), *The Inferno: A Story of Terror and Survival in Chile*, Madison: The University of Wisconsin Press.
Bächler, Maja (2013), *Inszenierte Bedrohung: Folter Im US-Amerikanischen Kriegsfilm 1979–2009*, Frankfurt: Campus.

Bacon, Henry (2015), *The Fascination of Film Violence*, Basingstoke: Palgrave Macmillan.
Balázs, Béla (2011), *Early Film Theory: Visible Man and the Spirit of Film*, Erica Carter (ed.) and Rodney Livingstone (trans.), New York: Berghahn.
Ballengee, Jennifer (2009), *The Wound and the Witness: The Rhetoric of Torture*, Albany: SUNY Press.
Barker, Jennifer M. (2009), *The Tactile Eye: Touch and the Cinematic Experience*, Berkeley: University of California Press.
Baron, Jaimie (2012), 'The Archive Effect: Archival Footage as an Experience of Reception', *Projections*, 6.2, pp. 102–20.
Barraza, Andrea López (2011), *Nuevo Cine Chileno 2005–2010*, PhD thesis at the Universidad de Chile.
Barril, Claudia and José M. Santa Cruz (2011), *El cine que fue: 100 años de cine chileno*, Santiago de Chile: Editorial Arcis.
Barthes, Roland [1957] (1991), 'The Face of Garbo', in Roland Barthes, *Mythologies*, New York: Farrar, Straus and Giroux, pp. 56–7.
Bass, Thomas A. (2008), 'Counterinsurgency and Torture', *American Quarterly*, 60, pp. 233–40.
Bazin, André [1958–1965] (2005), *What Is Cinema?*, Berkeley: University of California Press.
Bégin, Richard (2014), 'Ceci Est Mon Image, Livrée Pour Vous', presentation at *FilmForum*, Gorizia.
Bellafante, Ginia (2007), 'In the *24* World, Family Is the Main Casualty', *The New York Times*, 20 May, <https://www.nytimes.com/2007/05/20/arts/television/20Bell.html> (accessed 8 March 2020).
Belton, John (2014a), 'If Film is Dead, What is Cinema?', *Screen*, 55.4, pp. 460–70.
Belton, John (2014b), 'Psychology of the Photographic, Cinematic, Televisual, and Digital Image', *New Review of Film and Television Studies*, 12, pp. 234–46.
Bennett, Jill (2005), *Empathic Vision: Affect, Trauma, and Contemporary Art*, Stanford: Stanford University Press.
Bennett, Jill and Rosanne Terese Kennedy (2003), *World Memory: Personal Trajectories in Global Time*, Basingstoke: Palgrave Macmillan.
Benson-Allott, Caetlin (2009), '*Standard Operating Procedure*: Mediating Torture', *Film Quarterly*, 62, pp. 39–44.
Benson-Allott, Caetlin (2013), 'An Illusion Appropriate to the Conditions. *NO* (Pablo Larraín, 2012)', *Film Quarterly*, 66.3, pp. 61–3.
Berlant, Lauren (2004), *Compassion: The Culture and Politics of an Emotion*, New York: Routledge.
Beugnet, Martine (2012), *Cinema and Sensation: French Film and the Art of Transgression*, Edinburgh: Edinburgh University Press.
Bevan, Alex (2015), 'The National Body, Women, and Mental Health in *Homeland*', *Cinema Journal*, 54.4, pp. 145–55.

Beverley, John (2009), 'Torture and Human Rights: A Paradoxical Relationship?', *Hispanic Issues Online*, 5.1, <http://hdl.handle.net/11299/182849> (accessed 7 July 2018).
Bilbija, Ksenija, and Leigh A. Payne (2011), *Accounting for Violence: Marketing Memory in Latin America*, Durham, NC: Duke University Press.
Bisama, Álvaro (2011), '*Los Archivos del Cardenal*: El alfabeto en los huesos', *Qué Pasa*, 6 June, <http://www.quepasa.cl/articulo/cultura/2011/07/6-6210-9-los-archivos-del-cardenal-el-alfabeto-en-los-huesos.shtml/> (accessed 1 December 2019).
Blackman, Lisa (2008), *The Body: The Key Concepts*, Oxford: Berg.
Blackman, Lisa (2012), *Immaterial Bodies: Affect, Embodiment, Mediation*, London: SAGE.
Bloch-Elkon, Yaeli and Brigitte Nacos (2014), 'News and Entertainment Media: Government's Big Helpers in the Selling of Counterterrorism', *Perspectives On Terrorism Online* 8.5, pp. 18–32.
Blondheim, Menahem and Tamar Liebes (2011), 'Archaic Witnessing and Contemporary News Media', in Paul Frosh, and Amit Pinchevski (eds), *Media Witnessing: Testimony in the Age of Mass Communication*, Basingstoke: Palgrave Macmillan, pp. 112–32.
Boltanski, Luc (1999), *Distant Suffering: Morality, Media and Politics*, Cambridge: Cambridge University Press.
Bolter, David and Richard Grusin (1999), *Remediation: Understanding New Media*, Cambridge, MA: MIT Press.
Bordwell, David (1999), 'The Art Cinema as a Mode of Film Practice', in Leo Braudy and Marshall Cohen (eds), *Film Theory and Criticism: Introductory Readings*, New York: Oxford University Press, pp. 716–24.
Bordwell, David (2002), 'Intensified Continuity: Visual Style in Contemporary American Film', *Film Quarterly*, 55, pp. 16–28.
Bond, Lucy (2015), *Frames of Memory After 9/11: Culture, Criticism, Politics, and Law*, Basingstoke: Palgrave.
Bossay, Claudia (2009), 'Cineastas al rescate de la memoria reciente chilena', *Imagofagia*, 4.
Bourke, Joanna (2014), *The Story of Pain: From Prayer to Painkillers*, Oxford: Oxford University Press.
Bowcott, Owen, Oliver Holmes and Erin Durkin (2018), 'John Bolton threatens war crimes court with sanctions in virulent attack', *The Guardian*, 10 September, <https://www.theguardian.com/us-news/2018/sep/10/john-bolton-castigate-icc-washington-speech> (accessed 23 July 2019).
Boym, Svetlana (2001), *The Future of Nostalgia*, New York: Basic Books.
Bradshaw, Peter (2007), 'Rendition', *The Guardian*, 19 October, <https://www.theguardian.com/film/2007/oct/19/thriller> (accessed 7 July 2018).
Brewer, John (2010), 'Reenactment and Neo-Realism', in Iain McCalman and Paul A. Pickering (eds), *Historical Reenactment from Realism to the Affective Turn*, Basingstoke: Palgrave Macmillan, 2010, pp. 79–89.

Broderick, Mick and Antonio Traverso (2011), *Interrogating Trauma: Collective Suffering in Global Arts and Media*, London: Routledge.
Brodsky, Joseph (1995), *On Grief and Reason: Essays*, London: Hamish Hamilton.
Brody, Richard (2012), 'The Deceptive Emptiness of *Zero Dark Thirty*', *The New Yorker*, 19 December, <https://www.newyorker.com/culture/richard-brody/the-deceptive-emptiness-of-zero-dark-thirty> (accessed 7 July 2018).
Bronfen, Elisabeth (2012), *Specters of War: Hollywood's Engagement with Military Conflict*, New Brunswick, NJ: Rutgers University Press.
Brown, Bill (2001), 'Thing Theory', *Critical Inquiry*, 28, pp. 1–22.
Brown, Michelle and Nicole Rafter (2013), 'Genocide Films, Public Criminology, Collective Memory', *British Journal of Criminology*, 53.6, pp. 1017–32.
Brown, Tom (2012), *Breaking the Fourth Wall: Direct Address in the Cinema*, Edinburgh: Edinburgh University Press.
Brown, Wendy (1995), *States of Injury: Power and Freedom in Late Modernity*, Princeton: Princeton University Press.
Bruck, Connie (2015), 'The Inside War', *The New Yorker*, 22 June, <https://www.newyorker.com/magazine/2015/06/22/the-inside-war> (accessed 7 July 2018).
Bruni, Frank (2012), 'Bin Laden, Torture and Hollywood', *The New York Times*, 8 December, <https://www.nytimes.com/2012/12/09/opinion/sunday/bruni-bin-laden-torture-and-hollywood.html> (accessed 7 July 2018).
Brunsdon, Charlotte (2012), '"It's a Film": Medium Specificity as Textual Gesture in *Red Road* and *The Unloved*', *Journal of British Cinema and Television*, 9, pp. 457–79.
Bruzzi, Stella (2006), *New Documentary*, London: Routledge.
Bruzzi, Stella (2014), keynote 'Restaging History; Revisiting Pain: Re-enacting Trauma in Film and Television', at conference 'Voice and Silence: (Beyond) The Rhetoric of Pain', 15 November, Warwick University.
Buck-Morss, Susan (1989), *The Dialectics of Seeing: Walter Benjamin and the Arcades Project*, Cambridge, MA: MIT Press.
Burgoyne, Robert (2012), 'Embodiment in the War Film: Paradise Now and the Hurt Locker', *Journal of War and Culture Studies*, 5, pp. 7–19.
Burgoyne, Robert (2014), 'The Violated Body. Affective Experience and Somatic Intensity', in David LaRocca (ed.), *Zero Dark Thirty* in *The Philosophy of War Films*, Lexington: University Press of Kentucky, pp. 247–60.
Burucúa, José Emilio and Nicolás Kwiatkowski (2014), 'The Absent Double: Representations of the Disappeared', *New Left Review*, 87, pp. 97–113.
Butler, Judith (1997), *Excitable Speech: A Politics of the Performative*, London: Routledge.
Butler, Judith (2005), 'Photography, War, Outrage', *PMLA*, 120, pp. 822–7.
Butler, Judith (2007), 'Torture and the Ethics of Photography', *Environment and Planning D: Society and Space*, 25.6.
Butler, Judith (2010), *Frames of War: When Is Life Grievable?*, London: Verso.

Caldwell, Ryan Ashley (2012), *Fallgirls: Gender and the Framing of Torture at Abu Ghraib*, Farnham: Ashgate.
Cameron, Allan (2008), *Modular Narratives in Contemporary Cinema*, London: Palgrave Macmillan.
Carby, Hazel (2014), 'A Strange and Bitter Crop: The Spectacle of Torture', openDemocracy website, 10 November, <https://www.opendemocracy.net/en/article_2149jsp/> (accessed 1 December 2019).
Carter, Daniel (2014), 'Weapons of Disinformation', *Index on Censorship* 43.1, pp. 41–4.
Castonguay, James (2015), 'Fictions of Terror: Complexity, Complicity and Insecurity in "Homeland"', *Cinema Journal*, 54.4, pp. 139–45.
Cavallo, Ascanio and Carolina Díaz (2007), *Explotados y Benditos: Mito y Desmitificación del cine chileno de los 60*, Santiago de Chile: Uqbar.
Cavallo, Ascanio, Pablo Douzet and Cecilia Rodríguez (2007), *Huérfanos y perdidos: El cine chileno de la transición 1990–1999*, Santiago de Chile: Grupo Grijalbo Mondadori.
Cavallo, Ascanio and Gonzalo Maza (2010), *El Novísimo Cine Chileno*, Santiago de Chile: Uqbar Editores.
Cavanaugh, William T. (2006), 'Making Enemies: The Imagination of Torture in Chile and the United States', *Theology Today*, 63, pp. 307–23.
Cettl, Robert (2009), *Terrorism in American Cinema: An Analytical Filmography, 1960–2008*, Jefferson: McFarland & Co.
Chaudhuri, Shohini (2013), 'Documenting the Dark Side: Torture and the "War on Terror" in *Zero Dark Thirty*, *Taxi to the Dark Side*, and *Standard Operating Procedure*', *Screening the Past* 37.
Cheyre, Juan Emilio (2005), 'Ejército de Chile: El fin de una visión', *Estudios Públicos* 97, <https://anuariocdh.uchile.cl/index.php/ADH/article/view/13361/13634> (accessed 12 November 2019).
'Chile: Police Reforms Needed in the Wake of Protests. Excessive Force Against Demonstrators, Bystanders; Serious Abuse in Detention' (2019), *Human Rights Watch*, 26 November, <https://www.hrw.org/news/2019/11/26/chile-police-reforms-needed-wake-protests> (accessed 1 December 2019).
Chion, Michel (1994), *Audio-Vision: Sound on Screen*, New York: Columbia University Press.
Chion, Michel (1999), *The Voice in Cinema*, New York: Columbia University Press.
Chion, Michel (2009), *Film, A Sound Art*, New York: Columbia University Press.
Chun, Wendy Hui Kyong (2011), *Programmed Visions: Software and Memory*, Software Studies, Cambridge, MA: MIT Press.
CNN (2004), 'Pentagon Press Briefing', aired on 4 May, <http://transcripts.cnn.com/TRANSCRIPTS/0405/04/se.02.html> (accessed 8 July 2018).
Coll, Steve (2013), '"Disturbing" & "Misleading"', *The New York Review of Books*, 7 February, <http://www.nybooks.com/articles/2013/02/07/disturbing-misleading-zero-dark-thirty/> (accessed 8 July 2018).

Coll, Steve (2014), 'The Unblinking Stare: The Drone War in Pakistan', *The New Yorker*, 24 November, <https://www.newyorker.com/magazine/2014/11/24/unblinking-stare> (accessed 8 July 2018).

Collins, Cath (2008), 'State Terror and the Law – the (Re)Judicialization of Human Rights Accountability in Chile and El Salvador', *Latin American Perspectives*, p. 35.

Collins, Cath (2009), 'Prosecuting Pinochet: Late Accountability in Chile and the Role of the "Pinochet Case"', Santiago de Chile: Universidad Diego Portales/George Mason University, Center for Global Studies.

Collins, Cath (2010), 'Human Rights Trials in Chile during and after the "Pinochet Years"', *International Journal of Transitional Justice*, 4.

Connor, Steven, 'Sounding out Film' (2000), stevenconnor.com, <http://www.stevenconnor.com/soundingout/> (accessed 3 December 2013).

Cook, Pam (2005), *Screening the Past: Memory and Nostalgia in Cinema*, London: Routledge.

Coplan, Amy (2011), 'Understanding Empathy: Its Features and Effects', in Amy Coplan and Peter Goldie (eds), *Empathy: Philosophical and Psychological Perspectives*, New York: Oxford University Press, pp. 3–18.

Coplan, Amy and Peter Goldie (2011), 'Introduction', in Amy Coplan and Peter Goldie (eds), *Empathy: Philosophical and Psychological Perspectives*, New York: Oxford University Press, pp. ix–xlvii.

Corner, John (2007), 'Television Studies and the Idea of Criticism', *Screen*, 48.

Corro, Pablo (2012), *Retóricas del cine chileno: Ensayos con el realismo*, Santiago de Chile: Cuarto Propio.

Cortínez, Verónica and Manfred Engelbert (2013), 'El cine chileno de los sesenta: Clave para una cultura moderna', in Annette Paatz and Janett Reinstädler (eds), *Arpillera sobre Chile. Cine, teatro y literature antes y después de 1973*, Berlin: Edition Tranvía-Verlag Walter Frey, pp. 13–59.

Coulthard, Lisa (2009), 'Torture Tunes: Tarantino, Popular Music, and New Hollywood Ultraviolence', *Music and the Moving Image*, 2, pp. 1–6.

Creeber, Glen (2004), *Serial Television: Big Drama on the Small Screen*, London: BFI Publishing.

Creeber, Glen (2001), '"Taking Our Personal Lives Seriously": Intimacy, Continuity and Memory in the Television Drama Serial', *Media, Culture & Society*, 23, pp. 439–55.

Cubitt, Sean (2013), 'Archive Ethics', presentation at Symposium *Turn to the Archive! Ethics and the Making, Encountering, Imagining and Missing of the Archive*, London: Goldsmiths, 23 April.

Cusac, Anne-Marie (2009), *Cruel and Unusual: The Culture of Punishment in America*, New Haven: Yale University Press.

D'Aloia, Adriano (2012), 'Cinematic Empathy: Spectator Involvement in the Film Experience', in Dee Reynolds and Matthew Reason (eds), *Kinesthetic Empathy in Creative and Cultural Practices*, Bristol: Intellect.

Danner, Mark (2004), *Torture and Truth: America, Abu Ghraib, and the War on Terror*, New York: New York Review Books.

Danner, Mark and Hugh Eakin (2014), 'Our New Politics of Torture', *The New York Book Review*, 30 December, <http://www.nybooks.com/blogs/nyrblog/2014/dec/30/new-politics-torture/%3E> (accessed 21 March 2016).

Danzig, David (2012), 'Countering the Jack Bauer Effect', in Michael Flynn and Fabiola F. Salek (eds), *Screening Torture: Media Representations of State Terror and Political Domination*, New York: Columbia University Press, pp. 21–33.

Dargis, Manohla and A. O. Scott (2013), 'Movies in the Age of Obama', *The New York Times*, 16 January, <https://www.nytimes.com/2013/01/20/movies/lincoln-django-unchained-and-an-obama-inflected-cinema.html> (accessed 8 July 2018).

Darke, Chris (2015), 'Desert of the disappeared: Patricio Guzmán on *Nostalgia for the Light*', *BFI Film Forever*, 19 February, <https://www.bfi.org.uk/news-opinion/sight-sound-magazine/interviews/desert-disappeared-patricio-guzman-nostalgia-light> (accessed 1 December 2019).

Daum, Meghan (2015), 'Hollywood's Idealized View of CIA Officers Is No Substitute for Reality', *Los Angeles Times*, 2 January, <https://www.latimes.com/opinion/op-ed/la-oe-daum-maya-torture-report-20150102-column.html> (accessed 1 December 2019).

Dauphinée, Elizabeth (2007), 'Politics of the Body in Pain', *Security Dialogue* 38.2, pp. 139–55.

Davidson, Amy (2012), 'Three Senators and *Zero Dark Thirty*', *The New Yorker*, 20 December, <https://www.newyorker.com/news/amy-davidson/three-senators-and-zero-dark-thirty> (accessed 8 July 2018).

de Groot, Jerome (2011), '"Perpetually Dividing and Suturing the Past and Present": *Mad Men* and the Illusions of History', *Rethinking History*, 15, pp. 269–85.

de la Garza, Armida (2009), 'Realism and national identity in *Y Tu Mamá También*: an audience perspective', in Lúcia Nagib and Cecília Mello, C. (eds), *Realism in the audio-visual media*, London and New York : Palgrave Macmillan, pp. 108–18.

del Rosso, Jared (2015), *Talking About Torture: How Political Discourse Shapes the Debate*, New York: Columbia University Press.

de Luca, Tiago (2013), *Realism of the Senses in Contemporary World Cinema: The Experience of Physical Reality*, London: I. B. Tauris.

Déotte, Jean Louis (2000), 'El arte en la época de la desaparición', in Nelly Richard (ed.), *Políticas y Estéticas de la Memoria*, pp. 149–61.

Dershovitz, Alan (2004), 'Should the Ticking Bomb Terrorist Be Tortured? A Case Study in How a Democracy Should Make Tragic Choices', in Katherine Darmer, Robert Baird and Stuart Rosenbaum (eds), *Civil Liberties vs. National Security in a Post-9/11 World*, Amherst: Prometheus Books, pp. 189–214.

Devji, Faisal (2012), 'Torture at the Limits of Politics', in Michael Flynn and Fabiola F. Salek (eds), *Screening Torture: Media Representations of State Terror and Political Domination*, New York: Columbia University Press, pp. 239–55.

de Zárate, Verónica Valdivia Ortiz (2003), 'Terrorism and Political Violence During the Pinochet Years: Chile, 1973–1989', *Radical History Review*, pp. 182–90.

Didi-Huberman, Georges (2012), *Images in Spite of All: Four Photographs from Auschwitz*, Chicago: University of Chicago Press.

Diestro-Dópido, Mar (2017), 'Children of the coup: Chilean cinema after Pinochet', *Sight & Sound*, 27 June, <https://www.bfi.org.uk/news-opinion/sight-sound-magazine/comment/festivals/chilean-cinema-after-pinochet> (accessed 2 September 2019).

Doane, Mary Ann (2002), *The Emergence of Cinematic Time: Modernity, Contingency, the Archive*, Cambridge, MA: Harvard University Press.

Doane, Mary Ann (2007a), 'Indexicality: Trace and Sign: Introduction', *Differences: A Journal of Feminist Cultural Studies*, 18, pp. 1–6.

Doane, Mary Ann (2007b), 'The Indexical and the Concept of Medium Specificity', *Differences: A Journal of Feminist Cultural Studies*, 18, pp. 128–52.

Doane, Mary Ann (2009), 'Scale and the Negotiation of Cinematic Space', in Lúcia Nagib and Cecília Mello (eds), *Realism and the Audiovisual Media*, Basingstoke: Palgrave Macmillan, pp. 63–81.

Dorfman, Ariel (2007), 'Globalizing Compassion, Photography, and the Challenge of Terror', *CLCWeb: Comparative Literature and Culture*, 9.

Draper, Susana (2010), 'The Question of Awakening in Postdictatorship Times: Reading Walter Benjamin with Diamela Eltit', *Discourse*, 32, pp. 87–116.

Draper, Susana (2011), 'The Business of Memory: Reconstructing Torture Centers as Shopping Malls and Tourist Sites', in Ksenija Bilbija and Leigh A. Payne (eds), *Accounting for Violence: Marketing Memory in Latin America*, Durham, NC: Duke University Press.

Draper, Susana (2012), *Afterlives of Confinement: Spatial Transitions in Postdictatorship Latin America*, Pittsburgh: University of Pittsburgh Press.

Dreyfuss, Ben (2014), 'Obama: "We Tortured Some Folks"', *Mother Jones*, 1 August, <https://www.motherjones.com/politics/2014/08/obama-we-tortured-some-folks/> (accessed 1 December 2019).

DuBois, Page (1991), *Torture and Truth*, New York: Routledge.

Dunn, Timothy (2010), 'Torture, Terrorism, and *24*: What Would Jack Bauer Do?', in Timothy M. Dale and Joseph Foy (eds), *Homer Simpson Marches on Washington: Dissent through American Popular Culture*, Lexington: The University Press of Kentucky, pp. 171–84.

Dyer, Richard (1997), *White*, London: Routledge.

Dyer, Richard (2007), *Pastiche*, London: Routledge.

Eban, Katherine (2007), 'Rorschach and Awe', *Vanity Fair*, 17 July, <https://www.vanityfair.com/news/2007/07/torture200707> (accessed 8 July 2018).

Ebbrecht, Tobias (2007), 'Docudramatizing History on TV: German and British Docudrama and Historical Event Television in the Memorial Year 2005', *European Journal of Cultural Studies*, 10, pp. 35–53.

Ebert, Roger (2001), 'Errol Morris: Megatron, son of Interrotron', rogerebert.com, 30 January, <http://www.rogerebert.com/festivals-and-awards/errol-morris-megatron-son-of-interrotron> (accessed 16 March 2016).

Ebert, Roger (2005), 'Syriana', rogerebert.com, 8 December, <https://www.rogerebert.com/reviews/syriana-2005> (accessed 1 September 2019).

Eckstein, Barbara J. (1990), *The Language of Fiction in a World of Pain: Reading Politics as Paradox*, Philadelphia: University of Pennsylvania Press.

Eder, Jens (2006), 'Ways of Being Close to Characters', *Film Studies*, pp. 68–80.

Edgerton, Gary (2012), 'Brody Must Die', *CST Online*, 29 November <https://cstonline.net/brody-must-die-gary-r-edgerton/> (accessed 6 February 2016).

Edgerton, Gary and Edgerton, Katherine (2012), 'Pathologizing Post-9/11 America in *Homeland*: Private Paranoia, Public Psychosis', *Critical Studies in Television: The International Journal of Television Studies*, 7, pp. 89–92.

Elsaesser, Thomas (1993), 'Hyper-, Retro- or Counter-Cinema: European Cinema and Third Cinema between Hollywood and Art Cinema', in John King, Ana M. López, and Manuel Alvarado (eds), *Mediating Two Worlds: Cinematic Encounters in the Americas*, London: British Film Institute, pp. 119–35.

Elsaesser, Thomas (2009), 'World Cinema: Realism, Evidence, Presence', in Lúcia Nagib and Cecília Mello (eds), *Realism and the Audiovisual Media*, Basingstoke: Palgrave Macmillan, pp. 3–19.

Elsaesser, Thomas (2011), 'James Cameron's *Avatar*: Access for all', *New Review of Film and Television Studies*, 9, pp. 247–64.

Elsaesser, Thomas (2012), 'Digital Hollywood: Between Truth, Belief and Trust', in Thomas Elsaesser (ed.), *The Persistence of Hollywood*, New York: Routledge, pp. 308–18.

Elsaesser, Thomas (2016), *Film History as Media Archaeology: Tracking Digital Cinema*, Amsterdam: Amsterdam University Press.

Elsaesser, Thomas and Warren Buckland (2002), *Studying Contemporary American Film: A Guide to Movie Analysis*, London: Arnold.

Elsaesser, Thomas (2009), 'The Mind-Game Film', in Warren Buckland (ed.), *Puzzle Films: Complex Storytelling in Contemporary Cinema*, Chichester: Wiley-Blackwell, pp. 13–41.

Elsaesser, Thomas and Malte Hagener (2010), *Film Theory: An Introduction Through The Senses*, New York: Routledge.

Eltit, Diamela and Berenike Jung (2019), 'Pain and Writing: An Interview with Diamela Eltit', in Berenike Jung and Stella Bruzzi (eds), *Beyond the Rhetoric of Pain*, New York: Routledge.

Errázuriz, Luis Hernán and Gonzalo Leyva (2010), *El golpe estetico. Dictadura militar en Chile 1973–1989*, Santiago de Chile: Ocho libros.

Ernst, Wolfgang and Jussi Parikka (2013), *Digital Memory and the Archive*, Minneapolis: University of Minnesota Press.

Estévez, Antonella (2010), 'Dolores políticos: reacciones cinematográficas. Resistencias melancólicas en el cine chileno contemporáneo', *Aisthesis*, 47, pp. 15–32.

Estévez, Antonella (2011), 'Cine contemporáneo chileno: Joven cine chileno: En la movilización de los márgenes', in Claudia Barril and Jose M. Santa Cruz G (eds), *El cine que fue: 100 años de cine chileno*, Santiago de Chile: Arcis, pp. 75–83.

Executive Order No. 13,823 (2018), 'Protecting America Through Lawful Detention of Terrorists', *Federal Register*, 30 January, <https://www.federalregister.gov/d/2018-02261> (accessed 2 September 2019).

Fajardo, Marco (2006), *Contra Bachelet y otros: los militares que se opusieron al golpe*, Santiago de Chile: Editorial Quimantú.

Fallon, Kris (2013), 'Archives analog and digital: Errol Morris and documentary film in the digital age', *Screen* 54.1, pp. 20–43.

Faludi, Susan (2008), *The Terror Dream: Myth and Misogyny in an Insecure America*, New York: Picador.

Farrell, Michelle (2013), *The Prohibition of Torture in Exceptional Circumstances*, Cambridge: Cambridge University Press.

Filkins, Dexter (2012), 'Bin Laden, the Movie', *The New Yorker*, 17 December, <https://www.newyorker.com/magazine/2012/12/17/bin-laden-the-movie> (accessed 8 July 2018).

Filkins, Dexter (2017), 'The New C.I.A. Deputy Chief's Black-Site Past', *The New Yorker*, 3 February, <https://www.newyorker.com/news/news-desk/the-new-c-i-a-deputy-chiefs-black-site-past> (accessed 20 May 2018).

Fiske, Alan and Tage Rai (2014), *Virtuous Violence: Hurting and Killing to Create, Sustain, End, and Honor Social Relationships*, Cambridge: Cambridge University Press.

Flood, Maria (2019), 'Torture in Word and Image: Inhuman Acts in Resnais and Pontecorvo', *JCMS: Journal of Cinema and Media Studies*, 58.3, pp. 26–48.

Flores Delpino, Carlos (2007), *Excéntricos y Astutos. Influencia de la consciencia y uso progresivo de operaciones materiales en la calidad de cuatro películas chilenas realizadas entre 2001 y 2006*, Santiago de Chile: LOM.

Flynn, Michael and Fabiola F. Salek (2012), *Screening Torture: Media Representations of State Terror and Political Domination*, New York: Columbia University Press.

Foucault, Michel [1975] (1991), *Discipline and Punish: The Birth of the Prison*, London: Penguin.

Franco, Jean (2013), *Cruel Modernity*, Durham, NC: Duke University Press.

Frazier, Lessie Jo (2007), *Salt in the Sand: Memory, Violence, and the Nation-State in Chile, 1890 to the Present*, Durham, NC: Duke University Press.

Frosh, Paul and Amit Pinchevski (eds) (2011), *Media Witnessing: Testimony in the Age of Mass Communication*, Basingstoke: Palgrave Macmillan.

Gaines, Jane (1999), 'Political Mimesis', in Jane Gaines and Michael Renov (eds), *Collecting Visible Evidence*, Minneapolis: University of Minnesota Press, pp. 84–102.

Galt, Rosalind and Karl Schoonover (2010), *Global Art Cinema: New Theories and Histories*, New York: Oxford University Press.

Gauthier, Philippe (2014), 'What Will Film Studies Be? Film Caught between the Television Revolution and the Digital Revolution', *New Review of Film and Television Studies*, 12, pp. 229–33.

Goldberg, Elizabeth Swanson (2001), 'Splitting difference: global identity politics and the representation of torture in the counterhistorical dramatic film', in J. David Slocum (ed.), *Violence and American Cinema*, New York: Routledge, pp. 245–70.

Gómez-Barris, Macarena (2008), *Where Memory Dwells: Culture and State Violence in Chile*, Berkeley: University of California Press.

Gooch, Joshua (2014), 'Beyond Panopticism: The Biopolitical Labor of Surveillance and War in Contemporary Film', in David LaRocca (ed.), *The Philosophy of War Films*, Lexington: University Press of Kentucky, pp. 155–78.

Gordon, Avery (1997), *Ghostly Matters: Haunting and the Sociological Imagination*, Minneapolis: University of Minnesota Press.

Gordon, Avery (2009), 'The United States Military Prison: The Normalcy of Exceptional Brutality', in Phil Scraton and Jude McCulloch (eds), *The Violence of Incarceration*, London: Routledge.

Gordon, Nathan and William Fleisher (2011), *Effective interviewing and interrogation techniques*, London: Amsterdam Press.

Grajeda, Tony (2006), 'Picturing Torture: Gulf Wars Past and Present', in Andrew Martin and Patrice Petro (eds), *Rethinking Global Security: Media, Popular Culture, and The 'War on Terror'*, New Brunswick, NJ: Rutgers University Press, pp. 206–35.

Greenwald, Glen (2009), 'The Suppressed Fact: Deaths by U.S. Torture', *Salon*, 30 June, <https://www.salon.com/2009/06/30/accountability_7/> (accessed 8 July 2018).

Greenwald, Glen (2012), '*Zero Dark Thirty*: CIA hagiography, pernicious propaganda', *The Guardian*, 14 December, <https://www.theguardian.com/commentisfree/2012/dec/14/zero-dark-thirty-cia-propaganda> (accessed 8 July 2018).

Grusin, Richard (2010), *Premediation: Affect and Mediality after 9/11*, Basingstoke: Palgrave Macmillan.

Grusin, Richard (2014), 'Post-Cinematic Atavism', *SEQUENCE*, 1.

Guerin, Frances and Roger Hallas (2007), *The Image and the Witness: Trauma, Memory and Visual Culture*, London: Wallflower.

Gunning, Tom (2007a), 'Moving Away from the Index: Cinema and the Impression of Reality', *Differences: A Journal of Feminist Cultural Studies*, 18, pp. 29–52.

Gunning, Tom (2007b), 'To Scan a Ghost: The Ontology of Mediated Vision', *Grey Room*, 1, pp. 94–127.

Guynn, William (2016), *Unspeakable Histories: Film and the Experience of Catastrophe*, New York: Columbia University Press.

Haddu, Miriam and Joanna Page (2009), *Visual Synergies in Fiction and Documentary Film from Latin America*, Basingstoke: Palgrave Macmillan.

Hammond, Phil (2011), *Screens of Terror: Representations of War and Terrorism in Film and Television since 9/11*, Suffolk: Arima Publishing.

Hansen, Miriam (1987), 'Benjamin, Cinema and Experience: "The Blue Flower in the Land of Technology"', *New German Critique*, pp. 179–224.

Harris, Mark (1 October 2018), 'The Lie Generator: Inside the Black Mirror World of Polygraph Job Screenings', *Wired*, <https://www.wired.com/story/inside-polygraph-job-screening-black-mirror/?mbid=email_onsiteshare> (accessed 25 November 2018).

Harrison, Nicholas (2014), 'Yesterday's Mujahiddin: Gillo Pontecorvo's *The Battle of Algiers* (1966)', in Rebecca Weaver-Hightower and Peter Hulme (eds), *Postcolonial Film: History, Empire, Resistance*, New York, London: Routledge, pp. 23–46.
Hart, Stephen (2004), *A Companion to Latin American Film*, Woodbridge: Tamesis.
Hasian, Marouf A. (2014), 'Military Orientalism at the Cineplex: A Postcolonial Reading of *Zero Dark Thirty*', *Critical Studies in Media Communication*, 31, pp. 464–78.
Hayner, Priscilla (2002), *Unspeakable Truths: Facing the Challenge of Truth Commissions*, New York: Routledge.
Hediger, Vinzenz (2012), 'Lost in Space and Found in a Fold: Cinema and the Irony of Media', in Gertrud Koch, Volker Pantenburg and Simon Rothöhler (eds), *Screen Dynamics: Mapping the Borders of Cinema*, Wien: SYNEMA-Gesellschaft für Film und Medien.
Hennelly, Robert (2014), 'Evil Torturers Catch a Break: How America Got Distracted from a National Travesty', *Salon*, 24 December, <https://www.salon.com/2014/12/24/evil_torturers_catch_a_break_how_america_got_distracted_from_a_national_travesty/> (accessed 8 July 2018).
Henríquez, Roberto Bruna (2013), 'El cine chileno de ficción, la última conquista de Milton Friedman', *elmostrador*, 3 September, <http://www.elmostrador.cl/cultura/2013/09/03/el-cine-chileno-de-ficcion-la-ultima-conquista-de-milton-friedman/> (accessed 28 March 2016).
Hernandez, Julie Gerk (2010), 'The Tortured Body, the Photograph, and the US War on Terror', in Sophia A. McClennen and Henry James Morello (eds), *Representing Humanity in an Age of Terror*, West Lafayette: Purdue University Press, pp. 174–86.
Hersh, Seymour (2004), 'Torture at Abu Ghraib. American Soldiers Brutalized Iraqis. How Far Up Does the Responsibility Go?', *The New Yorker*, 10 May, <https://www.newyorker.com/magazine/2004/05/10/torture-at-abu-ghraib> (accessed 8 July 2018).
Hirsch, Marianne (2001), 'Surviving Images: Holocaust Photographs and the Work of Postmemory', *The Yale Journal of Criticism*, 14, pp. 5–37.
Hirsch, Marianne (2008), 'The Generation of Postmemory', *Poetics Today*, 29, pp. 103–28.
Hoby, Hermione, '*Zero Dark Thirty*: Jason Clarke Confesses', *The Guardian*, 18 January 2013.
Höglund, Johan (2014), *The American Imperial Gothic: Popular Culture, Empire, Violence*, Farnham: Ashgate.
Holdsworth, Amy (2011), *Television, Memory and Nostalgia*, Basingstoke: Palgrave Macmillan.
Holloway, David (2008), *9/11 and the War on Terror*, Edinburgh: Edinburgh University Press.

'Homeland – Creating the Opening Titles Music' (2012), YouTube video by film-musicreporter.com with Sean Callery, 26 August, <https://www.youtube.com/watch?v=Bmt7rhwXHkI&index=8&list=PL2cp47gnY-DqNgaepTvN-RoBktAoC3YdcW> (accessed 5 February 2016).

Horowitz, Jason (2001), 'Breaking Down the Situation Room' *The Washington Post Online*, 5 May, <http://www.washingtonpost.com/wp-srv/lifestyle/style/situation-room.html> (accessed 8 July 2018).

Hughey, Matthew (2014), *The White Savior Film: Content, Critics, and Consumption*, Philadelphia: Temple University Press.

Hutchings, Peter J. (1999), 'Spectacularizing Crime: Ghostwriting the Law', *Law and Critique*, 10, pp. 27–48.

Hutchings, Peter J. (2012), 'Entertaining Torture, Embodying Law', *Cultural Studies*, 27, pp. 49–71.

Huyssen, Andreas (2003), *Present Pasts: Urban Palimpsests and the Politics of Memory*, Stanford: Stanford University Press.

Illanes, María Angélica O. (2002), *La batalla de la memoria: Ensayos históricos de nuestro siglo: Chile, 1900–2000*, Santiago de Chile: Planeta/Ariel.

'Imagen Latente' (nd), *Cinechile* <http://cinechile.cl/pelicula/imagen-latente/> (accessed 30 November 2019).

'INDH presenta querella por torturas en Talca y tribunal la declara admisible' ('Chile's National Institut of Human Rights files complaint about torture in Talca and court declares it admissible') (2016), *INDH*, 22 March, <https://www.indh.cl/indh-presenta-querella-por-torturas-en-talca-y-tribunal-la-declara-admisible/> (accessed 1 December 2019).

Insunza, Andrea and Javier Ortega (2014), *Los Archivos del Cardenal 2. Casos Reales*, Santiago de Chile: Catalonia.

Jacobs, Ben (2015), 'Donald Trump on waterboarding: "Even if it doesn't work they deserve it"' *The Guardian*, 24 November, <https://www.theguardian.com/us-news/2015/nov/24/donald-trump-on-waterboarding-even-if-it-doesnt-work-they-deserve-it> (accessed 8 July 2018).

Jacobsen, Udo and Sebastián Lorenzo (2009), *La imagen quebrada, palabras cruzadas: Apuntes y notas (provisorias) sobre el ensayo fílmico (en Chile)*, Valparaíso: Fuero de Campo.

'Jean Baudrillard: "Der viralen Gewalt der Globalisierung widerstehen"' ['J.B. "Resisting the viral violence of globalisation"'] (2002), *Der Standard*, 18 March, <https://www.derstandard.at/story/896686/jean-baudrillard-der-viralen-gewalt-der-globalisierung-widerstehen> (accessed 1 December 2019).

Jeffries, Dru H. (2014), 'Comics at 300 Frames Per Second: Zack Snyder's *300* and the Figural Translation of Comics to Film', *Quarterly Review of Film and Video*, 31, pp. 266–81.

Jelin, Elizabeth, Judy Rein and Marcial Godoy-Anativia (2003), *State Repression and the Labors of Memory*, Minneapolis: University of Minnesota Press.

Jocelyn-Holt, Alfredo (2000), *Espejo retrovisor: Ensayos histórico-políticos 1992–2000*, Santiago de Chile: Planeta.

Jones, J. R. (n.d.), 'No', *Chicago Reader*, <http://www.chicagoreader.com/chicago/no/Film?oid=8618363> (accessed 9 March, 2015).
Jung, Berenike (2010), *Narrating Post-9/11 Action Cinema*, Wiesbaden: VS Verlag für Sozialwissenschaften.
Jung, Berenike (2015), 'History, Fiction and the Politics of Corporeality in Pablo Larraín's Dictatorship Trilogy', in Jennie Carlsten and Fearghal McGarry (eds), *Film, History and Memory*, Basingstoke: Palgrave, pp. 118–33.
Jung, Berenike (forthcoming), 'Surface Meanings: A Media Archaeological Analysis of *NO* (Pablo Larraín, 2012)', *Cinergie Libri*.
Jung, Berenike (forthcoming), '"Within the Limits of the Possible." Realist Aesthetics in Larraín's Dictatorship Trilogy', in Laura Hatry (ed.), *ReFocus: The Films of Pablo Larraín*, Edinburgh: Edinburgh University Press.
Kahana, Jonathan (2010), 'Speech Images: *Standard Operating Procedure* and the Staging of Interrogation', *Jump Cut*, 52.
Kahn, Paul W. (2008), *Sacred Violence: Torture, Terror, and Sovereignty*, Ann Arbor: University of Michigan Press.
Kahn, Paul W. (2011), 'Torture and the Dream of Reason', *Social Research* 78, pp. 759–62.
Kansteiner, Wulf (2002), 'Finding Meaning in Memory: A Methodological Critique of Collective Memory Studies', *History and Theory*, 41, pp. 179–97.
Kantaris, Geoffrey and Rory O'Bryen (2013), *Latin American Popular Culture: Politics, Media, Affect*, Woodbridge: Tamesis Books.
Kaplan, E. Ann (2005), *Trauma Culture: The Politics of Terror and Loss in Media and Literature*, New Brunswick, NJ: Rutgers University Press.
Kaplan, E. Ann (2011), 'Empathy and Trauma Culture: Imaging Catastrophe', in Amy Coplan and Peter Goldie (eds), *Empathy: Philosophical and Psychological Perspectives*, New York: Oxford University Press, pp. 255–76.
Kapur, Jyotsna (2009), 'Fear on the Footsteps of Comedy: Childhood and Paranoia in Contemporary American Cinema', *Visual Anthropology*, 22.1, pp. 44–51.
Kara, Selmin (2014), 'Beasts of the Digital Wild: Primordigital Cinema and the Question of Origins', *Sequence*, 1.4.
Kerr, Paul (2010), *'Babel's network narrative: packaging a globalized art cinema'*, *Transnational Cinemas*, 1:1, pp. 37–51.
King, John (1990), *Magical Reels: A History of Cinema in Latin America*, London: Verso.
Klein, Naomi (2008), *The Shock Doctrine: The Rise of Disaster Capitalism*, London: Penguin.
Kleinhans, Chuck (2009), 'Imagining Torture', *Jump Cut*, 51.
Klubock, Thomas Miller (2003), 'History and Memory in Neoliberal Chile: Patricio Guzman's *Obstinate Memory* and *The Battle of Chile*', *Radical History Review*, 85, pp. 272–81.
Kramer, Lawrence (2009), 'Forensic Music: Channeling the Dead on Post-9/11 Television', in Michele Byers and Val Marie Johnson (eds), *The CSI Effect: Television, Crime, and Governance*, Lanham: Lexington Books.

Kopytoff, Igor (1986), 'The Cultural Biography of Things. Commoditization as Process', in Arjun Appadurai (ed.), *The Social Life of Things: Commodities in Cultural Perspective*, Cambridge: Cambridge University Press, pp. 64–91.

Kristeva, Julia (1982), *Powers of Horror: An Essay on Abjection*, New York: Columbia University Press, p. 2.

Kurzon, Dennis (1998), *Discourse of Silence*, Amsterdam: J. Benjamins.

Labanyi, Jo (2010), 'Doing Things: Emotion, Affect, and Materiality', *Journal of Spanish Cultural Studies*, 11, pp. 223–33.

LaCapra, Dominick (2001), *Writing History, Writing Trauma, Parallax*, Baltimore: Johns Hopkins University Press.

Landsberg, Alison (2004), *Prosthetic Memory: The Transformation of American Remembrance in the Age of Mass Culture*, New York: Columbia University Press.

Landy, Marcia (2005), '*Rome Open City* (1945), Roberto Rossellini', in Jeffrey Geiger, R. L. Rutsky (eds), *Film Analysis. A Norton Reader*, New York, London: W. W. Norton & Company, 400–21.

LaRocca, David (2014), 'Introduction', in David LaRocca (ed.), *The Philosophy of War Films*, Lexington: University Press of Kentucky, pp. 1–78.

'Las 40 frases macabras del tirano' (2013), *The Clinic Online*, 3 September, <http://www.theclinic.cl/2013/09/03/para-los-que-celebran-las-40-frases-macabras-del-tirano/> (accessed 3 July 2018).

Laverty, Christopher (2009), 'Body of Lies: Mark Strong in Huntsman', Clothes on Film.com, 4 November, <https://clothesonfilm.com/body-of-lies-mark-strong-in-huntsman/> (accessed 2 September 2019).

Lavery, David (2006), '"No more unexplored countries": the early promise and disappointing career of time-lapse photography', *Film Studies*, 9, pp. 1–8.

Leach, Joan (2011), 'Scientific Witness, Testimony, and Mediation', in Paul Frosh and Amit Pinchevski (eds), *Media Witnessing: Testimony in the Age of Mass Communication*, Basingstoke: Palgrave Macmillan, pp. 182–97.

Leimbacher, Irina (2009), 'Facetime', *Film Comment*, XLV, pp. 52–7.

Lemann, Nicholas (2010), 'Terrorism Studies: Social scientists do counterinsurgency', *The New Yorker*, 26 April, <https://www.newyorker.com/magazine/2010/04/26/terrorism-studies> (accessed 8 July 2018).

Liñero, Germán (2010), *Apuntes para una historia del video en Chile*, Santiago: Ocho libros.

Lithwick, Dahlia (2015), 'Amicus: Throwing Away the Key. Has the Supreme Court Turned Its Back on Guantánamo?', *Amicus*, 14 March, <http://www.slate.com/articles/podcasts/amicus/2015/03/the_supreme_court_turns_away_two_cases_involving_alleged_torture_at_guantanamo.html> (accessed 8 July 2018).

Little, William G. (2014), '*24*: Time, Terror, Television', *Journal of Popular Film and Television*, 42, pp. 2–15.

'*Los Archivos del Cardenal* llega a Uruguay, Venezuela y Estados Unidos' (2015), teleseries.cl, 14 April, <http://teleseriescl.blogspot.co.uk/2015/04/los-archivos-del-cardenal-llega-uruguay.html> (accessed 5 February 2016).

'Los casos de la vicaria. Las historias reales que inspiran la serie *Los Archivos del Cardenal*', Research And Publications Center (CIP) of the Diego Portales University, <http://www.casosvicaria.cl/> (accessed 7 July 2018).

Lury, Karen (2005), *Interpreting Television*, London: Oxford University Press.

Lyon, David (2009), 'Surveillance, Power, and Everyday Life', in Chrisanthi Avgerou, Robin Mansell, Danny Quah and Roger Silverstone (eds), *The Oxford Handbook of Information and Communication Technologies*, Oxford: Oxford University Press.

Maira, Carolina Cerda (2011), 'Desgarrador final de temporada de *Los 80* consigue 35 puntos de rating', *La Tercera*, 21 December.

Manovich, Lev (1998), 'To Lie and to Act: Cinema and Telepresence', in Thomas Elsaesser and Kay Hoffmann (eds), *Cinema Futures: Cain, Abel or Cable?: The Screen Arts in the Digital Age*, Amsterdam: Amsterdam University Press, pp. 189–99.

Margulies, Ivone (1996), *Nothing Happens: Chantal Akerman's Hyperrealist Everyday*, Durham, NC: Duke University Press.

Marks, Jonathan H. (2010), 'The Logic and Language of Torture', in Sophia A. McClennen and Henry James Morello (eds), *Representing Humanity in an Age of Terror*, West Lafayette: Purdue University Press, pp. 58–74.

Marks, Laura U. (2000), *The Skin of the Film: Intercultural Cinema, Embodiment, and the Senses*, Durham, NC: Duke University Press.

Marks, Laura U. (2002), *Touch: Sensuous Theory and Multisensory Media*, Minneapolis: University of Minnesota Press.

Martin-Jones, David (2013), 'Archival Landscapes and a Non-Anthropocentric "Universe Memory"', *Third Text*, 27, pp. 707–22.

'Más de dos mil personas en proyección de *Los Archivos del Cardenal* repletaron explanada del museo' (2012), Museo de la Memoria website, 13 October, <http://www.museodelamemoria.cl/un-post-de-prueba-para-empezar-las-cosas/> (accessed 6 February 2016).

Masiello, Francine (2001), *The Art of Transition: Latin American Culture and Neoliberal Crisis*, Durham, NC: Duke University Press.

Matheou, Demetrios (2013), 'The Body Politic: Pablo Larraín on *Post Mortem*', *BFI Film Forever*, 29 January, <http://www.bfi.org.uk/news-opinion/sight-sound-magazine/interviews/body-politic-pablo-larra-on-post-mortem> (accessed 21 March 2016).

Mayer, Jane (2007), 'The Black Sites. a Rare Look inside the C.I.A.'s Secret Interrogation Program', *The New Yorker*, 13 August, <https://www.newyorker.com/magazine/2007/08/13/the-black-sites> (accessed 8 July 2018).

Mayer, Jane (2007), 'Whatever It Takes. The Politics of the Man Behind *24*', *The New Yorker*, 19 February, <https://www.newyorker.com/magazine/2007/02/19/whatever-it-takes> (accessed 8 July 2018).

Mayer, Jane (2012), 'Zero Conscience in *Zero Dark Thirty*', *The New Yorker*, 14 December, <https://www.newyorker.com/news/news-desk/zero-conscience-in-zero-dark-thirty> (accessed 8 July 2018).

Mayer, Jane (2014), 'The Unidentified Queen of Torture', *The New Yorker*, 18 December, <https://www.newyorker.com/news/news-desk/unidentified-queen-torture> (accessed 8 July 2018).

Mazzetti, Mark, Matthew Rosenberg and Charlie Savage (2017), 'Trump Administration Returns Copies of Report on C.I.A. Torture to Congress', *New York Times*, 2 June, <https://www.nytimes.com/2017/06/02/us/politics/cia-torture-report-trump.html> (accessed 22 May 2018).

McClintock, Anne (2009), 'Paranoid Empire: Specters from Guantánamo and Abu Ghraib', *Small Axe*, 13, pp. 50–74.

McCoy, Alfred (2012), 'Beyond Susan Sontag: The Seduction of Psychological Torture', in Michael Flynn and Fabiola F. Salek (eds), *Screening Torture: Media Representations of State Terror and Political Domination*, New York: Columbia University Press, pp. 119–52.

McNamara, Laura A. (2007), 'Notes on an Ethnographic Scandal: Seymour Hersh, Abu Ghraib and the Arab Mind', *Anthropology News*, 48, pp. 4–5.

McSweeney, Terence (2014), *The 'War on Terror' and American Film: 9/11 Frames Per Second, Traditions in American Cinema*, Edinburgh: Edinburgh University Press.

Meek, Allen (2010), *Trauma and Media: Theories, Histories, and Images*, New York: Routledge.

Melley, Tim (2012), *The Covert Sphere: Secrecy, Fiction, and the National Security State*. Ithaca: Cornell University Press.

Melley, Tim (2015), 'Zero Dark Democracy', in John N. Duvall (ed.) *Narrating 9/11: Fantasies of State, Security, and Terrorism*, Baltimore: Johns Hopkins University Press, pp. 17–39.

Mestrovic, Stjepan (2012), 'Documenting the Documentaries on Abu Ghraib: Facts Versus Distortion', in Michael Flynn and Fabiola F. Salek (eds), *Screening Torture: Media Representations of State Terror and Political Domination*, New York: Columbia University Press, pp. 273–91.

Middleton, Jason (2010), 'The Subject of Torture: Regarding the Pain of Americans in *Hostel*', *Cinema Journal*, 49, pp. 1–24.

Minh-ha, T. T. (2016), 'The Image and the Void', *Journal of Visual Culture*, 15(1), pp. 131–40.

Mirzoeff, Nicholas (2006), 'Invisible Empire: Visual Culture, Embodied Spectacle, and Abu Ghraib', *Radical History Review*, pp. 21–44.

Mishra, Pankaj (2018), 'The crisis in modern masculinity', *The Guardian*, 17 March, <https://www.theguardian.com/books/2018/mar/17/the-crisis-in-modern-masculinity> (accessed 14 November 2019)

Mitchell, W. J. T. (2011), *Cloning Terror: The War of Images, 9/11 to the Present*, Chicago: University of Chicago Press.

Mitnick, Gilda Waldman (2009), 'Chile: La persistencia de las memorias antagónicas', *Política y Cultura*, pp. 211–34.

Mizejewski, Linda (1993) 'Picturing the female dick: *The Silence of the Lambs* and *Blue Steel*', *Journal of Film and Video* 45.2/3, pp. 6–23.

Montañez, María Soledad and David Martin-Jones (2013), 'Uruguay Disappears: Small Cinemas, Control Z Films, and the Aesthetics and Politics of Auto-Erasure', *Cinema Journal*, 53.1, pp. 26–51.
Morell, Michael (2012), 'Message from the Acting Director: *Zero Dark Thirty*', CIA.gov, 21 December, <https://www.cia.gov/news-information/press-releases-statements/2012-press-releasese-statements/message-from-adcia-zero-dark-thirty.html> (accessed 29 March 2016).
Morris, Errol (2004), 'Eye Contact: "Interrotron"', errolmorris.com, <http://www.errolmorris.com/content/eyecontact/interrotron.html> (accessed 22 January 2016).
Morris, Errol (2007), 'Will the *Real* Hooded Man Please Stand Up', *The New York Times*, 15 August, <https://opinionator.blogs.nytimes.com/2007/08/15/will-the-real-hooded-man-please-stand-up/> (accessed 8 July 2018).
Morris, Errol (2008), 'Play It Again, Sam (Re-Enactments, Part One)', *The New York Times*, 3 April, <https://opinionator.blogs.nytimes.com/2008/04/03/play-it-again-sam-re-enactments-part-one/> (accessed 8 July 2018).
Morris, Errol (2008), 'Play It Again, Sam (Re-Enactments, Part Two)', *The New York Times*, 10 April, <https://opinionator.blogs.nytimes.com/2008/04/10/play-it-again-sam-re-enactments-part-two/> (accessed 8 July 2018).
Morris, Errol (2008), 'The Most Curious Thing', *The New York Times*, 19 May, <https://opinionator.blogs.nytimes.com/2008/05/19/the-most-curious-thing/> (accessed 8 July 2018).
Moses, Rafael (1985), 'Empathy and Dis-Empathy in Political Conflict', *Political Psychology*, 6.1, pp. 135–39.
Mouesca, Jacqueline (1988), *Plano secuencia de la memoria de Chile: Veinticinco años de cine chileno (1960–1985)*, Santiago de Chile: Ediciones del Litoral.
Mouesca, Jaqueline and Carlos Orellana (2010), *Breve historia del cine chileno: Desde sus orígenes hasta nuestros días*, Santiago de Chile: LOM.
Moulian, Tomás (1997), *Chile Actual: Anatomía de un mito*, Santiago, Chile: ARCIS Universidad: LOM Ediciones.
Mulvey, Laura (2006), *Death 24x a Second: Stillness and the Moving Image*, London: Reaktion Books.
Nacos, Brigitte (2011), 'The Image of Evil: Why Screen Narratives of Terrorism and Counterterrorism Matter in Real Life Politics and Policies', in Phil Hammond (ed.), *Screens of Terror: Representations of War and Terrorism in Film and Television since 9/11*, Suffolk: Arima Publishing.
Nagib, Lúcia (2011), *World Cinema and the Ethics of Realism*, London: Continuum.
Nagib, Lúcia and Cecília Mello (2009), *Realism and the Audiovisual Media*, Basingstoke: Palgrave Macmillan.
Nagib, Lúcia, Christopher Perriam and Rajinder Kumar Dudrah (2012), *Theorizing World Cinema*, London: I. B. Tauris.
Negra, Diane and Jorie Lagerwey (2015), 'Analyzing *Homeland*: Introduction', *Cinema Journal*, 54.4, pp. 126–31.

Neroni, Hilary (2009), 'The Nonsensical Smile of the Torturer: Documentary Form and the Logic of Enjoyment', *Studies in Documentary Film*, 3, pp. 245–57.

Newcomb, Horace (2007), *Television: The Critical View*, New York: Oxford University Press.

Newcomb, Horace M. and Paul M. Hirsch (1983), 'Television as a Cultural Forum: Implications for Research', in Horace Newcomb (ed.), *Television: The critical view*, pp. 561–73.

'News Conference by the President, 4/29/2009' (2009), *Obama White House*, 30 April, <https://obamawhitehouse.archives.gov/the-press-office/news-conference-president-4292009> (accessed 1 December 2019).

Nichols, Bill (1991), *Representing Reality: Issues and Concepts in Documentary*, Bloomington: Indiana University Press.

Nichols, Bill (2005), 'The Voice of Documentary', in Alan Rosenthal and John Corner (eds), *New Challenges for Documentary*, Manchester: Manchester University Press, pp. 17–33.

Nichols, Bill (2008), 'Documentary Reenactment and the Fantasmatic Subject', *Critical Inquiry*, 35, pp. 72–89.

Nichols, Bill (2010), 'Feelings of Revulsion and the Limits of Academic Discourse', *Jump Cut*, 52.

Nichols, Bill (2013), 'Irony, Cruelty, Evil (and a Wink) in the Act of Killing', *Film Quarterly*, 67, pp. 25–9.

Niemeyer, Katharina (2014), *Media and Nostalgia: Yearning for the Past, Present and Future*, Basingstoke: Palgrave-Macmillan.

'NO según M.A. Garretón: es la basura ideológica más grande que he visto' (2012), *Emol*, 23 August, <http://www.emol.com/noticias/magazine/2012/08/23/557085/manuel-antonio-garreton-contra-la-pelicula-no.html> (accessed 9 July 2018).

Nowak, Magdalena (2011), 'The Complicated History of Einfühlung', *ARGUMENT*, 1, pp. 301–26.

Nowell-Smith, Geoffrey (2005), 'Bicycle Thieves (1948), Vittoria De Sica', in Jeffrey Geiger, R. L. Rutsky (eds), *Film Analysis. A Norton Reader*, New York, London: W. W. Norton & Company, pp. 422–38.

Nussbaum, Emily (2011), '*Homeland*: The Antidote for *24*', *The New Yorker*, 29 November, <https://www.newyorker.com/culture/culture-desk/homeland-the-antidote-for-24> (accessed 8 July 2018).

Oyarzún, Pablo (2009), *La Letra Volada: Ensayos sobre literatura*, Santiago de Chile: Ediciones Universidad Diego Portales, Colección Huellas.

Odin, Roger (2007), 'Reflections on the Family Home Movie as Document: A Semio-Pragmatic Approach', in Karen L. Ishizuka and Patricia R. Zimmermann (eds), *Mining the Home Movie: Excavations in Histories and Memories*, Berkeley: University of California Press, pp. 255–71.

Odorico, Stefano (2014), '"That Would Be Wrong": Errol Morris and His Use of Home Movies (as Metalanguages) in Feature Documentaries', in Laura Rascaroli, Barry Monahan and Gwenda Young (eds), *Amateur filmmaking: The Home Movie, the Archive, the Web*, London: Bloomsbury.

O'Hehir, Andrew (2013), 'Pick of the Week: This Is How You Overthrow a Dictator', *Salon*, 15 February, <https://www.salon.com/2013/02/15/pick_of_the_week_this_is_how_you_overthrow_a_dictator/> (accessed 8 July 2018).
Olick, Jeffrey K., Vered Vinitzky-Seroussi and Daniel Levy (2011), *The Collective Memory Reader*, New York: Oxford University Press.
O'Regan, Tom (2012), 'Transient and Intrinsically Valuable in Their Impermanence: Television's Changing Aesthetic Norms', *LOLA*, 3, <http://www.lolajournal.com/3/tv.html> (accessed 8 July 2018).
Orgeron, Devin and Marsha Orgeron (2007), 'Megatronic Memories: Errol Morris and the Politics of Witnessing', in Frances Guerin and Roger Hallas, *The Image and the Witness: Trauma, Memory and Visual Culture*, London: Wallflower, pp. 238–52.
Osiel, Mark (2006), *The Mental State of Torturers: Argentina's Dirty War*, Oxford: Oxford University Press.
Ossa, Vanessa, 'Sleeping Threats: The Enemy as Sleeper Agent in Post-9/11 Threat Communication', unpublished PhD dissertation submitted 2019, University of Tübingen.
Page, Joanna (2009), 'Digital Mimicry and Visual Tropes: Some Images from Argentina', in Miriam Haddu and Joanna Page (eds), *Visual Synergies in Fiction and Documentary Film from Latin America*, Basingstoke: Palgrave Macmillan, pp. 197–217.
Page, Joanna (2017), 'Neoliberalism and the Politics of Affect and Self-Authorship in Contemporary Chilean Cinema', in Maria M. Delgado, Stephen M. Hart, Randal Johnson (eds), *A Companion to Latin American Cinema*, Chichester: Wiley-Blackwell, pp. 269–84.
Paglen, Trevor (2016), 'Invisible Images. Your Pictures Are Looking at You', *The New Inquiry*, 8 December, <https://thenewinquiry.com/invisible-images-your-pictures-are-looking-at-you/> (accessed 2 September 2019).
Palacios, José Miguel (2012), 'Archivos Sin Archivo: Sobre el acontecimiento histórico y la images de lo real en *Los Archivos del Cardenal*', *la Fuga* 14, <http://www.lafuga.cl/archivos-sin-archivo/574> (accessed 5 February 2016).
Palacios, José Miguel (2012), 'The Problems of Fiction', *The Brooklyn Rail*, 6 November, <http://brooklynrail.org/2012/11/film/the-problems-of-fictionpablo-larran-with-jos-miguel-palacios> (accessed 5 February 2016).
Parikka, Jussi (2012), *What Is Media Archaeology?*, Cambridge: Polity Press.
Patai, Raphael (1973), *The Arab Mind*, New York: Charles Scribners and Sons.
Peebles, Stacey (2014), 'Lenses into War: Digital Vérité in Iraq War Films', in David LaRocca (ed.), *The Philosophy of War Films*, Lexington: University Press of Kentucky, pp. 133–54.
Peirano, Maria (2013), 'Towards a 'cosmopolitan' national film industry: Contemporary Chilean Cinema at International Film Festivals', presentation at *Screen*, Glasgow.
Penfold-Mounce, Ruth (2015), 'Corpses, Popular Culture and Forensic Science: Public Obsession with Death', *Mortality*, pp. 1–17.

Perkins, V. F. (1991), *Film as Film: Understanding and Judging Movies*, London: Penguin Books.
Peters, John Durham (2001), 'Witnessing', *Media, Culture & Society*, 23, pp. 707–23.
Philipose, Liz (2007), 'The Politics of Pain and the Uses of Torture', *Signs: Journal of Women in Culture & Society*, 32, pp. 1047–71.
Pick, Zuzana (1990), 'Chilean Documentary Continuity and Disjunction', in Julianne Burton (ed.), *The Social Documentary in Latin America*, Pittsburgh: University of Pittsburgh Press, pp. 109–30.
Pino-Ojeda, Walescka (2009), 'Latent Image: Chilean Cinema and the Abject', *Latin American Perspectives*, 36, pp. 133–46.
Piotrowska, Agnieszka (2014), '*Zero Dark Thirty* – "War Autism" or a Lacanian Ethical Act?', *New Review of Film and Television Studies*, 12, pp. 143–55.
Pisters, Patricia (2010), 'Logistics of Perception 2.0: Multiple Screen Aesthetics in Iraq War Films', *Film-Philosophy*, 14, pp. 232–52.
Pitzer, Andrea (2017), *One Long Night: A Global History of Concentration Camps*, New York: Little, Brown and Company.
Plantinga, Carl (1999), 'The Scene of Empathy and the Human Face on Film', in Carl R. Plantinga and Greg M. Smith (eds), *Passionate Views: Film, Cognition and Emotion*, Baltimore: Johns Hopkins University Press, pp. 239–55.
Poblete, Juan (2004), 'New National Cinemas in a Transnational Age', *Discourse*, 26, pp. 214–34.
Podalsky, Laura (2011), *The Politics of Affect and Emotion in Contemporary Latin American Cinema. Argentina, Brazil, Cuba, and Mexico*, Basingstoke: Palgrave Macmillan.
Pomerance, Murray (2013), 'Talking Space in Vertigo', *Movie A Journal of Film Criticism*, 4.
Portales, Felipe (2004), *Los Mitos De La Democracia Chilena*, Santiago de Chile: Catalonia.
Pribram, E. Deidre (2011), *Emotions, Genre, and Justice in Film and Television: Detecting Feeling*, New York: Routledge.
Prince, Stephen (2015), 'Reviewed Work(s): Terrorism TV: Popular Entertainment in Post-9/11 America by Stacy Takacs.' *Cinema Journal*, 54.4, pp. 178–82.
Purse, Lisa (2017), 'Ambiguity, ambivalence and absence in Zero Dark Thirty', in L. Purse and C. Hellmich (eds) *Disappearing War. Interdisciplinary Perspectives on Cinema and Erasure in the Post-9/11 World*. Edinburgh: Edinburgh University Press, pp. 131–48.
Quijada, Gonzalo Leiva (2013), 'El Golpe Estético de la dictadura', *The Clinic*, 6 September, <https://www.theclinic.cl/2013/09/06/el-golpe-estetico-de-la-dictadura/> (accessed 6 February 2016).
Quinlivan, Davina (2009), 'Breath Control: The Sound and Sight of Respiration as Hyperrealist Corporeality in *Breaking the Waves*', in Lúcia Nagib and Cecília Mello (eds), *Realism and the Audiovisual Media*, Basingstoke: Palgrave Macmillan, pp. 152–63.

Quinlivan, Davina (2014), *The Place of Breath in Cinema*, Edinburgh: Edinburgh University Press.
Rancière, Jacques (2008), *The Future of the Image*, London: Verso.
Rancière, Jacques (2009), *The Emancipated Spectator*, London: Verso.
Rancière, Jacques (2010), *Dissensus: On Politics and Aesthetics*, London: Continuum.
Reading, Anna (2011), 'Globital Witnessing: Mobile Memories of Atrocity and Terror from London and Iran', in Katharina Hall and Kathryn Jones (eds), *Constructions of Conflict: Transmitting Memories of the Past in European Historiography, Culture, and Media*, Bern: Peter Lang, pp. 73–90.
Reading, Anna (2013), 'Generative Memory: Gender, Digital Media and Roma Memory of the Holocaust.' Keynote at conference 'Memories of Conflict, Conflicts of Memory', 12–13 February, Senate House, University of London.
Rejali, Darius (2007), *Torture and Democracy*, Princeton: Princeton University Press.
Rejali, Darius (2012), 'Movies of Modern Torture as Convenient Truths', in Michael Flynn and Fabiola F. Salek (eds), *Screening Torture: Media Representations of State Terror and Political Domination*, New York: Columbia University Press, pp. 219–37.
Reyes G., Myriam, Federico Aguirre and Oliver Bauer (1999), *Tortura durante la transición a la democracia*, Santiago de Chile: LOM.
Reynolds, Dee and Matthew Reason (2012), *Kinesthetic Empathy in Creative and Cultural Practices*, Bristol: Intellect.
Ribeiro de Menezes, Alison (2019), 'Memory Beyond the Anthropocene: The Tactile Rhetorics of Patricio Guzmán's *Nostalgia de la luz* and *El botón de nácar*', in Berenike Jung and Stella Bruzzi (eds), *Beyond the Rhetoric of Pain*, London: Routledge.
Richard, Nelly (1998), *Residuos y Metáforas: Ensayos de Crítica Cultural sobre el Chile de la transición*, Santiago de Chile: Cuarto Propio.
Richard, Nelly (2000a), *Políticas y Estéticas de la Memoria*, Santiago de Chile: Cuarto Propio.
Richard, Nelly (2000b), 'The Reconfigurations of Post-Dictatorship Critical Thought', *Journal of Latin American Cultural Studies*, 9.
Richard, Nelly (2004), *Cultural Residues*, Minneapolis: University of Minnesota Press.
Richard, Nelly and Jorge Arrate (2005), 'Las derrotas son completas solo cuando los vencidos olvidan las razones por las que lucharon', *Revista Cultural*, November.
Ricœur, Paul (2004), *Memory, History, Forgetting*, Chicago: University of Chicago Press.
Riechmann, Deb (2016), 'Torture is illegal, but there's the issue of Appendix M', Business Insider.com, 11 March, <https://www.businessinsider.com/ap-torture-is-illegal-but-theres-the-issue-of-appendix-m-2016-3?r=US&IR=T> (accessed 23 November 2018).

Rodowick, David Norman (2007), *The Virtual Life of Film*, Cambridge, MA: Harvard University Press.

Rodríguez, Juan Carlos (2013), 'Framing ruins. Patricio Guzmán's Postdictatorial Documentaries', *Latin American Perspectives, Special Issue: Political Documentary Film and Video in the Southern Cone (1950s–2000s)*, 40, pp. 131–44.

Rohter, Larry (2013), 'One Prism on the Undoing of Pinochet', *New York Times*, 10 February, <https://www.nytimes.com/2013/02/10/movies/oscar-nominated-no-stirring-debate-in-chile.html> (accessed 8 July 2018).

Rohter, Larry (2013), 'Pablo Larraín and His Unintentional Trilogy', *The New York Times*, 8 January, <https://carpetbagger.blogs.nytimes.com/2013/01/08/pablo-larrain-and-his-unintentional-trilogy/> (accessed 23 November 2019).

Rojas, Sergio (2015), 'Profunda superficie: El pasado no cabe en la historia', Centre for Iberian and Latin American Visual Studies (CILAVS), 30 April, London: Birkbeck University.

Rombes, Nicholas (2013), '*Zero Dark Thirty* and the New History', *Filmmaker Magazine*, 29 January, <http://filmmakermagazine.com/64175-zero-dark-thirty-and-the-new-history/#.VvARDmSLRcw> (accessed 21 March 2016).

Romney, Jonathan (2009), 'Staying alive', *Sight and Sound*, 19.5, pp. 46–7.

Rosenberg, Carol (2019), 'Guantánamo Trials Grapple With How Much Evidence to Allow About Torture', *New York Times*, 5 April, <https://www.nytimes.com/2019/04/05/us/politics/guantanamo-trials-torture.html> (accessed 1 October 2019).

Rosenberg, Matthew (2017), 'Gina Haspel, C.I.A. Deputy Director, Had Role in Torture', *New York Times*, 2 February, <https://www.nytimes.com/2017/02/02/us/politics/cia-deputy-director-gina-haspel-torture-thailand.html> (accessed 22 May 2018).

Rosenstone, Robert (2012), *History on Film/Film on History*, New York: Pearson.

Saavedra Cerda, Carlos Alberto and Horta, Luis (2013), *Intimidades Desencantadas: La poética cinematográfica del dos mil*, Santiago de Chile: Editorial Cuarto Propio.

Sample, Mark (2008), 'Virtual Torture: Videogames and the War on Terror', *Game Studies*, 8.

Sands, Philippe (2008), *Torture Team: Deception, Cruelty and the Compromise of Law*, London: Allen Lane.

Sarlo, Beatriz (2005), *Tiempo pasado: Cultura de la memoria y giro subjetivo*, Buenos Aires: Siglo Veintiuno Editores Argentina.

Savage, Charlie (2016), 'Harsher Security Tactics? Obama Left Door Ajar, and Donald Trump Is Knocking', New York Times, 13 November, <https://www.nytimes.com/2016/11/14/us/politics/harsher-security-tactics-obama-left-door-ajar-and-donald-trump-is-knocking.html> (accessed 22 May 2018).

Saxton, Libby (2007), 'Secrets and Revelations: Off-Screen Space in Michael Haneke's *Caché* (2005)', *Studies in French Cinema*, 7, pp. 5–17.

Scarry, Elaine (1985), *The Body in Pain: The Making and Unmaking of the World*, New York: Oxford University Press.

Schillings, Sonja (2016), *Enemies of All Humankind: Fictions of Legitimate Violence*, Lebanon, NH: Dartmouth College Press.
Schmöller, Verena (2009), *Kino in Chile – Chile im Kino. Die chilenische Filmlandschaft nach 1990*, Aachen: Shaker Media.
Schoonover, Karl (2012), *Brutal Vision: The Neorealist Body in Postwar Italian Cinema*, Minneapolis: University of Minnesota Press.
Schultz, Fred (2013), 'Exclusive: USNI Interview with Kathryn Bigelow', USNI News website, 22 February, <http://news.usni.org/2013/02/22/exclusive-usni-interview-with-kathryn-bigelow%3E> (accessed 20 March 2016).
Scott, A. O. (2009), 'Neo-Neo Realism', *New York Times*, 17 March, <https://www.nytimes.com/2009/03/22/magazine/22neorealism-t.html> (accessed 8 July 2018).
Semán, Ernesto (2014), 'The Torture Consensus in U.S. Democracy. Learning from Latin America's Democratic Transition', *nacla*, 19 December, <https://nacla.org/news/2014/12/19/torture-consensus-us-democracy> (accessed 26 March 2015).
Shapiro, Michael (2009), *Cinematic Geopolitics*, London: Routledge.
Shapiro, Stephen (2015), 'Homeland's Crisis of Middle-Class Transformation', *Cinema Journal* 54, No. 4, Summer, pp. 152–8.
Shaviro, Steven (1993), *The Cinematic Body*, Minneapolis: University of Minnesota Press.
Shaviro, Steven (2003), 'Straight from the Cerebral Cortex: Vision and Affect in *Strange Days*', in Deborah Jermyn and Sean Redmond (eds), *The Cinema of Kathryn Bigelow: Hollywood Transgressor*, London: Wallflower Press, pp. 159–77.
Shaviro, Steven (2016), 'Post-Continuity: An Introduction', in Julia Leyda and Shane Denson (eds), *Post-Cinema: Theorizing 21st-Century Film*, Falmer, Sussex: REFRAME, pp. 51–64
Shaw, Deborah (2003), *Contemporary Cinema of Latin America: Ten Key Films*, New York: Continuum.
Shaw, Deborah (2014), 'Transnational Latin American Film and the Languages of Art Cinema', presentation at the University of Warwick.
Shaw, Tony (2015), *Cinematic Terror: A Global History of Terrorism on Film*, London: Bloomsbury.
Shue, Henry and David Luban (2012), 'Mental Torture: A Critique of Erasures in U.S. Law', *Georgetown Law Journal*, 100, pp. 823–63.
Simms, Karl (2003), *Paul Ricoeur*, London: Routledge.
Slifkin, Meredith (2014), 'Melodrama, the Americans, and the Global Television Imaginary', *Cineaction*, 94.
Slotkin, Richard (1998), *Gunfighter Nation: The Myth of the Frontier in Twentieth-Century America*, Norman: University of Oklahoma Press.
Slowik, Michael (2014), 'Controlling Terror: The Representation of December 7th and September 11th in Film', *Quarterly Review of Film and Video*, 31, pp. 692–706.

Smith, Damon (2012), 'Pablo Larraín, *Post Mortem*', *Filmmaker Magazine*, 11 April, <https://filmmakermagazine.com/43874-pablo-larrain-post-mortem/> (accessed 26 November 2015).

Smith, Greg (2003), *Film Structure and the Emotion System*, Cambridge: Cambridge University Press.

Smith, Jonathan (2014), 'The Luckiest Man: Errol Morris's *A Brief History of Time* and *The Pride of the Yankees*', *Quarterly Review of Film and Video*, 32, pp. 193–207.

Smith, Murray (1997), '*The Battle of Algiers:* Colonial Struggle and Collective Allegiance', in J. David Slocum, *Terrorism, Media, Liberation*. New Brunswick, NJ: Rutgers University Press, pp. 94–110.

Smith, Murray (2011), 'Empathy, Expansionism, and the Extended Mind', in Amy Coplan and Peter Goldie (eds), *Empathy: Philosophical and Psychological Perspectives*, New York: Oxford University Press, pp. 99–117.

Sznajder, Mario and Luis Roniger (2009), *The Politics of Exile in Latin America*, Cambridge: Cambridge University Press.

Sobchack, Vivian (2004a), *Carnal Thoughts: Embodiment and Moving Image Culture*, Berkeley: University of California Press.

Sobchack, Vivian (2004b), 'The Charge of the Real: Embodied Knowledge and Cinematic Consciousness', in Vivian Sobchak, *Carnal Thoughts: Embodiment and Moving Image Culture*, Berkeley: University of California Press, pp. 258–85.

Sontag, Susan (1977), *On Photography*, New York: Farrar, Straus and Giroux.

Sontag, Susan (1991), *Illness as Metaphor*, London: Penguin.

Sontag, Susan (2003), *Regarding the Pain of Others*, London: Hamish Hamilton.

Sontag, Susan (2004), 'Regarding the Torture of Others', *The New York Times*, 23 May, <https://www.nytimes.com/2004/05/23/magazine/regarding-the-torture-of-others.html> (accessed 8 July 2018).

Sorkin, Amy Davidson (2018), 'Gina Haspel and the Enduring Questions About Torture', *The New Yorker*, 10 May, <https://www.newyorker.com/news/our-columnists/gina-haspel-and-the-enduring-questions-about-torture> (accessed 8 July 2018).

Soto, Elizabeth R. (2014), '(Un)Veiling Bodies: A Trajectory of Chilean Post-Dictatorship Documentary', unpublished PhD thesis, University of Warwick.

Soufan, Ali H. (2011), *The Black Banner. The Inside Story of 9/11 and the War Against al-Qaeda*, London, New York: W. W. Norton & Company.

Sprengler, Christine (2009), *Screening Nostalgia: Populuxe Props and Technicolor Aesthetics in Contemporary American Film*, New York: Berghahn Books.

Stadler, Jane (2013), 'Affectless Empathy, Embodied Imagination, and *The Killer Inside Me*', *Screening the Past* 37, <http://www.screeningthepast.com/2013/10/affectless-empathy-embodied-imagination-and-the-killer-inside-me/> (accessed 1 December 2019).

Stanitzek, Georg (2009), 'Reading the Title Sequence (Vorspann, Générique)', *Cinema Journal* 48.4, pp. 44–58.

Steenberg, Lindsay and Yvonne Tasker (2015) '"Pledge Allegiance": Gendered Surveillance, Crime Television, and "Homeland"', *Cinema Journal*, 54.4, pp. 132–8.

Steenberg, Lindsay (2013), *Forensic Science in Contemporary American Popular Culture: Gender, Crime, and Science*, New York: Routledge.

Stern, Steve (2010), *Reckoning with Pinochet: The Memory Question in Democratic Chile, 1989–2006*, Durham, NC: Duke University Press.

Stevens, Dana (2008), 'Glossy Torture: Russell Crowe and Leonardo Dicaprio in *Body of Lies*', *Slate*, 10 October, <http://www.slate.com/articles/arts/movies/2008/10/glossy_torture.html> (accessed 8 July 2018).

Stewart, Garrett (2007), *Framed Time. Toward a Postfilmic Cinema*, London and Chicago: University of Chicago Press.

Stewart, Garrett (2014), 'War Pictures: Digital Surveillance from Foreign Theater to Homeland Security Front', in David LaRocca (ed.), *The Philosophy of War Films*, Lexington: University Press of Kentucky, pp. 107–31.

Stock, Ann Marie (1997), *Framing Latin American Cinema. Contemporary Critical Perspec-tives*, Minneapolis: University of Minnesota Press.

Straw, Mark (2010), 'The Guilt Zone: Trauma, Masochism and the Ethics of Spectatorship in Brian De Palma's *Redacted* (2007)', *Continuum*, 24, pp. 91–105.

Sundquist, Eric J. (2007), 'Witness without End?', *American Literary History*, 19, pp. 65–85.

Talen, Julie (2002), '*24*: Split Screen's Big Comeback', *Salon*, 14 May, <https://www.salon.com/2002/05/14/24_split/> (accessed 8 July 2018).

Taub, Ben (2019), 'Guantánamo's Darkest Secret', *The New Yorker*, 15 April, <https://www.newyorker.com/magazine/2019/04/22/guantanamos-darkest-secret> (accessed 3 October 2019).

Taub, Ben (2018), 'The spy who came home: why an expert in counterterrorism became a beat cop', *The New Yorker*, 7 May, <https://www.newyorker.com/magazine/2018/05/07/the-spy-who-came-home> (accessed 3 October 2019).

ten Brink, Joram and Joshua Oppenheimer (2012), *Killer Images: Documentary Film, Memory and the Performance of Violence*, London: Wallflower.

Tal, Tzvi (2012), 'Memoria y Muerte. La dictadura de Pinochet en las Películas De Pablo Larraín: *Tony Manero* (2007) y *Post Mortem* (2010)', *Nuevo Mundo: Mundos Nuevos*, 29 March, <http://nuevomundo.revues.org/62884?lang=en> (accessed 6 February 2015).

'Terrorism and civil liberty: Is torture ever justified?' (2007), *The Economist*, 20 September, <https://www.economist.com/international/2007/09/20/is-torture-ever-justified> (accessed 8 July 2018).

Thomson, David (2012), '*Zero Dark Thirty* Has All the Depth of a John Wayne Movie', *The New Republic*, 21 December, <https://newrepublic.com/article/111312/zero-dark-thirty-review-old-fashioned-revenge-movie> (accessed 21 March 2016).

Timm, Trevor (2015), 'CIA's Torture Experts Now Use Their Skills in Secret Drones Program', *The Guardian*, 29 April, <https://www.theguardian.com/commentisfree/2015/apr/29/cias-torture-experts-now-use-their-skills-in-secret-drones-program> (accessed 8 July 2018).

Tomasulo, Frank (1996), 'I'll See It When I Believe It', in Vivian Sobchack (ed.), *The Persistence of History: Cinema, Television and the Modern Event*, New York: Routledge, pp. 69–90.

Traverso, Antonio and Tomás Crowder-Taraborrelli (2013), 'Political Documentary Cinema in the Southern Cone', *Latin American Perspectives*, 40, pp. 5–22.

Traverso, Antonio (2018), 'Post-Dictatorship Documentary in Chile: Conversations with Three Second-Generation Film Directors', *Humanities*, 7.1.

Trejo Ojeda, Roberto (2009), *Cine, Neoliberalismo y Cultura: Crítica de la economía política del cine chileno contemporáneo*, Santiago de Chile: Editorial Arcis.

Trejo Ojeda, Roberto (2011), 'El cine chileno en la primera década del siglo XXI: el agotamiento ideológico de una estrategia de resarrollo material', in Claudia Barril and José Santa Cruz (eds), *El cine que fue: 100 años de cine chileno*, Santiago de Chile: Editorial Arcis, pp. 84–101.

Troncoso, Alfredo Barría (2011), *El espejo quebrado: Memorias del cine de Allende y la Unidad Popular*, Santiago de Chile: Uqbar Editores.

United Nations General Assembly (10 December 1984), *Convention Against Torture and Other Cruel, Inhuman or Degrading Treatment or Punishment*, United Nations, Treaty Series, vol. 1465, p. 85, <http://www.refworld.org/docid/3ae6b3a94.html> (accessed 24 May 2018).

United States Department of Defense (2002), 'News Transcript DoD News Briefing – Secretary Rumsfeld and Gen. Myers', US Department of Defense archive website, 12 February, <https://archive.defense.gov/Transcripts/Transcript.aspx?TranscriptID=2636> (accessed 21 September 2019).

United States Office of the Press Secretary (2014), 'Press Conference by the President', *The White House*, 1 August, <https://obamawhitehouse.archives.gov/the-press-office/2014/08/01/press-conference-president> (accessed 22 May 2018).

Ulloa, Gabriela (2014), 'Canal 13 lideró el rating con final de *Los 80*: Se confirma séptima Temporada', biobiochile.com, 13 January, <https://www.biobiochile.cl/noticias/2014/01/13/canal-13-lidero-el-rating-con-final-de-los-80-se-confirma-septima-temporada.shtml> (accessed 1 December 2019).

Urrutia, Carolina (2009), 'Turistas. Inventarios', *laFuga* 10, <http://www.lafuga.cl/turistas/379> (accessed 14 November 2019).

Urrutia, Carolina (2010), 'Hacia una política en tránsito: Ficción en el cine chileno (2008–2010)', *Aisthesis*, 47, pp. 33–44.

Urrutia, Carolina (2012), '*NO*. Más alegre que la alegría', *laFuga*, <http://www.lafuga.cl/no/571> (accessed 8 July 2018).

Urrutia, Carolina (2013), *Un Cine Centrífugo: Ficciones Chilenas 2005–2010*, Santiago de Chile: Cuarto Propio.

van Raalte, Christa. 'Intimacy, "truth" and the gaze: The double opening of *Zero Dark Thirty*', *Movie: A Journal of Film Criticism* 7, pp. 23–30.

Verdugo, Patricia (2004), *De la tortura no se habla: Agüero versus Meneses*, Santiago de Chile: Editorial Catalonia.

Verheul, Jacobus (2010), 'Paranoia and Preemptive Violence in *24*', in Leah Murray (ed.), *Politics and Popular Culture*, Newcastle Upon Tyne: Cambridge Scholars Publishing, pp. 137–47.
Villarroel, Mónica (2005), *La voz de los cineastas: Cine e identidad chilena en el umbral del milenio*, Santiago de Chile: Cuarto Propio.
Villarroel, Mónica and Isabel Mardones (2012), *Señales contra el olvido: Cine chileno recobrado*, Santiago de Chile: Cuarto Propio.
Virilio, Paul (1989), *War and Cinema: The Logistics of Perception*, London: Verso.
Walker, Janet (2005), *Trauma Cinema: Documenting Incest and the Holocaust*, Berkeley: University of California Press.
Walsh, Rachel (2011), 'What Stories We Tell When We Talk About Torture: Mapping the Geopolitics of Compassion and the Post-Abu-Ghraib National Family in *24*: Redemption and Rendition', *Environment and Planning D-Society & Space*, 29, pp. 150–68.
West, Mark (2012), 'Close Reading of the Homeland Title Sequence', Mark Peter West blog, 20 March, <http://markpeterwest.blogspot.de/2012/03/close-reading-of-homeland-title.html> (accessed 23 May 2018).
Westwell, Guy (2011a), 'In Country: Mapping the Iraq War in Recent Hollywood Combat Movies', in Phil Hammond (ed.), *Screens of Terror: Representations of War and Terrorism in Film and Television since 9/11*, Suffolk: Arima Publishing, pp. 19–37.
Westwell, Guy (2011b), 'The Hurt Locker (2008)', *Mapping Contemporary Cinema*, <http://www.mcc.sllf.qmul.ac.uk/?p=446> (accessed 9 March 2015).
Westwell, Guy (2012), 'Zero Dark Thirty', *Sight and Sound* 23, pp. 86–7.
Westwell, Guy (2014), *Parallel Lines: Post-9/11 American Cinema*, New York: Columbia University Press.
White, Rob (2009), 'Heaven Knows We're Digital Now', *Film Quarterly*, 62, pp. 4–5.
Williams, Andrew (2012), *A Very British Killing: The Death of Baha Mousa*, London: Jonathan Cape.
Williams, Andrew (2019), 'Atrocity and the Pain in Law' in Berenike Jung and Stella Bruzzi (eds), *Beyond the Rhetoric of Pain*, London: Routledge.
Williams, Linda (1993), 'Mirrors without Memories: Truth, History, and the New Documentary', *Film Quarterly*, 46, pp. 9–21.
Williams, Linda (2010), 'Cluster Fuck: The Forcible Frame in Errol Morris's *Standard Operating Procedure*', *Camera Obscura*, 25, pp. 29–67.
Winn, Peter (2007), 'El pasado está presente. Historia y memoria en el Chile contemporáneo', in Anne Pérotin-Dumon (ed.), *Historizar el pasado vivo en América Latina*, <http://www.historizarelpasadovivo.cl/downloads/winn.pdf> (accessed 16 March 2016).
Winter, Jessica and Lily Rothman (2013), 'Art of Darkness', *Time*, 181, pp. 24–31.
Wolf, Mark (1999), 'Subjunctive Documentary: Computer Imaging and Simulation', in Jane Gaines and Michael Renov (eds), *Collecting Visible Evidence*, Minneapolis: University of Minnesota Press, pp. 274–98.

Wolf, Naomi (2013), 'A letter to Kathryn Bigelow on *Zero Dark Thirty*'s apology for torture', *The Guardian*, 4 January, <https://www.theguardian.com/commentisfree/2013/jan/04/letter-kathryn-bigelow-zero-dark-thirty> (accessed 8 July 2018).

Wolff, Michael (2012), 'The truth about *Zero Dark Thirty*: this torture fantasy degrades us all', *The Guardian*, 24 December, <https://www.theguardian.com/commentisfree/2012/dec/24/zero-dark-thirty-torture-bigelow-boal> (accessed 8 July 2018).

Wright, Sarah (2013), 'Tough Love: Fernando Guzzoni's *Carne de Perro* (2012)', presentation at 'Chile on Film: One-day Symposium on Chilean Cinema', Anglia Ruskin University, Cambridge.

Yehuda, Rachel, Stephanie Mulherin Engel, Sarah R. Brand, Jonathan Seckl, Sue M. Marcus and Gertrud S. Berkowitz (2005), 'Transgenerational effects of posttraumatic stress disorder in babies of mothers exposed to the World Trade Center attacks during pregnancy', *The Journal of Clinical Endocrinology & Metabolism* 90.7, pp. 4115–18.

Zavattini, Cesare (1953), 'Some Ideas on the Cinema', *Sight and Sound* 23.2, pp. 50–61.

Zielinski, Siegfried (2006), *Deep Time of the Media: Toward an Archaeology of Hearing and Seeing by Technical Means*, Cambridge, MA: MIT Press.

Zimmer, Catherine (2011), 'Caught on Tape? The Politics of Video in the New Torture Film', in Aviva Briefel and Sam J. Miller (eds), *Horror after 9/11: World of Fear, Cinema of Terror*, Austin: University of Texas Press, pp. 83–106.

Zivin, Erin Graff (2012), 'Seeing and Saying: Towards an Ethics of Truth in José Saramago's Ensaio Sobre a Lucidez', *SubStance*, 41, pp. 109–23.

Žižek, Slavoj (2013), 'Zero Dark Thirty: Hollywood's Gift to American Power', *The Guardian*, 25 January, <https://www.theguardian.com/commentisfree/2013/jan/25/zero-dark-thirty-normalises-torture-unjustifiable> (accessed 8 July 2018).

Filmography

The titles of films in Spanish are given first in the original, followed by their English titles, except when the Spanish title was used in world release. If no English title was readily available, a translation is offered in square brackets. The director(s) and year the film was released are noted in brackets after the film title/translation.

11'09"01 – September 11 (Youssef Chahine et al., 2002)
24 (Fox, 2001–10)
Amnesia (Gonzalo Justiniano, 1994)
Auge/Maschine I, II, III/Eye/Machine I, II, III (Harun Farocki, 2001–2003)
Avatar (James Cameron, 2009)
La battaglia di Algeri/Battle of Algiers (Gillo Pontecorvo, 1966)
Ladri di Biciclette/Bicycle Thieves (Vittorio de Sica, 1948)
Body of Lies (Ridley Scott, 2008)
Camp X-Ray (Peter Sattler, 2014)
Carne de Perro/Dogflesh (Fernando Guzzoni, 2012)
Chile, la memoria obstinada/Chile, Obstinate Memory (Patricio Guzmán, 1997)
Death and the Maiden (Roman Polanski, 1994)
El chacal de Nahueltoro/Jackal of Nahueltoro (Miguel Littin, 1969)
El caso Pinochet/The Pinochet Case (Patricio Guzmán, 2001)
El diario de Agustín/Agustin's Newspaper (Ignacio Agüero, 2008)
Fahrenheit 9/11 (Michael Moore, 2004)
Fernando ha vuelto/Fernando is Back (Silvio Caiozzi, 1998)
¿Fernando ha vuelto a desaparecer?/Has Fernando Disappeared Again? (Silvio Caiozzi, 2006)
Fighting Terror with Torture (2015, BBC1)
Full Metal Jacket (Stanley Kubrick, 1987)
Garage Olimpo/Olympic Garage (Marco Bechis, 1999)
Homeland (Showtime, 2011–20)
Imagen Latente/Latent Image (Pablo Perelman, 1987)
La batalla de Chile/The Battle of Chile (Patricio Guzmán, 1975–9)
La Danza de la Realidad/The Dance of Reality (Alejandro Jodorowsky, 2013)
La Flaca Alejandra (Carmen Castillo/Guy Girard, 1994)
La historia oficial/The Official Story (Luis Puenzo, 1985)
La Luna en el Espejo/The Moon in the Mirror (Silvio Caiozzi, 1990)

Largo viaje / A Long Journey (Patricio Kaulen, 1967)
Los Archivos del Cardenal [The Cardinal's Archives] (TVN, 2011–14)
Los 80 [The Eighties] (Canal 13, 2008–14)
Machuca (Andres Wood, 2004)
Miguel, San Miguel (Matías Cruz, 2012)
Missing (Costa-Gavras, 1982)
Nuit et brouillard / Night and Fog (Alain Resnais, 1955)
NO (Pablo Larraín, 2012)
Nostalgia de la luz / Nostalgia for the Light (Patricio Guzmán, 2010)
Pena de Muerte / Death Penalty (Tevo Díaz, 2012)
Post Mortem (Pablo Larraín, 2010)
Prófugos / Fugitives (2011– present, HBO Latin America)
Rendition (Gavin Hood, 2007)
Roma città aperta / Rome, Open City (Roberto Rossellini, 1945)
Salvador Allende (Patricio Guzmán, 2004)
Saturday Night Fever (John Badham, 1977)
Standard Operating Procedure (Errol Morris, 2008)
Syriana (Stephen Gaghan, 2005)
The Act of Killing (Joshua Oppenheimer, 2012)
The Battle of Algiers (Gillo Pontecorvo, 1966)
Boys of Abu Ghraib (Luke Moran, 2014)
The Thin Blue Line (Errol Morris, 1988)
The Unknown Known (Errol Morris, 2013)
Tony Manero (Pablo Larraín, 2008)
Tres tristes tigres / Three Sad Tigers (Raúl Ruiz, 1969)
United 93 (Paul Greengrass, 2006)
Valparaíso mi amor [Valparaíso my love] (Aldo Francia, 1969)
V for Vendetta (James McTeigue, 2005)
Vice (Adam McKay, 2018)
Zero Dark Thirty (Kathryn Bigelow, 2012)

Index

24, 17, 33, 72, 74–82, 87n
9/11
    footage, 27–8, 31–2
    post, 4, 11, 17, 74, 78, 83, 85
    World Trade Center, 27–8
    see also terrorism
9′11″01, 5

Aaron, Michele, 12
abject, 10, 81, 94, 117, 180
Abu Ghraib, 2–3, 7, 17, 19n, 24, 31, 54, 83, 105, 109–10, 113, 116–18, 120–1, 203
    Boys of Abu Ghraib, 64, 69
    images, 1–2, 14, 16–17, 25, 31, 54, 109–11, 114–15, 120, 122–3, 127–8, 196, 202
    see also archive; black sites
acousmêtre see sound
affect, 42, 117, 149, 197, 200
    body genres, 44
    experience, 98, 104, 181, 191
    affective economy, 180
    affective space, 198
    affective turn, 13, 18–19
Afghanistan, 7, 47n, 107
Ahmed, Sara, 18
Allende, Salvador, 5, 158–60, 162–3, 170n–1n, 173, 175, 192n
al-Qaida, 24, 42, 47n, 79
ambivalence *see* double binds; *see* narration
Améry, Jean, 134
amnesty, 6, 8–9, 133, 141
Amnesty International, 8
Anable, Aubrey, 132
animation, 138, 174
apparatus (cinematic), 84, 182, 185; *see also* dispositif
archive, 14, 19, 28, 91, 95, 115, 163, 177, 187, 190–2, 201–2
    Abu Ghraib archive, 110

archive material, 14, 31, 90, 92, 102, 181, 186–7
    footage, 31–2, 83, 87, 90, 92, 103, 186, 202
Arendt, Hannah, 37
Art Cinema, 155–6
aura, 144, 178, 181
authenticity, 51, 95, 97, 146, 168, 172, 174–6, 186, 191, 200

Ballengee, Jennifer, 17, 52
Baron, Jaimie, 19, 191
    archival effect, 191
Barthes, Roland, 41, 124, 174, 180
Battle of Algiers, 11, 70n, 106n, 167
Baudrillard, Jean, 66, 196, 203n,
Bégin, Richard, 115
Benjamin, Walter, 178, 203; *see also* optical unconscious, 203
Bennett, Jill, 200–1; *see also* empathic vision
Benson-Allott, Caetlin, 122, 185, 187; *see* archive
Bernal, Gael García, 137, 186
Berríos, Violeta, 177, 180
Beugnet, Martine, 189
Bigelow, Kathryn, 17, 24, 42–5, 48n, 85, 89n, 176
bin Laden, Osama, 24–7, 33, 39–41, 43–4, 57, 65, 66
black sites, 4–5, 30–1, 67, 109; *see also* Abu Ghraib
blackmail, 112–13
Body of Lies, 17, 57, 59, 67
Bordwell, David, 66
Bourke, Joanna, 10
Boym, Svetlana *see* nostalgia
Boys of Abu Ghraib, 64, 69
Bronfen, Elisabeth, 115
Brown, Wendy, 97

Bruzzi, Stella, 191; *see* documentary
Burgoyne, Robert, 41, 45, 49n, 66
Butler, Judith, 47n, 63, 111, 113, 165, 191, 198, 203

Camp X-Ray, 64, 69
Canclíni, García, 155
Carne de Perro, 18, 140–3, 145–8, 199
Cavanaugh, William T., 4
censorship, 4, 95, 135, 138, 153
Chacabuco, 177, 181
Chaudhuri, Shohini, 22n, 33
Chile
  coup, 4–5, 10, 15, 90, 95, 133, 136, 140, 158–64
  cultural blackout, 95
  see also dictatorship; NO-campaign; Truth Commission
Chilean Cinema, 18, 98, 132, 135–6, 140, 153–5, 157, 165, 167–8, 196
  audience, 99, 154–5
  distribution, 98, 153, 196
  industry, 154
  New Chilean Cinema, 154, 167
Chion, Michel, 144–5; *see also acousmêtre*
Chun, Wendy, 200
CIA, 3, 5, 7–8, 24–5, 28–9, 31–2, 34, 36, 39–40, 44, 53, 55, 57, 60–1, 65, 67–8, 75, 79–83, 85–6, 110, 202
Connor, Steven, 134
Cortínez, Verónica and Engelbert, Manfred, 18, 154
Creeber, Glen, 73
CSI, 91, 93–4

Danner, Mark, 85, 118, 128n
Dauphinée, Elizabeth, 18
detenidos desaparecidos see disappeared
Díaz, Tevo *see Pena de Muerte*
dictatorship, 1–3, 6, 9–10, 14, 16–17, 20n, 21n, 22n, 90, 95, 99, 103–4, 132–3, 135–7, 145, 161, 164–6, 168, 176–7, 198
  post-dictatorship, 8, 132–3, 137, 180, 185
  digital
  deterioration, 86, 173
  images, 114–15, 120, 122–3, 172–3
  media, 115, 173, 200
  metadata, 121–2, 126, 173, 200
  ontology, 122
  pre-digital, 102, 122
  turn, 10, 19, 114, 172
disappeared; 10, 14, 67, 93, 100, 134, 137, 160, 163, 176–81, 195n
  Lonquén, 93–5
  photographs of, 93
dispositif, 172, 202
Doane, Mary Ann, 147, 173
documentary, 2, 14, 16–17, 24, 51, 67, 90–2, 102, 105, 109, 111, 128, 138, 153, 156, 177, 179, 186, 188, 190–2, 195n, 197
  re-enactments, 31–2, 120–7, 138, 141, 163, 176, 186, 192
Dorfman, Ariel, 5
double binds, 17, 24, 27, 32, 34, 104
drones, 3, 7, 57, 59–61, 69, 82–3, 89n
DuBois, Page, 17, 51–2
Dyer, Richard, 190; *see also* whiteness

El botón de nácar, 176
El caso Pinochet, 179
Elsaesser, Thomas, 24, 32, 199; *see also* double bind
Eltit, Diamela, 1
embodiment, 51–2, 164
emotions, 12–13, 18, 54, 96, 104, 135–6, 143, 149, 156, 189–90, 197
empathy, 12, 97, 126, 135, 146, 190, 193n
  empathic identification, 135, 198
  empathic vision, 95, 126, 135, 149, 200
  scene of, 39
enhanced interrogation *see* torture
epistemology, 10, 18, 80, 85, 133, 200
  crisis, 32, 57, 80, 82, 84, 133, 168
  interrogation, 85, 122, 168, 172
  visual, 17–18, 45, 90, 133, 168, 200
  epistemological strategy, 2, 19, 51, 105, 128, 157, 165, 185, 196–201
Ernst, Wolfgang, 185; *see also* media archaeology
evidence, 2, 6–10, 14, 27, 31, 67, 72, 75, 79, 84, 86, 92–4, 105, 110–12, 114, 116–17, 119–20, 123, 127, 134–5, 160, 167–8, 174–5, 179–82, 184, 197, 199–200

INDEX

destruction, 7–8, 22n, 95, 191
  see also documentary; testimony

Farocki, Harun
  operational images, 66, 202
faux footage, 139, 184, 191
FBI, 7, 67, 75, 85
film festivals, 153–5, 157
forensics, 93–5
Foucault, Michel, 51–2, 68, 198

Garage Olimpo, 161
gaze, 13, 41–2, 54, 59, 63, 65–6, 68–9, 85, 94–5, 111, 115, 119, 126–8, 145, 149, 160–2, 177, 181, 199, 202–3
  panoptic, 63, 65–6, 115
  see also surveillance; witness
Goldberg, Elizabeth Swanson, 54
Gómez-Barris, Macarena, 2, 18
Grusin, Richard, 77, 115, 199
  premediation, 77
  remediation, 66, 172, 185, 195n
Guantánamo, 3, 6–8, 24, 31, 44, 74–5, 109, 196; *see also* black sites
Gunning, Tom, 174, 192n
Guzmán, Patricio *see Nostalgia de la luz*
Guzzoni, Fernando *see Carne de Perro*

Halbwachs, Maurice, 97
haptics
  haptic images, 29, 34, 146–7, 149, 174, 199
  haptic visuality, 18, 146
  sensual mode, 18, 132, 135, 141, 146
Haspel, Gina, 8, 31
Hersh, Seymour, 18, 112–13
Hirsch, Marianne, 96–7, 101, 107n, 111
  postmemory, 96, 98
historical figures, 185; *see also NO*; Rumsfeld, Donald; Trump, Donald; bin Laden, Osama
Hofstadter, Richard, 76
home videos *see* video
Homeland, 17, 23n, 69, 72, 76, 78–86, 88n, 89n, 92, 202
Hussein, Saddam, 46n, 83

impunity, 5–6, 9, 14, 133, 138, 141, 165, 169n, 175; *see also* amnesty

indexicality, 28, 149, 156, 172–3, 180, 198, 200; *see also* photography
International Criminal Court, 7
interrogation, 7–8, 24, 26, 34–7, 41, 56, 60, 62, 74–5, 85, 116, 124, 166
intensified continuity, 66
Iraq, 2, 4, 27, 45, 59, 64, 67, 109, 116–17, 119, 125; *see also* Abu Ghraib

Jodorowsky, Alejandro, 165–6, 176
junta, 94, 104; *see also* dictatorship

Kahn, Paul W., 11
Kramer, Lawrence, 74

La Danza de la Realidad, 18, 165–6, 176, 202
La historia oficial, 141, 169n
Landsberg, Alison, 96–7
  prosthetic memory, 96–9
landscape, 153–4, 177, 189, 198, 200
LaRocca, David, 14
Larraín, Pablo, 18, 136, 154–5, 157, 160–1, 168, 175, 183–5, 187, 202
Latin American cinema, 92, 155
  hybridity, 13, 91, 155, 197
  magical realism, 166
Los, 80, 17, 72, 90, 101–4, 105n, 202
Los Archivos del Cardenal, 17, 72, 87, 90–5, 98–102, 104, 107n, 141, 163, 201
Lury, Karen, 74
lynching postcards, 4, 112–13

Machuca, 16
Marks, Laura U., 18, 146–7, 190; *see also* haptics
Martin-Jones, David, 154
masculinity, 62, 76, 85
Mayer, Jane, 44
McClintock, Anne, 4, 110, 113
McNamara, Laura, 112, 119
media
  archaeology, 182, 185
  history in Chile, 90, 94, 103, 189–90
  landscape, 3, 19, 128, 176
  manipulation, 3, 67, 111, 122, 173, 185, 196
  memory, 87, 101
mediation, 28, 50–1, 77, 106, 120, 127, 141, 162, 167, 196, 199–201

Melley, Tim, 8, 49n
    cultural imaginary, 8, 75
melodrama, 72, 101, 104, 180, 184, 199
memory
    collective, 72, 97, 179
    mémoire involontaire, 175
    public, 2, 9, 84, 90, 98, 103, 137, 191
    studies, 50, 177
mental health, 81, 83
mise-en-abyme, 40
Mitchell, James and Jessen, Bruce, 75
Mitchell, W. J. T., 110; *see also* Abu Ghraib Archive
Mohammed, Khalid Sheikh, 35
Morris, Errol, 17, 109, 111, 116, 118–24, 126–8, 130n–1n
    Interrotron, 118–19, 126–7, 130n
Moulian, Tomas, 20n, 132
Mulvey, Laura, 124, 174
Museo de la Memoria y de los Derechos Humanos, 10, 179; *see also* memory

Nagib, Lucia, 156, 190
narration, 34–5, 42, 81, 109, 120, 123–4, 127, 156, 177
narrative
    perpetrator, 126, 132, 149
    revisionist, 9, 132
neoliberalism, 5, 135
    neoliberal, 18, 95, 99, 132, 135, 157, 164
neorealism, 153–7, 162, 167–8
    corporeality, 157, 164, 167
    ethics of, 14, 57, 62, 66, 84, 135, 155–6
Newcomb, Horace, 72, 80, 88n
Nichols, Bill, 47n, 92, 116, 120, 126, 138
    discourse of sobriety, 92
NO, 18, 136–8, 148, 182–90, 193n, 194n, 201
NO campaign, 136–7, 183–5, 187–8
non-fiction *see* documentary
nostalgia, 104, 148, 187, 189–90
    nostalgic mode, 19, 101, 104, 189–90
    see also archive
Nostalgia de la luz, 14, 18, 107n, 148, 176–82, 190, 195n, 198, 202
Nuit et brouillard, 11, 106n

Obama, Barack, 6, 8, 32–3, 57, 81, 84, 118
objectivity, 11, 19, 122, 174
Odin, Roger, 189

ontology, 11, 19, 122, 174; *see also* indexicality
orientalism *see* race
Osiel, Mark, 37

Paglen, Trevor, 67
pain
    emotional, 15, 53, 197
    event, 10, 134
    social, 47n, 73, 98–9, 196, 199
palimpsest, 177, 184, 201
paranoia, 74, 76, 82–3
Parikka, Jussi, 185
Payne, Leigh A., 143
Peirano, Maria, 154
Pena de Muerte, 18, 138–9, 141, 173, 175, 192, 198
Penfold-Mounce, Ruth, 94
perpetrators, 21n, 37, 39, 47n, 65, 97–9, 110–12, 119, 126, 132–3, 141, 143, 149, 152n, 174
Peters, John Durham, 51; *see also* witnessing
Philipose, Liz, 113
photography
    photographic metadata, 121–2, 126, 173, 200
Pinochet, Augusto, 4, 9–10, 102–3, 133, 139, 173–4, 183, 185, 187; *see also* dictatorship
Pino-Ojeda, Walescka, 100
Piotrowska, Agnieszka, 48n
Pisters, Patricia, 66, 171n
Plantinga, Carl, 39
Poblete, Juan, 155, 189
    supplementarity, 155, 189
Pomerance, Murray, 40
Post Mortem, 18, 136, 148, 157–8, 160–4, 175, 184, 192, 197
postcolonial, 55, 61
post-dictatorship *see* dictatorship
postmodern, 19, 128, 175, 183, 185
post-traumatic stress disorder (PTSD) *see* trauma
Prince, Stephen, 75, 88n
Purse, Lisa, 39

Quart, Alissa, 60
Quinlivan, Davina, 18, 146–7; *see also* haptics

race
  orientalism, 33, 55, 112
  Other, 62, 202
  racial discourse, 20n, 56, 113–14
  whiteness, 41
  see also Western
Rancière, Jacques, 12, 34, 134, 156
realism, 76, 124, 153, 155–7, 166, 168
  realist aesthetics, 18, 153–7
  realist mode, 31, 168, 169n
referendum see NO campaign
Rejali, Darius, 11, 26, 47n, 76, 88n, 112
rendition, 3, 7, 31, 110
Rendition, 11, 17, 26, 53–7, 60–3, 65, 67–9, 70n, 199, 202
Richard, Nelly, 18, 95, 135, 143
Ricœur, Paul, 90
Rogin, Michael, 8
Rojas, Sergio, 95
Roma città aperta, 11, 70n, 167, 171n
Rombes, Nicholas, 43
Rosen, Philip, 192n
Rosenstone, Robert, 2, 25, 134, 191
Rumsfeld, Donald, 109, 116–20, 130n

Salvador Allende, 179
Sarlo, Beatrice, 97
Saturday Night Fever, 164
Scarry, Elaine, 17, 26, 30, 34–5, 47n
Schoonover, Karl, 54, 156–7, 162, 167–8
screens, 31, 43, 50 63, 66–7, 75, 86, 172
Senate report see Truth Commission
Shaviro, Steven, 42, 45, 66, 79, 198–9
Smith, Murray, 39
Sontag, Susan, 64, 87n, 104, 114, 125, 151n, 202; see also photography
sound
  acousmêtre, 142–5
  footage, 84
  soundscape, 28, 142–3, 145, 175
spectacle, 27, 31–2, 46n, 52, 74, 110, 113–14, 184, 202
spectatorship, 13, 52, 111, 124, 135, 140
  embodied spectator, 135, 202
Standard Operating Procedure, 17, 109, 120–1, 125, 201
Stern, Steve, 9; see also memory
Strange Days, 42, 45

subjectivity, 13, 34, 42, 51, 84, 126, 142
sublime, 58, 99
Sundquist, Eric J., 28, 97; see also memory
surveillance, 29–30, 57–9, 61, 63, 66, 68–9, 74–5, 78, 80–2, 88n, 114–15, 196, 200, 202; see also drones
survivor, 8, 20n, 66, 95–6, 99, 106n, 133–4, 141, 148, 161, 177
Syriana, 60–1, 63–4, 69, 199

technology
  CGI, 172
  digital, 10, 114, 187
  objectivity of, 50–1, 67, 81–2, 123, 128, 138, 149
television
  cultural forum, 72, 101
  historical event, 93, 101, 104
  televisuality, 87
  see also title sequence
temporality, 76–7, 100, 102, 123, 126, 157, 180–2, 189, 197
  duration, 156, 174–5, 181
  long take, 28, 119, 155, 157–61
  time-lapse, 176, 177, 181–2, 198
terrorism, 3, 5, 27, 37, 44, 61, 66, 75, 83, 116, 134, 196, 203n
  counterterrorism, 37, 82
  terrorist, 3–4, 6–7, 27, 29, 31, 34–6, 56–7, 59, 70n, 74, 76, 79, 81, 83, 117, 196
testimony, 9, 21n, 26, 35, 50–1, 93, 111, 120, 125–6, 137–8, 179, 190
The Unknown Known, 17, 109, 116, 119
Thin Blue Line, 128
title sequence, 23n, 74, 78–9, 83–5, 89n, 91–2, 95, 102, 121–2
  narrative image, 23n, 74
Tony Manero, 18, 136, 140–1, 148, 164–5, 184–5, 197
torture
  bureaucracy, 36–8, 54, 60, 76
  centres, 2, 4, 10, 107, 133
  clean, 3, 20n
  debates, 5, 10, 12, 25–7, 31, 44, 90, 101
  definition, 5, 7
  enhanced interrogations, 7–8, 26, 60, 74
  folklore, 35–6, 47n, 76

torture *(cont.)*
  history, 1, 20n, 140
  memos, 7, 21n, 65, 88n
  as narrative shortcut, 19n, 74, 76, 109
  performance of, 26, 52, 60, 77, 114–15, 127
  programme, 8, 25, 28, 85, 171n
  psychological, 6, 137
  as punishment, 3, 6, 32, 36, 56, 60, 63
  rhetorical function, 52
  as spectacle, 27, 31–2, 52, 74, 114
  tropes, 11, 28, 63–4, 89n; omniscient narrator fallacy, 35
  as utility, 25–7, 36, 44
Torture Report *see* Truth Commission
touch *see* haptics
trauma, 28, 66, 69, 80–1, 85, 96
  PTSD, 81, 100, 145
Trump, Donald, 7
Truth Commission, 8–10, 137
  Comisión Asesora para la calificación de Detenidos Desaparecidos, Ejecutados Políticos y Víctimas de Prisión Política y Tortura (Valech II), 9
  La Comisión Nacional sobre Prisión Política y Tortura / The National Commission on *Committee Study of the Central Intelligence Agency's Detention and Interrogation Program* (Torture Report/Senate Report on Torture), 7, 25, 109–10, 114, 121
  La Comisión Nacional sobre Verdad y Reconciliación (Rettig report), 9
  Political Imprisonment and Torture Report) (Valech report), 9, 21n

UN Convention Against Torture and Other Cruel, Inhuman or Degrading Treatment or Punishment (UNCAT), 6–7
United, 93, 28, 39
Urrutia, Carolina, 140, 164, 184

Vice, 65, 201

victim, 6, 9, 11–12, 17, 31, 34–7, 39, 51, 53–4, 59, 63–5, 70n, 71n, 94, 98–100, 107n112, 118, 125, 126, 134, 139, 145, 149, 151n–2n, 163–4, 193n, 199
  identification with, 11–12, 17, 34, 98
  re-victimisation, 9
  voices of, 64–5, 125–6
video, 7, 57, 59, 79, 82, 102, 110, 112–13, 118, 121–2, 137, 184, 186–9, 196
  home video, 102, 122
visibility, 3, 24, 57, 66, 113, 140, 180, 196–7, 199
vision
  failure, limits of, 84, 86, 119, 139, 161, 167
  lack of, 29, 40, 43, 64, 66
  panoptic surveillance, 63
  regime of, 13, 42, 69, 181–2, 199
  searching for, control, 30

Walsh, Rachel, 11, 54
war
  films, 14, 44–5, 53, 65–6
  Iraq, 45, 116, 120
  War on Terror, 4, 66, 72, 78, 116
  warfare, 3, 59, 65–7, 82, 110, 115, 172
Westwell, Guy, 27, 33, 39, 47n–8n
whiteness *see* race
Williams, Linda, 44, 127–8
Williams, Raymond, 132, 150n, 198
  structures of feeling, 135–6
Winn, Peter, 21n
witness, 17, 42–3, 50–4, 57, 68, 93, 97, 115, 119, 167
  ethical, 51
  mediated, 17, 50–1
  public, 51–2
  Western audience as, 3, 23n, 27–8, 32, 37–40, 42–3, 53–6, 58, 60–5, 69, 76, 93, 104, 113–14, 143, 173

Zero Dark Thirty, 2, 17, 24–7, 31–40, 42–5, 46n–9n, 53–5, 65–9, 76, 86, 104, 176, 183, 169n–202
Žižek, Slavoj, 2, 5, 25, 37

EU representative:
Easy Access System Europe
Mustamäe tee 50, 10621 Tallinn, Estonia
Gpsr.requests@easproject.com